Development Economics

T0300397

Since the inception of development economics in the post-World War II period, most of its proponents have prescribed the adoption of western institutions as the path for prosperity – the unequivocal solution for poverty, illiteracy, hunger, inequality, and violence in the world. Seventy years of attempts, or at least the pretense thereof, to reproduce the western model in completely different historical and cultural contexts have proven to be no more than a mirage for most.

Faced with this scenario, why do economists insist on the ideas of development, convergence, and emulation of the lifestyle of western countries? Is it possible to disassociate development from multidimensional instability, dependency, subordination, and exploitation? Is the current social, political, ecological, and economic organized destabilization observed in the western countries a model to follow, a desirable end of history? These questions raised earlier by some fellow economists have become ever more pressing in the present context of generalized instability. This book questions how ethical and professionally responsible it is for economists to continue to undiscerningly prescribe miraculous one-size-fits-all market-oriented models to solve socio-economic problems everywhere. The contributors of this edited volume invite the readers to consider these questions and further similar inquiries in the future.

The chapters in this book were originally published as a special issue of the *Review of Political Economy*.

Natalia Bracarense is Associate Professor of Economics at North Central College, Naperville, USA, and an ATER at SciencesPo Toulouse, France. Specialised in International Political Economy and History of Economic Thought, Dr. Bracarense analyses the historical unfolding of development policies implemented in several countries to inform economic theory towards a framework that views economic transformation as a non-linear and non-teleological process.

Louis-Philippe Rochon is Full Professor of Economics at Laurentian University, Sudbury, Canada. He is the Editor-in-Chief of the *Review of Political Economy* and the founding Editor (now Emeritus) of the *Review of Keynesian Economics*. He has published over 150 books and journal articles and written or edited over 30 books.

Development Economics

Aptly or Wrongly Named?

Edited by
Natalia Bracarense and Louis-Philippe Rochon

Routledge
Taylor & Francis Group

LONDON AND NEW YORK

First published 2022
by Routledge
4 Park Square, Milton Park, Abingdon, Oxon, OX14 4RN

and by Routledge
605 Third Avenue, New York, NY 10158

Routledge is an imprint of the Taylor & Francis Group, an informa business

© 2022 Taylor & Francis

British Library Cataloguing-in-Publication Data
A catalogue record for this book is available from the British Library

ISBN13: 978-1-032-21210-4 (hbk)
ISBN13: 978-1-032-21211-1 (pbk)
ISBN13: 978-1-003-26730-0 (ebk)

DOI: 10.4324/9781003267300

Typeset in Minion Pro
by codeMantra

Publisher's Note
The publisher accepts responsibility for any inconsistencies that may have arisen during the conversion of this book from journal articles to book chapters, namely the inclusion of journal terminology.

Disclaimer
Every effort has been made to contact copyright holders for their permission to reprint material in this book. The publishers would be grateful to hear from any copyright holder who is not here acknowledged and will undertake to rectify any errors or omissions in future editions of this book.

Contents

Citation Information

The chapters in this book were originally published in the *Review of Political Economy*, volume 33, issue 1 (2021). When citing this material, please use the original page numbering for each article, as follows:

Chapter 6

Keynes on State and Economic Development
Fábio Henrique Bittes Terra, Fernando Ferrari Filho and Pedro Cezar Dutra Fonseca
Review of Political Economy, volume 33, issue 1 (2021) pp. 88–102

Chapter 7

Capital Flows to Latin America (2003–17): A Critical Survey from Prebisch's Business Cycle Theory
Roberto Lampa
Review of Political Economy, volume 33, issue 1 (2021) pp. 103–125

Chapter 8

Institutions and Development From a Historical Perspective: the Case of the Brazilian Development Bank
Alex Wilhans Antonio Palludeto and Roberto Alexandre Zanchetta Borghi
Review of Political Economy, volume 33, issue 1 (2021) pp. 126–144

Chapter 9

Institutional Change in Nepal: Liberalization, Maoist Movement, Rise of Political Consciousness and Constitutional Change
Kalpana Khanal and Natalia Bracarense
Review of Political Economy, volume 33, issue 1 (2021) pp. 145–166

For any permission-related enquiries please visit:
http://www.tandfonline.com/page/help/permissions

Notes on Contributors

Douglas Alencar Federal University of Pará, Belem, Brazil.

Roberto Alexandre Zanchetta Borghi Institute of Economics, University of Campinas (Unicamp), Brazil.

Natalia Bracarense North Central College, Naperville, USA.

Gustavo Britto Federal University of Minas Gerais, Belo Horizonte, Brazil.

Fernando Ferrari Filho National Council of Scientific and Technological Development (CNPq), Brasilia, Brazil; Federal University of Rio Grande do Sul, Porto Alegre, Brazil.

Pedro Cezar Dutra Fonseca National Council of Scientific and Technological Development (CNPq), Brasilia, Brazil; Federal University of Rio Grande do Sul, Porto Alegre, Brazil.

Celso Furtado University of Cambridge, UK.

Frederico G. Jayme Federal University of Minas Gerais, Belo Horizonte, Brazil.

Kalpana Khanal Nichols College, Dudley, USA.

Roberto Lampa CONICET (National Scientific and Technical Research Council), Buenos Aires, Argentina; Institute of Higher Social Studies (IDAES), University of San Martin (UNSAM), Buenos Aires, Argentina.

Pedro Loureiro University of Cambridge, Centre of Latin American Studies, Department of Politics and International Studies (CLAS-POLIS) and Fitzwilliam College – Cambridge, UK.

Marcos Vinícius Isaias Mendes Institute of International Relations, University of Brasília, Brazil; Institute of Sociology, Goethe University Frankfurt, Germany.

Alex Wilhans Antonio Palludeto Institute of Economics, University of Campinas (Unicamp), Brazil.

Fernando Rugitsky Department of Economics, University of São Paulo, Brazil.

Alfredo Saad-Filho Department of International Development, King's College London, UK.

Fábio Henrique Bittes Terra Federal University of ABC, São Paulo, Brazil; PPGE-UFU, Uberlandia, Brazil; National Council of Scientific and Technological Development (CNPq), Brasilia, Brazil.

The Aptly or Wrongly Named Development Economics: An Introduction to New Perspectives and Models

Natalia Bracarense

Introduction

Since the inception of development economics in the post-World War II period, most of its proponents have prescribed the adoption of western institutions as the path for prosperity; the unequivocal solution for poverty, illiteracy, hunger, inequality, and violence in the world. Seventy years of attempts, or at least the pretense thereof, to reproduce the western model in completely different historical and cultural contexts have proven to be no more than a mirage for most.

Theoretically, the shortcomings are many. To name a few: development has been viewed as a linearly staged path to a determined end: the market economies of the United States and Western Europe (Furtado [1973] 2021; Loureiro, Rugitsky, and Saad Filho 2021); institutions are treated as structures, that is, emptied of their substance as ongoing processes (Waller 1988; Khanal and Bracarense 2021); and the relationship between development and institutions are seen as unidirectional (i.e., from structure to development), ignoring that 'development' (i.e., cultural, economic, and social factors) also influences institutions (Bracarense 2012; Palludeto and Borghi 2021).

In practice, the failures are not fewer. The level of inequality among and within countries, for instance, has a tendency to skyrocket (Furtado [1974] 2021). While world leaders resistlessly face the pressures of a conceivable environmental collapse, famine provokes violence and massive emigration waves (Reuveny and Moore 2009). The setbacks are not only present in countries that have actively engaged with development policies aimed at replicating the western capitalism, both developmentalist and neoliberal, such as Argentina (Lampa 2021), Brazil (Alencar, Jayme, and Britto 2021; Mendes 2021), Nepal (Khanal and Bracarense 2021), Mexico (Molina and Peach 2005), India (Borooah 2005), Bolivia (Bracarense and Gil-Vasquez 2018). They are also felt by a large part of the population of countries like Greece (Kaplanoglou and Rapanos 2018), Portugal (Ferreira 2008), and the United States (Peach and Adkisson 2020).

Faced with this scenario, why do economists insist on the ideas of development, convergence, and emulation of the lifestyle of western countries? Is it possible to disassociate development from multidimensional instability, dependency, subordination, and exploitation? Is the current social, political, ecological and economic organized destabilization observed in the western countries a model to follow, a desirable end of history? Questions earlier raised by some of our fellow economists, but ever more pressing in the present context of generalized instability. In fact, how ethical and professionally responsible is it for economists to continue to undiscerningly prescribe miraculous *one-size-fits-all* market-oriented models to solve socio-economic problems everywhere?

The articles in this volume invite the readers to consider these questions and further similar inquiries in the future. On that note, the volume starts with two unpublished articles by Celso Furtado, one of the most remarkable Latin American economists of his generation, whose thought has influenced policymakers and social movements in the region since the 1950s (Loureiro, Rugitsky, and Saad Filho 2021). Furtado's ([1973] 2021) first piece presents his views of underdevelopment and dependence vis-à-vis the reconfiguration of international division of labor prompted by multinational corporations, who had then just started to outsource their capacities to non-industrialized countries. Furtado foresees that this new configuration does not promote development, but rather reinforces a heterogeneous process of industrialization, where there is an incongruence between the productive capacities of traditional manufacturing goods for the majority of the population and luxury goods for the consumption of the elites who wish to mimic the patterns of consumption of industrialized countries. For Furtado, this diversification is one of defining feature of capitalism and requires an income which is highly concentrated. This tendency leads him to conclude that the process of development recommended by traditional economists becomes the very source for the perpetuation and reproduction of inequality and dependency of peripheral countries.

In the second article, Furtado ([1974] 2021) discusses the impossibility for underdeveloped countries to emulate the pattern of development of countries in the core of the market system. According to him, the impossibility is due to both the structural inequality on which the market economy depends, as described in his first paper, and the constraints delineated by natural resources. The exclusion of the big majority of the population of the Third World of the fruits of the present form of development, therefore, is not a simple accident, but rather a necessary condition to cope with the increasing inelasticity in the supply of non-renewable resources. Consequently, the style of life created by industrial capitalism will always be a preserve, accessible only to a minority, as any attempt to generalize such a style of life would precipitate a collapse of the system as a whole. The inevitability of this outcome leads the author to argue that economic models that assume away the imbalance and heterogeneity of distribution, assume away the defining feature of the world economy. In effect, Furtado ([1974] 2021) insists that 'it is now apparent that what we have been calling *economic development*—namely a policy aiming at bridging the gap between the standards of living of the poor and rich countries—is nothing more than a myth' intended to maintain current conditions of exploitation and dependency. Namely, 'the notion of linear progress and the closely related myth of economic development provided a meta-narrative holding the capitalist system together ideologically and anchoring economic thought' (Loureiro, Rugitsky, and Saad Filho 2021). The author, then, prompts countries, who have been subordinated to industrial capitalism to reimagine 'development' through a bottom-up, democratic process in order to escape the dependency trap.

Furtado's original papers are followed by Pedro Loureiro, Fernando Rugitsky, and Alfredo Saad Filho's (2021) article, which presents the Brazilian economist, analyzes and places his two unpublished contributions in theoretical and historical context, and emphasizes their current relevance. Regarding the latter point, the authors focus on two of Furtado's contributions: firstly, his call for a disaggregated analysis of production and consumption and, secondly, his invitation to democratically rethink 'development'.

With relation to the first point, Furtado argues that enabling economic theory to grasp sectorial heterogeneity results in models that more realistically deal with the conditions of subordinated countries, showing results that contradict 'common wisdom'. For instance, 'higher rates of economic growth tend to imply aggravation of both external dependence and internal exploitation,' deepening existent inequalities rather than promoting economic and social prosperity (Furtado [1974] 2021). Other papers in this volume supports the observation, Douglas Alencar, Frederico G. Jayme and Gustavo Britto (2021) and Marcos V. I. Mendes

(2021), for instance, present results that contradict predictions expected from traditional economic models.

Discussing the matter of exchange rates, balance of payment constraint growth, and income distribution, Alencar, Jayme, and Britto (2021) elaborate a Post-Kaleckian model to analyze the impact of wage-led and profit-led regimes on economic growth in Brazil. The applied research shows that, when external constraints and distribution considerations are included in the model, context-specific results that contradict 'generally accepted ideas' (i.e., exchange rate misalignments) may emerge. For example, between 1960 and 2011, despite its negative impact on investment and productivity growth, real exchange rate devaluation in Brazil boosted the economic growth through the export channel.

Mendes's analysis of Brazilian academic and practical participation on the new digital economy, on the other hand, reinforces Furtado's concerns that industrialization and technological advancement are incapable to lead a country like Brazil to catch up with core countries of industrial capitalism. Effectively, combining a bibliometric analysis with literature review, Mendes points out that the potential negative effects of current trends in global value chains and investments brought up by digitalization on the Brazilian economy is twofold. First, it may dislocate foreign direct investment from the information and communication technology sector back to developed countries. Second, it may increase the technological requirements on Brazil's software industry to an unachievable level, leading to a loss of international competitiveness and eventually to a deindustrialization in this sector. That is, economic advancement and the increased productivity that it brings along may, more often than not, lead to economic divergence and increased global inequality.

The insistence on basing economic models and policy on ideals of convergence is even more startling when the history of economic thought shows that questions of increasing inequality, even within rich countries, have long been tackled by some economists. John Maynard Keynes's evaluation of negative impacts of untamed industrial capitalism on the distribution of the fruits of increased productivity is well known. Why is Keynes differentiation between economic growth and technical advancement, on one hand, and development, on the other, often ignored? Fabio H. Terra, Fernando Ferrari Filho, and Pedro Cezar Fonseca (2021) show that, for John Maynard Keynes (1932), development did not unfold naturally from the evolution of market institutions but had to rather be actively and collectively pursued. Keynes's faith on State bureaucracy and technocracy prompted him to propose an *Agenda*, where the State would lead socialization of investment and the euthanasia of the rentier in favor of the establishment of full employment (Keynes 1936, chapter 24). Subsequently, once economic concerns, such as inequality and unemployment, were lifted from the mind of all members of society, individuals could abandon their love for money and occupy their minds with higher concerns, pertaining the art of life itself (Keynes 1932).

While most economists today are not familiar with most, if not all, of Keynes's work, Furtado, along with others economists in the post-WWII peripheral countries, believed that Keynes and his followers had made important contributions to economics, but, that economic theory needed to deal with historical specificities if it were to understand the reality of poor countries (Sunna 2015; Boianovsky 2010). Keynes focused mostly on the center of industrial capitalism to build his theory with no claim of universality (Crotty 1990). It is, thus, not a surprise that his vision of development as 'the stage where humankind overcomes its economic concerns, which are no longer a major problem for the general populace' is not non-teleological.[1]

---

[1] Teleological is used here in an analogous way to Thorstein Veblen's perspective, where teleological means an understanding that history unfolds towards a determined end (Hodgson 2001).

That brings us to the great importance of Furtado's second contribution to current debates: intellectual, social, and political autonomy are necessary to think what we mean by 'development' and how to redesign the means and goals of social prosperity (Loureiro, Rugitsky, and Saad Filho 2021). He believed that historical specificity and non-teleological framework are fundamental to rethinking and redesigning societal goals other than emulation of rich countries. Along these lines, Raúl Prebisch—a mentor and then colleague, despite theoretical and personal disagreements, of Furtado at the United Nations Economic Commissions to Latin America and the Caribbean—vents 'Keynes had gone only half the distance in explaining the dilemma of countries outside the core economies' (Prebisch 1947 *cited by* Dosman 2009, p. 218).

Prebisch was an important contributor to Latin American Structuralism and a strong advocate of an economic theory that grasps the historical specificities of peripheral countries. Specialized in business cycles and determined to analyze the impact of international monetary structures on Latin American economies, Prebisch incorporated the existent asymmetries between developed and underdeveloped countries to the economic debate. In the sixth paper of this volume, Roberto Lampa (2021) reintroduces Raúl Prebisch's contributions to discussions of monetary hegemony and currency hierarchy to show that, in Latin America, monetary authorities have perceived liberalization of capital flows as detrimental to economic development due to its volatility and consequent instability. As international liquidity increases, incoming capital is, thus, not converted into productive investment, but rather left idle instead. As a result, capital inflows from core countries yield an interest to their investors, without a counterpart benefit to the peripheral host countries. In his conclusion, Lampa echoes Prebisch by questioning the validity of traditional economic development theory and calling for the elaboration of context-specific policy prescriptions in Latin America to revert this situation and confront the dominance of the dollar.

Prebisch, much like Keynes, however, trusted an important role to bureaucracy and technocracy as the receptacle of 'development' and to a State Agenda (Keynes) or Programming (Prebisch) as a 'locus of conciliation between the democratic wills, government intentions, society's needs, and technical knowledge to execute the public policies' (Terra, Ferrari Filho, and Fonseca 2021). Furtado ([1974] 2021), on the other hand, hints at the weaknesses and hindrances of a top-down agenda, which underestimates the role played by the general population in determining how history unfolds; that is, institutional transformation involves interactive actions between agents and structures (Lawson 1997). He calls, therefore, for a democratic, i.e., bottom-up redefinition of, not only how to achieve societal prosperity, but more importantly, what it looks like. In other words, understanding institutions as processes entails a multidimensional and multidirectional interaction between agents and structures.

Alex W. A. Palludeto and Roberto A. Z. Borghi (2021), authors of the eight paper of this volume, discuss the interactive action between the Brazilian Development Bank (BNDES), economic theory, and Brazilian economic agents from 1952 until the present. It becomes evident that while BNDES had an institutional role in promoting development in Brazil, it was also influenced by the country's economic performance and by the many swings—between liberal and developmentalist mindsets—in economic policy in the past five decades. This article defies the theoretical view of new institutional economics—the new consensus in development theory and policy (Tamanaha 2015)—regarding the relation between institutions and development as unidirectional, which neglects the impact of social actors and realities on institutions. The historical analysis, moreover, demonstrates that the institutional capabilities of the BNDES to promote development were curbed during periods of economic liberalization—contradicting policies prescription that favor market-oriented policies to foster economic prosperity.

The final paper of the volume studies Nepal's experience with both liberal and developmentalist policies in the past century from a feminist institutionalist perspective to demonstrate that policies based on universal models tend to fall short from reducing inequality and social injustice (Khanal and Bracarense 2021). Regardless of their nature (liberal or developmentalist) the polices sustained by these models tend to benefit specific groups at the expenses of parts of the population whose subordination, at least initially, is not necessarily related to the process of commodification. Embracing the reformulation of Karl Polanyi's ([1944] 2001) theory proposed by feminist institutionalism (Waller and Jennings 1991; Fraser 2014), the paper discusses Nepal's 1996–2006 Maoist Revolution as a triple movement and the need for a critical economic theory able to grasp with the social, environment, political, and economic complexities of the 21st century.

The papers in this special volume shed light on the current relevance of the discussions around the meaning of development as well as forms of breaking away from cultural, economic and political dependency. Not only people in subordinated positions across and within nations continue to resist the negative impact of markets on their livelihood and struggle for their social wellbeing, but also the western model has shown clear signs of economic, social, political, and ecological exhaustion. Rethinking and redesigning the meaning of, and means to achieve, societal prosperity seems, thus, propitious. One needs not to abandon the love of money to enjoy the art of life itself if they never acquired a taste for its adoration. Hence, regarding social transformation as an open-ended, non-teleological process is crucial to renounce ideals of mimicking core countries and independently reimagine the various ways social prosperity may resemble and how they may be achieved.

Finally, I would like to acknowledge all the authors who contributed to the volume as well as those who responded to all related calls for papers. I would also like to recognize Steve Pressman for the continued support and mentorship throughout this project as well as Louis-Philippe Rochon for the final motivation and push to complete it. To conclude, I extend special thanks to all the referees, who voluntarily contributed to the production of this volume, as well as all members of Taylor and Francis and universities staff and faculty who supported and guided the authors.

References

Alencar, D., F. Jayme, and G. Britto. 2021. 'Growth, Distribution, and External Constraints: A Post-Kaleckian Model Applied to Brazil.' *Review of Political Economy* 33 (1).

Boianovsky, M. 2010. 'A View from the Tropics: Celso Furtado and the Theory of Economic Development in the 1950s.' *History of Political Economy* 42 (2): 221–266.

Borooah, V. 2005. 'Caste, Inequality, and Poverty in India.' *Review of Development Economics* 9 (3): 399–414.

Bracarense, N. 2012. 'Development Theory and the Cold War: The Influence of Politics on Latin American Structuralism.' *Review of Political Economy* 24 (3): 375–398.

Bracarense, N., and K. Gil-Vasquez. 2018. 'Bolivia's Institutional Transformation: Contact Zones, Social Movements, and the Emergence of an Ethnic Class Consciousness.' *Journal of Economic Issues* 52 (3): 615–636.

Crotty, J. 1990. 'Keynes on the Stages of Development of the Capitalist Economy: The Institutional Foundation of Keynes's Methodology.' *Journal of Economic Issues* 24 (3): 761–780.

Dosman, E. 2009. *The Life and Times of Raúl Prebisch*. London: McGill-Queen's University Press.

Ferreira, L. 2008. 'Persistent Poverty: Portugal and the Southern European Welfare Regime.' *European Societies* 10 (1): 49–71.

Fraser, N. 2014. 'Can Society be Commodities all the Way Down? Post-Polanyian Reflections on Capitalist Crisis.' *Economy and Society* 43 (4): 541–558.

Furtado, C. 2021 [1973]. 'Underdevelopment and Dependence: the Fundamental Connections.' *Review of Political Economy* 33 (1).

Furtado, C. 2021 [1974]. 'The Myth of Economic Development and the Future of the Third World.' *Review of Political Economy* 33 (1).

Hodgson, G. 2001. 'The Evolution of Capitalism from the Perspective of Institutional and Evolutionary Economics.' In *Capitalism in Evolution: Global Contentions—East and West*, edited by G. M. Hodgson, M. Itoh, and N. Yokokawa. Northampton, MA: Edward Elgar.

Kaplanoglou, G., and V. Rapanos. 2018. 'Evolutions in Consumption Inequality and Poverty in Greece: the Impact of the Crisis and Austerity Policies.' *The Review of Income and Wealth* 61 (1): 105–126.

Keynes, J. 1932. *Essays in Persuasion, edited by John Maynard Keynes*. New York: Harcourt, Brace and Company.

Keynes, J. 1936. *The General Theory of Employment, Interest and Money*. London: Macmillan.

Khanal, K., and N. Bracarense. 2021. 'Institutional Change in Nepal: Liberalization, Maoist Movement, Rise of Political Consciousness and Constitutional Change.' *Review of Political Economy* 33 (1).

Lampa, R. 2021. 'Capital Flows to Latin America (2003-2017): A Critical Survey from Prebisch's Business Cycle Theory.' *Review of Political Economy* 33 (1).

Lawson, T. 1997. *Economics and Reality*. London: Routledge.

Loureiro, P., F. Rugitsky, and A. Saad Filho. 2021. 'Celso Furtado and the Myth of Economic Development: Rethinking Development from Exile.' *Review of Political Economy* 33 (1).

Mendes, M. 2021. 'The Limitations of International Relations Regarding MNCs and the Digital Economy: Evidence from Brazil.' *Review of Political Economy* 33 (1).

Molina, D., and J. Peach. 2005. 'Mexico's Changing Distribution of Income.' *Journal of Economic Issues* 39 (2): 419–427.

Palludeto, A., and R. Borghi. 2021. 'Institutions and Development from a Historical Perspective: the Case of the Brazilian Development Bank.' *Review of Political Economy* 33 (1).

Peach, J., and R. Adkisson. 2020. 'Regional Income Inequality in the United States: 1969-2017.' *Journal of Economic Issues* 54 (2): 341–348.

Polanyi, K. 2001 [1944]. *The Great Transformation*. Boston, MA: Beacon Press.

Reuveny, R., and W. Moore. 2009. 'Does Environmental Degradation Influence Migration? Emigration to Developed Countries in the Late 1980s and 1990s.' *Social Science Quarterly* 90 (3): 461–479.

Sunna, C. 2015. 'Raúl Prebisch and the Keynesian Theory in Latin America.' In *Economic Development and Global Crisis: The Latin American Economy in Historical Perspective*, edited by Jose Luis Cardoso, Maria Cristina Marcuzzo, and M.E. Romero Sotelo, New York City, NY: Routledge.

Tamanaha, B. 2015. 'The Knowledge and Policy Limits of New Institutional Economics on Development.' *Journal of Economic Issues* 49 (1): 89–109.

Terra, F., F. Ferrari Filho, and P. Fonseca. 2021. 'Keynes on State and Economic Development.' *Review of Political Economy* 33 (1).

Waller, W. 1988. 'Radical Institutionalism: Methodological Aspects of the Radical Tradition.' *Journal of Economic Issues* 23 (3): 667–674.

Waller, W., and A. Jennings. 1991. 'A Feminist Institutionalist Reconsideration of Karl Polanyi.' *Journal of Economic Issues* 25 (2): 485–497.

Underdevelopment and Dependence: The Fundamental Connections*

Celso Furtado

May I start with an observation from modern history: the social formations characterized by great disparities in the spread of modern technology, sharp inequalities in labour productivity between urban and rural areas, a rather stable proportion of the population living at a physiological subsistence level, and increasing masses of underemployed people in the urban zones – i.e., the underdeveloped economies – are a particular feature of the way industrial capitalism has been growing and spreading from its inception. The industrial revolution took place inside an expanding commercial economy, in which foreign trade certainly was the most profitable economic activity. It was the combined impact of the sharp reduction in the cost of long distance transportation and of the insertion into commerce of a flow of new consumer goods springing from industry that gave rise to a new and complex system of international division of labour, provoking a profound reallocation of resources in different areas of the world. The study of underdevelopment starts with the identification of particular types of structures created in the areas where the new system of international division of labour allowed increases in the net product through changes in the use of the labour power already available.

My basic hypothesis is the following: underdevelopment was originally characteristic of economies in which an increase in labour productivity was largely the result of reallocation of resources aimed at obtaining static comparative advantages in international trade. Technical progress – partly in the form of more efficient methods of production and partly in the form of the introduction of new consumption goods – and the correlated process of capital accumulation which took place in those countries leading the industrial revolution, opened the way to significant increases in labour productivity in other areas, through geographical specialization. The latter type of increase in productivity can be obtained either without significant changes in the techniques of production (as in the case of tropical agriculture), or with significant changes but in the guise of an 'enclave' (as in the case of mineral production). The shift from subsistence agriculture into commercial agriculture does not necessarily presuppose a shift from traditional into modern agriculture. But if caused by foreign trade, such a shift generally entails a significant rise in the productivity of labour. Certainly the additional surplus may be fully appropriated from outside, as in the typical case of the colonial economy, but it may also be partially or mainly appropriated domestically. When this was the case, the surplus remaining in the country was basically used to finance a rapid diversification in the consumption habits of the ruling classes through the import of new products. It

*Originally published as: Furtado, C. 1973. 'Underdevelopment and Dependence: The Fundamental Connections.' *Centre of Latin American Studies Working Papers* 17.

was this particular use of the additional surplus that gave rise to the social formations that we now identify as underdeveloped economies.

Thus, from its inception, industrial capitalism caused certain countries (those leading the process of industrialization) to specialise in activities where technical progress, under the form of more efficient productive methods, penetrated rapidly whilst causing others to specialise in activities where such a form of technical progress was negligible, or to engage in a process of depletion of non-renewable natural resources. The 'law of comparative advantages' provided a valid justification for this international specialization but concealed the fact of the extremely uneven diffusion of progress in the techniques of production, as well as the fact that the new surplus created in the periphery was not geared to the process of capital accumulation. The surplus was mainly used to finance the diffusion in the periphery of the new patterns of consumption originating in the centre of the emerging world economic system.

Therefore, the relations between 'central' and 'peripheral' countries in the framework of the global system created by the international division of labour have been much more complex than appears from conventional economic analysis. A fundamental aspect often overlooked is the fact that the peripheral countries were rapidly transformed into importers of new consumer goods which were the fruit of capital accumulation and technical progress in the central countries. This process of adopting new patterns of consumption was bound to be a very uneven one as the additional surplus remained basically in the hands of a restricted minority, whose relative size depended on the agrarian structure, the relative abundance of land and labour, control of trade by foreigners or natives, the role of the state, and similar factors. Generally speaking, the benefits of the increase in productivity were appropriated by a small minority, a fact which permitted a sharp increase in the income available for the consumption of the privileged groups. Furthermore, the process of reallocation of resources and complementary capital formation (opening of new lands, building of feeder roads, rural construction, etc.,) required few imported inputs. When a completely new infrastructure had to be built, as in the case of the railroads, foreign financing would be the rule. Finally, the importing trade was in the hands of foreign firms seeking to make a profit out of the novelties introduced into the local market. Therefore, the importation of consumer goods for the privileged groups was bound to increase rapidly. The ultimate result of all this was the creation in the periphery of a cultural dualism that would make the elites feel exiled even in their own countries.

The existence of a ruling class tied up with consumption patterns similar to those in countries where the level of capital accumulation was much higher and geared to a culture focusing on technical progress became the basic factor in the evolution of the peripheral countries. If we bear in mind this fact – and I assume that it is grounded on historical evidence – we realize that in the study of underdevelopment the precedence of analysis at the level of production *vis-à-vis* analysis at the level of circulation frequently alluded to in the Marxian literature, does not hold. To grasp the origins of underdevelopment and to comprehend the process of reproduction of its structure, it is necessary to focus simultaneously on the process of production (reallocation of resources producing an additional surplus and the appropriation of such a surplus) and on the process of circulation (adoption of new patterns of consumption copied from countries at higher levels of capital accumulation, which in its turn generates cultural dependence). There is no doubt that the key to understanding the appropriation of the additional surplus obtained through foreign trade is the study of the institutional matrix determining the internal social relations of production. However, the utilization of such a surplus, which is the key to understanding the reproduction of the social formation, will be strongly influenced by the process of cultural domination operating at the level of the external relations of circulation.

Let us call *modernization* this process of adoption of more sophisticated patterns of consumption (private and public) which occurs without the corresponding process of capital accumulation and technical progress in productive methods. The larger the scope of modernization (and this includes military as well civilian forms of consumption) the stronger tends to be the pressure to increase the surplus, either expanding exports or increasing the rate of exploitation, that is the proportion of the surplus in the net product. In other words: due to the fact that pressure towards the adoption of new patterns of consumption is kept very high (it stems from technical progress, the accumulation of capital, and the consequent diversification of consumption, going on in the central countries) the internal social relations of production are shaped in such a way that the surplus is maximized. When the country reaches the point of diminishing returns in the traditional agricultural exporting sector and/or faces a decline in the terms of trade, tensions in the balance of payments are bound to show up on an increasing scale.

The significance of the modernization process in the shaping of an underdeveloped economy will be fully apparent in a more advanced phase, that is, when the country gets into the process of industrialization; namely, when it starts building up a new apparatus of production catering to the internal market. In effect, the techniques embodied in the equipment imported will not be related to the level of capital accumulated but to the demand profile (the degree of diversification of consumption) of the modernized sector of the society. It is this particular orientation of technical progress and its lack of connection with the degree of capital previously accumulated that gives a specific character to underdevelopment in the phase of industrialization. By requiring the adoption of capital-intensive methods of production, it strongly contributes to keeping real wages at subsistence levels. This allows the rate of exploitation to augment with increases in productivity. Because dependence shapes the behaviour of social groups appropriating the surplus in such a way that the social inequalities tend to increase as a consequence of capital accumulation, one can speak of it as the prime mover in the process of reproducing the social formations characteristic of underdevelopment. Approaching the problem from another angle: in the underdeveloped economies, the major factor governing income distribution, and therefore relative prices and the real wage rate in the industrial sector, seems to be the pressure generated by modernization to keep up with the rich countries' moving patterns of consumption. From this pressure stems both the need for a rapid diversification of consumption and the orientation of the technology adopted. It is this, and not the elastic supply of labour, that determines the differential between the industrial wage rate and the wage rate in the subsistence sector and keeps such a differential stable. In fact, in spite of the abundance of labour, certain sectors of the industrial working class have succeeded in organizing, and in substantially increasing this differential. Thus, it is more exact to say that, given the level of organization of the working class, the pressure towards modernization determines the relative size of the surplus appropriated by the ruling classes.

The industrialization of a peripheral country tends to take the form of local manufacturing of those consumer goods which were previously imported, as is well known by all students of the so-called process of import substitution. Now, the mix of the basket of consumer goods determines, within relatively narrow margins, the productive methods to be adopted, and ultimately the relative intensity of capital and labour used in the system of production. Thus, if the production of wage goods increases, abundant resources (land and unskilled labour) are bound to be used more, and scarce resources (capital, skilled labour, foreign exchange) used less than if the production of the sophisticated goods imported to the modernized minority expands. To enhance the consumption of rich people – and this holds also for the developed countries – means in general to introduce new products in the basket of consumer goods, which implies paying for more research and development; whereas the increase in the consumption of the poor is mainly a problem of spreading the use of already known products whose production most probably is in a phase of increasing returns. There is a close correlation between the degree of diversification of the basket of consumer goods on the one hand, and the level of capital accumulated per employed person and the complexity of the techniques of production on the other. The higher the average per capita income of a country, the more diversified the basket of consumer goods of its average inhabitant, and the higher the amount of capital accumulated per employed person in that country. I submit, even if I am not in a position to demonstrate it now, that the same applies to the sectors of a society with different levels of income.

The process of transplanting consumption patterns, generated by the system of international division of labour imposed by the countries leading the process of industrialization, gave rise to economic systems where technical progress was first assimilated at the level of the demand for consumption goods, that is through the absorption of a flow of new products which are imported before being locally produced. Therefore, dependence may exist in the absence of direct foreign investment and is conceivable even in the relations of a socialist country with capitalist countries commanding the flow of new products and the techniques required to produce them, providing that the socialist country has been transformed into a cultural satellite.

I would go further and submit that a similar type of cultural colonization has played an important role in changing the nature of class relations in the more advanced capitalist countries. The idea, stated by Marx, that an increasingly acute process of class struggle, within the framework of the capitalist economy, would be a decisive factor in the making of a new society, can only make sense if we admit that the relevant social classes are able to generate independent visions of the world and are culturally autonomous in a significant way. In fact, in the *18th Brumaire of Louis Bonaparte*, Marx identified the small holders of French agriculture as an independent social class playing a decisive role precisely because they had their own culture. In the more advanced capitalist countries class cultural autonomy has been progressively destroyed and replaced by the hegemony of a culture geared to the forms of consumption of the upper income group. Once trapped in this situation, the working class tends to lose its cultural creativity and ideological autonomy. In other words, as soon as the ultimate objective of the worker is the attainment on the standard of living of the bourgeoisie, he behaves as a satellite of the dominant culture of the capitalist society.

In the case of the peripheral countries the process of cultural colonization stems from an alliance of the local ruling classes, interested in maintaining a high rate of exploitation, with the external groups controlling the international economy, mainly interested in enlarging the markets for the new products of the central countries. Once this connection had been established, the doors were open to the introduction of all the forms of 'unequal exchange' which historically typify the relationship between underdeveloped and developed countries. But to isolate them from the global process of cultural colonization is to miss the essentials of the problem.

In the empty spaces of the temperate zone, agricultural production for the world market developed in competition with similar production in the central countries engaged in rapid industrialization, using similar techniques. Abundance and quality of natural resources allowed for the creation of a sizable surplus per person employed, even if the wage rate had to be high to attract immigrants from areas of similar climate, mainly Europe. The way such a surplus was domestically appropriated, and the relative number of the privileged minority depended on the historical conditions prevailing in each particular area. Nevertheless, insofar as it came to be used to finance the adoption of the new patterns of consumption produced by industrialization abroad, a process of modernization took place. Dependence in this case does exist in the absence of the social formation that we have called underdevelopment. It is rooted in a persistent disparity between the level of consumption (including eventually part of the working-class consumption) and the level of capital incorporated into the productive apparatus. In this particular type of dependent economy, when industrialization gets into full swing, penetration of the multinational corporations is bound to be very rapid because of the sophistication of the technology generally required. The cast of Argentina has demonstrated that if, because of particular historical conditions, a belated process of industrialization is oriented towards import substitution, the economy will know periods of acute tension in the balance of payments alternating with others of protracted growth. The causes of such a situation are many and complex: domestic demand tends to compete for the traditional exporting agricultural surplus; the relative amount of imported input in global production tends to augment; the surplus appropriated from outside (by the multinational corporations) tends also to increase in relative terms; finally, the possibility of exporting cheap labour does not exist. As population increases, from such a situation may in the long run emerge a social formation akin to those prevailing in the typical underdeveloped countries. It seems quite evident that dependence is a phenomenon of a higher order than underdevelopment: if the transition from underdevelopment to development is hard to be conceived – out of historical accident – the inverse process seems a rather probable path in the particular above-mentioned case of aggravation of dependence.

At its inception, dependence took the form of a split in the demand for consumer goods. It was the process of industrialization, aimed at the substitution of imports that reproduced the split in the structure of the productive apparatus, characterized by the coexistence of capital-intensive industries, catering to the modernized minority, with traditional activities (rural and urban) catering to the mass of the population and to foreign markets. For the economist looking at an underdeveloped economy as a closed system, this phenomenon appears as a 'disequilibrium at the factors' level' provoked by fixed coefficients in the production function, that is by the 'inadequacy' of the technology being absorbed. He does not realize that the real phenomenon results from a global process that permeates all the relevant economic and social decisions in the peripheral country. If the patterns of consumption of the modernized minority have to keep up with those prevailing and rapidly evolving in the central countries, no policy aimed at 'adapting' the technology can alter the situation.

Putting things in a nutshell: to miniaturize in a peripheral country the industrial system of a contemporary developed economy (and this is what the process of import substitution in conditions of dependence tends to do), in other words, the industrial system of a country where the accumulation of capital has reached a much higher level is to create an apparatus of production with two sectors, each one geared to a very different level of technology. This problem was not present in the pre-industrialization phase because the diversification in the consumption of the modernized minority was covered by the additional surplus created by static comparative advantage in foreign trade. Therefore, in the phase of industrialization the so-called 'disequilibrium at the factors' level' is inherent to the condition of dependence and cannot be overcome if dependence is going to remain. Furthermore, taking into account that dependence is permanently reinforced through the introduction of new products whose production requires the use of more sophisticated techniques and higher levels of capital accumulation, it becomes evident that industrialization will only proceed if the rate of exploitation increases, that is, if income distribution keeps concentrating. In such conditions, growth tends to rely heavily on the ability of the ruling classes to force the majority of the population to accept increasing social inequality.

Rapid industrial growth, in the conditions of dependence, implies an intense absorption of technical progress in the form of new products and the new processes required to produce them. In the advanced phase of industrialization, technical progress is no more a matter of importing a certain type of equipment, but more a question of having access to the flow of innovations pouring from the central countries. Such conditions make it easy for the branches of multinational corporations to supersede the local firms, particularly in the industries geared to the social sectors whose demand is diversifying more rapidly.

More precisely: such a diversified demand would never be satisfied out of local production if the flow of technical innovations had to be paid at market prices. Access to a certain flow of technical innovations constitutes a necessary condition for growth based on the imitation of the patterns of consumption created in the central countries, and the new techniques are controlled by firms that find it more advantageous to expand throughout the world than to sell their present and future 'know how'. Working on the basis of blueprints and using amortized technology, multinational corporations can overcome some of the constraints imposed by the relative smallness of local markets and lack of external economies prevailing in the underdeveloped countries. Certainly, it will be particularly easy in countries with a sizable population and an abundance of natural resources. Accordingly, a precondition for keeping the momentum going in the process of industrialization oriented towards imitation of the patterns of consumption in the rich countries is the cooperation of the multinational corporation. Other channels of transmission of the technical progress required by this type of industrialization are more expensive and less accessible.

Thus, in the advanced phase of industrialization, control of the productive apparatus by foreign firms tends to increase and dependence becomes directly rooted into the

process of production. However, direct control by foreign groups of the system of decisions at the production level is not a necessary outcome of the evolution of dependence.
A strong local bourgeoisie or even a state bureaucracy may share in the control of the
productive apparatus and even maintain a dominant position in it. This makes it
easier to accept tighter social controls, which may be badly needed in the face of increasing social inequalities. But the presence of local groups, private or public, controlling
decisions at the production level, does not mean leas dependence, as long as the
system keeps reproducing the new patterns of consumption originating in the central
countries, just as if it were determined by a genetic code that cannot be changed from
inside the country. Experience has demonstrated that no social group sharing in the
appropriation of a surplus generated in the framework of dependence seems motivated
to play a politically autonomous role requiring a basic change in the cultural vision of the
process of development.

Certainly, things in real life are much more complex than any theoretical scheme can
suggest. As a rule, industries catering to the mass of the population (textiles, food,
leather) were the first to develop, both because they are technically simpler, and the
market for such goods is larger. But, with a wage rate determined at the beginning by
the living conditions prevailing in subsistence agriculture, the implantation of such
industries did not substantially change the general pattern of the underdeveloped
economy. This block of industries competes, to a large extent, with local handicraft activities; hence, their impact on the employment pattern is bound to be limited, as well as the
feedback effect on domestic demand. This explains the typical growth curve of the so-
called first phase of industrialization in the underdeveloped countries: namely, sharp
increase succeeded by a rapid tendency to levelling off. It is in the phase of 'import substitution', when the new industries cater for the expanding market of the modernized
minority, that a complete industrial system starts to emerge. But the smallness of the
local market may appear, in this phase, like an insurmountable barrier. High protection
and subsidies are not always sufficient to offset diseconomies of scale and the lack of
externalities. Furthermore, the share of the surplus appropriated from outside tends to
increase with the rapid penetration of the multinational corporations. Such a situation,
characterized by a slowing-down in the rate of growth and alarming pressure on the
balance of payments has been attributed, particularly in the United Nations publications,
to an 'exhaustion' of the process of import substitution. But behind these symptoms one
can easily detect a deep disparity – if compared with the developed countries – between
the life-style of the higher groups and the level of capital accumulation reached by the
country. This disparity was not an obstacle to growth in the phase of international specialization: in fact, it was an outcome of growth in the framework of a particular social
formation. Moreover, during the first phase of industrialization the main problem
seemed to be how to finance the new investments, a problem that found a solution in
importing capital, inflation and other ways. The real difficulties did show up only in
the more advanced phase of industrialization. How to overcome them has been the
main concern of the more industrialized underdeveloped countries in the last ten
years. As the smallness of the local markets was the most visible aspect of the
problem, schemes of regional integration were envisaged and presented as a definitive
solution. By enlarging the scope of the process of import substitution, they brought

about middle-term solutions without going to the roots of the problem, which is irrelevant to the size of the country, stemming directly from the process of dependence.[1]

Certainly, the growth of the multinational corporations is bound to introduce important changes in the peripheral economies, opening a new phase in their evolution. It is quite obvious, for instance, that the increasing costs in foreign exchange of the production geared to the domestic markets provokes additional tensions in the balance of payments of the respective country. This may block the process of industrialization, but most probably will force 'corrective' changes in the general orientation such a process. The extraordinary flexibility of the multinational corporations has been instrumental in finding solutions to the new problems, while preserving the local social structures. As a consequence of such readjustments a new system of international division of labour has been framed. Transactions between branches and the headquarters of the multinational corporations are replacing or complementing the traditional forms of international trade, which enables the peripheral countries to pay for their increasing requirements of technology with cheap labour. The forms of the new type of underdeveloped economy, growing on the basis of exports of cheap labour embodied in industrial products produced by foreign firms for foreign markets, are still in the making. However, given the proportion of the surplus appropriated from outside, there are no reasons to expect a reduction in the rate of exploitation as long as the ruling classes continue to synchronize the evolution of their consumption to the rich countries. In other words: if the general conditions generated by dependence are continued, the outward-oriented industrialization can only succeed if labour is cheap, that is, if the rate of exploitation remains high.

We can now see the continuity throughout the different phases of underdevelopment, that is, how the underdeveloped structure once created can reproduce itself. From the system of international division of labour, imposed by the countries leading the industrial revolution, came a surplus in foreign exchange that allowed the local ruling classes of other countries (peripheral to the system) – where no industrialization was taking place – to accede to the diversifying patterns of consumption produced by the intense process of technical progress and capital accumulation in the central countries. As a consequence, the peripheral countries increased the rate of exploitation without reduction in the real wage rate and independently of assimilation of new techniques of production and capital accumulation. Once a new demand profile was produced in the peripheral country and the exporting sector entered a phase of diminishing returns, industrialization started under the guise of import substitution. But having to miniaturize industrial systems derived from an advanced process of capital accumulation, and having to catch up with the ever-diversifying panoply of consumer goods, the peripheral countries had to

---

[1] More definitive solutions are coming now from different directions: (a) an effort to increase the rate of exploitation coupled with a speeding-up of the consumption expenditures financed out of the surplus; a higher rate of profit (particularly in the durable consumer goods industries), caused by economies of scale, fosters the inflow of foreign capital (so-called Brazilian model); (b) an effort to steer the industrial process towards foreign markets in the framework of a new system of international division of labour governed by the multinational corporations; (c) a reshuffle of the patterns of consumption and the resources available for capital formation. The last way does presuppose substantive changes at the political level, being only conceivable as part of a global effort aiming at ending the process of dependence. The first two ways make it possible to reconcile an increasing rate of exploitation with expansion of employment in the industrial sector, which brings about an increase in the average wage rate. Furthermore, the first one is only viable in countries with a large population and abundance of land, which makes the second the most easy to be generalized. Combinations of both are now being tried in many underdeveloped countries, the results ranging from proclaimed 'miracles' to frustrating failures.

increase their rates of exploitation: namely, enter into a process of concentration of income. Furthermore, the increasing cost of technology, coupled with the speeding-up of technical progress, opened the door to the penetration of multinational corporations, that accelerated and enlarged the diffusion of the new patterns of consumption, i.e., tightened up the process of dependence.

The essentials of the whole process are: the traditional institutional matrix geared to the concentration of wealth and income; the historical conditions represented by the emerging systems of international division of labour fostering foreign trade as a function of the interests of the economies leading the industrial revolution; the increase in the rate of exploitation, and the use of the additional surplus by the ruling classes causing a cultural split through modernization; the orientation of the process of industrialization as a function of the interests of the modernized minority creating the conditions to keep the real wage rate at subsistence level; the increasing cost of the technology required to keep up, through local production, with the patterns of consumption of the rich countries, which in turn fostered the control of the apparatus of production by the multinational corporations; the need to face up to the increasing cost in foreign exchange of the productive process catering to the domestic market forcing the export of cheap labour in the guise of manufacture products.

Underdevelopment is rooted in a specific connexion, created in a particular historical setting, between an internal process of exploitation and an external process of dependence. The more intense the inflow of new patterns of consumption, the more concentrated income tends to become. Thus if external dependence increases, the internal rate of exploitation also has to go up. Higher rates of economic growth tend to imply aggravation of both external dependence and internal exploitation. Therefore, higher rates of growth, far from reducing underdevelopment, tend to make it more acute, as it entails increasing social inequalities.

May I say, to conclude, that underdevelopment, to be comprehended, must be envisaged as a process, namely as a set of forces mutually determined and self-reproducing in time. Through it, capitalism has succeeded in spreading over important areas of the world, with a minimum of disruption of the traditional social structures prevailing in such areas. Its role in the building of the present world economic system has been fundamental, and its present dynamism is considerable: new forms of underdeveloped economies fully industrialized and/or oriented towards the export of manufactured products, are only now emerging. It is indisputable that it is a permanent feature of the capitalist system. Fundamental changes that might occur in the immediate future are likely to be caused by the social tensions begot by the increasing economic inequalities, not the lack of dynamism of the economic system.

Cambridge, November 1973

The Myth of Economic Development and the Future of the Third World*

Celso Furtado

Myths have exercised a strong rule over the human mind striving to understand the social reality. From Rousseau's dream of *le bon sauvage* to Marx's idea of the withering of the state, from Malthus' population principle to the Walrasian idea of a general equilibrium, the social scientists have always sought support in some postulate deeply rooted in their systems of value.

An example of this tendency to myth worship is given by the literature on economic development of the last quarter of a century: 90 per cent of it is grounded on the implicit idea that economic development, such as has been practiced in the countries that led the industrial revolution, can be universalized; more precisely: that the standards of consumption presently enjoyed by the population of the industrialized countries could be shared by the masses of population living and rapidly expanding in the Third World, provided that they work hard and behave well.

Aiming at translating such myth into operational norms, the economists have been scheming on capital accumulation and its interactions with an abstract technical progress, conceived out of any social context; on inter-temporal decisions concerning consumption and savings in abstract, and similar exercises. They never felt concerned about the cultural consequences of a boundless process of capital accumulation and still less about the long-term impact of economic decisions geared to private interest on the physical environment. And because they cling so much to such myths, the economists have been brought down to such a dramatic volte-face. Indeed, nothing less than the big depression of the thirties was necessary to stop the economists worshipping Say's law. The energy problem that has been brewing over the last ten years and now come to the fore may force the development economists to a volte-face as dramatic as that of the thirties.

The irritation provoked among most of the economists by the study *The Limits to Growth* prepared at the MIT for the Club of Rome is a clear indication that the profession begins to feel uneasy about the models built on the postulates of the mechanics of individual self-interest.[1]

I am far from espousing either the implicit conclusions or all the methodological features of this study, but I recognise its paramount importance for bringing into the open very fundamental problems that the development economist has been trying to ignore.

*Originally published as: Furtado, C. 1974. 'The Myth of Economic Development and the Future of the Third World.' *Centre of Latin American Studies Working Papers* 16.
[1] *The Limits to Growth*, D. H. Meadows, Dennis L. Meadows, Jørgen Randers, William W. Behrens III (Universe Books, New York 1972), and J. W. Forrester, *World Dynamics* (Cambridge, Mass., 1971).

And the information it conveys permits us to raise a set of questions that go deep into the problems of the future of the underdeveloped countries. Thanks to it, we now have, for the first time, the results of a systematic attempt aiming at disclosing the behaviour of the world economy as a whole over a long period of time. To be sure, highly elaborated and reliable models picturing the behaviour of national economies were already available.

In the last twenty years, a series of models have been built in the United States, aiming to forecast the long-term trends of the US economy and going into details on the probable trends of the demand for natural non-renewable resources. The Pallay Report of 1951 initiated a series of studies concerned with *resources for the future*. However, the projections submitted by such studies are based on the implicit hypothesis that the world outside of the United States is unbounded. Thus, the ultimate objective has been to anticipate how *dependent* the United States will be vis-à-vis the resources of this limitless world, and to appraise the impact on the prices of the main raw materials of other industrial nations' expanding demands.

Drawing on such studies, the US Department of the Interior has been publishing alarming data on the increasing dependence of the American economy on external supplies of basic materials. Of the 13 principal mineral products required by the economy, they say, all with one exception (phosphates) will depend on foreign sources for more than 50 per cent of the local supply, before the end of the century. In 1985, that is in eleven years, 9 of the 13 products will already depend for local supply more on external than on internal sources, whereas in 1970 only 5 were in such situation. A product like copper, a traditional item in American exports, and up to 1970 relying strictly on local production, at the end of the century will depend on foreign sources for almost 60 per cent of its supply. Sulphur, another conspicuous item of American exports, will be in an identical situation. But the most dramatic change concerns oil: from the biggest world exporter, the United States has become of the great importers. The data of the Minister of the Interior disclosed that the US imports of oil will most probably reach in 1985 a level four times higher than that of 1970, and at the end of the century eight times higher. Such were the trends before the recent explosion of oil prices. If we take into account the increase in prices, the projected value of the American imports of oil for 1985 would be twice as big as the total value of the American imports in 1970.

As a matter of fact, the study of the Club of Rome is not concerned with the problem of the progressive utilization by the industrial economies of the underdeveloped countries' reserves of natural resources, nor yet with the consequences for the latter countries of the predatory use of such resources. Attention was focused, in a straightforward manner, on this other question: what will happen if all the countries of the world pursue their present growth policies, and actually succeed in keeping their economies growing? The answer to this question leaves no room for ambiguity. Indeed, pressure on non-renewable natural resources and pollution of the environment will rise to such a point (or alternatively: the cost of controlling pollution will be so high) that the whole system will inexorably break down. Furthermore, the nature of the system is such (the past the present and the future are deeply interlocked) that the present main trends cannot be easily altered. The future has already been shaped (to an important extent) by decisions made in the past or being made today aiming at short-term objectives. Thus, pollution that has to be faced in the future is an offspring of decisions made in past years; the supply of labour at the end of the century has already been established by the rate of birth in recent years, and so on.

Information about all these questions has been available for some time, and the methodology underlying the projections does not entail great novelties. The breakthrough stems from the fact that for the first time an economic system at a planetary scale has been built. The convenient hypothesis of a limitless outer environment has been dropped, and this very fundamental stop brought to the fore a simple truth that modern man strives to elude, namely: the unescapable fact that the civilization process, most particularly the variant of this process engendered by the industrial revolution, has an acutely predatory character. The hard fact of life is that in our civilization creation of economic *value*, as a very general rule, provokes irreversible processes of degradation of the physical world. To quote one of the few economists who has cared about this problem—Professor Georgescu-Rogen—

> Some economists have alluded to the fact that man can neither create nor destroy matter or energy – a truth which follows from the First Law of Thermodynamics. Yet no one seems to have been struck by the question – "what then does the economic process do?" All that we find in the cardinal literature is an occasional remark that man can produce only utilities, a remark which actually accentuates the puzzle ... Let us consider the economic process as a whole and view it only from the purely physical viewpoint. What we must note first of all is that this process is a partial process, is circumscribed by a boundary across which matter and energy are exchanged with the rest of the material universe. The answer to the question of what this material process does is simple: it neither produces nor consumes matter-energy; it only absorbs matter-energy and throws it out continuously. We may trust that even the fiercest partisan of the position that natural resources have nothing to do with value will admit in the end that there is a difference between what goes into the economic process and what comes out of it ... From the viewpoint of thermodynamics, matter-energy enters the economic process in a state of *low entropy* and comes out of it in a state of *high entropy*.[2]

To express in a few words what Prof. Georgescu-Roegen said: through the economic process man transforms available or free energy, over which he has almost complete command, into unavailable or bound energy which he cannot possibly use. And such a process is an irreversible one. The immediate impulse of the man born in this century of dazzling progress is to react: such dooming prophecies have been frequent among the economists from the times of the dismal science, but the facts are there: technical progress has coped with all such problems and economic growth has been proceeding steadily. Moreover, this is the first time we deal with a global closed system, whereas the old quarrels between optimists and pessimists stemmed from fragmentary observation. To state the issue clearly: man's continuous tapping of natural resources is a cumulative process and only now are we prepared to measure its long-run repercussions. Acceleration of technical progress by itself will not make our civilization less predatory; indeed it could accelerate the tapping of non-renewable resources and the flow of polluting waste.

But it is not my intention to elaborate on this fundamental yet remote problem of the destiny of our civilization. Man's psychology is such that he cannot be consistently interested in problems that outrange a rather shallow time horizon. My problem is much more immediate: I am concerned with the global trends of the world economy, focusing

---

[2]Nicholas Georgescu-Roegen, The Entropy Law and the Economic Problem. Distinguished Lecture Series No. 1, University of Alabama, 1970.

on them from the viewpoint of the underdeveloped countries. Looking at the model from this angle we immediately realize its lack of realism. In fact, it appears highly doubtful whether a model that reflects the behaviour of the industrialized countries could be used to project the long-run trends of the process of industrialization at a planetary scale. In other words: the structure of the model has been built on the basis of information drawn on the process of industrialization of the countries which are now highly industrialized. The authors are very explicit on this point: 'The basis of the method', they say, 'is the recognition that the *structure* of any system – the many circular, inter-locking, sometimes time-delayed relationships among its components – is often just as important in determining its behaviour as the individual components themselves' (p. 31). And they add later on: ' ... high level of aggregation is necessary at this point to keep the model understandable ... National boundaries are not recognized. Distribution inequalities of food, resources, and capital are included implicitly in the data but they are not calculated explicitly nor graphed in the output'.

The relevant question to be raised is the following: do we have sufficient knowledge of the structure of the world economy in order to project its main trends on the long run? For example: can we accept as meaningful a statement like this: 'as the rest of the world economy develops economically, it will follow basically the US pattern of consumption'? (p. 109). The uncritical acceptance of such a postulate reveals an absolute ignorance of what has been specific to the underdeveloped countries from the inception of the industrial revolution. It forces us to think about underdevelopment as a feature of the so-called young countries; to conceive the development process as a sequence of necessary phases à la Rostow. This doctrine has exercised a strong rule over public opinion in the industrialized countries, but it is in contradiction with the empirical knowledge we now have of the underdeveloped countries.

Underdevelopment is certainly a very complex problem. But it has nothing to do with the fact that a country or a society is old or young. It can better be described as a series of imbalances caused by technological heterogeneity introduced by a certain type of external relation which always involves dependency. When the system of international division of labour created by the Industrial Revolution emerged, certain countries specialized in activities where technical progress penetrated rapidly and others specialized either in activities where technical progress was negligible, or in simple exploitation of non-renewable natural resources. The fact that trade was profitable to both types of countries concealed the extremely uneven diffusion of technical progress. Two types of economies came out from this process: economies producing and controlling technology and exporting manufactures, and economies where technical progress penetrated from outside, mainly as a flow of new consumption products, and exporting raw materials. The asymmetrical relations prevailing between these two types of economies are responsible for the perpetuation of underdevelopment.

Doubtless we are far from having a complete knowledge of underdevelopment as a self-perpetuating process. But we know enough about it to doubt that the evolution of the underdeveloped economies will reproduce the past evolution of the present-day industrialized economies. Indeed, the process of industrialization of the countries in the periphery of the capitalist world, which took place in the last quarter of a century – industrialization based on import substitution to the benefit of small minorities and on the exploitation of cheap labour in exporting industries – such a process has been fundamentally distinct from the forms of industrialization of the dominant centres of the world economy. But, it was this latter pattern, pictured in the statistics of the developed economies covering this century up to 1970, that was reproduced in the structure of the model.

Industrialization in the leading capitalist countries – industrialization during the advanced phase of capitalism – has been based on an intense diffusion of the benefits of technical progress, that is, on the building up of mass consumption markets. Such a process of industrialization took place inside the framework of national economies and brought about an increase in the cost of labour (in terms of final product) parallel to the rise in labour productivity. In other words: the pattern of functional income distribution remained stable. Whether in an early period of the development of the capitalist economies the share of labour in net income decreased or increased, is a problem to which we have no easy answer. But it can be demonstrated on the basis of empirical evidence that, in the course of the last one hundred years, a parallel expansion in the real wage rate and in labour productivity at a national level has been a main feature of industrial capitalism. Because income tends to remain highly concentrated – as concentrated as it was a century ago when average productivity was much lower – the development of such economies relies heavily on the introduction of new products. In effect, if the average propensity to consume of high-income people is not to decline, a flow of new products – that is, more sophisticated forms of satisfying human necessities – must be poured into the markets. On the other hand, expansion of mass consumption, consequent on the increase in real wages, opens the door to economies of scale, the second prime mover of the industrial economies.

The recent experience of countries like Brazil and Mexico has demonstrated that such a model of industrialization is far from being reproduced in the periphery of the capitalist world. Adoption of the life style of the rich countries by the ruling minorities of the peripheral countries requires so acute a concentration of income that the process of industrialization tends to be basically different. It takes the form of 'import substitution', that is the local manufacturing of the same articles which were previously imported. Now, the quality of the basket of consumer goods determines, within relatively narrow margins, the productive processes to be adopted, and ultimately, the relative intensity of capital and labour used in production. Thus, the peripheral country getting into full industrialization is bound to face a slow absorption of labour in the sectors where productivity is increasing. Consequently, the wage rate is bound to remain stable, even in the sectors benefitting from rapid productivity increase, while the income of the propertied groups and other privileged people sharing in the surplus increases in absolute and relative terms.

Thus, industrialization tends to foster income concentration in the peripheral economies. In other words: in order to keep the pattern of consumption of the rich minorities diversifying, industrial technology has to be geared to the most sophisticated processes coming out in the highly capitalized economies, notwithstanding the much lower level of capital accumulation of the peripheral country. In effect, because 5 per cent of the Brazilian population is enjoying the highly diversified forms of consumption corresponding to an average income of 4,000 dollars in a rich country, whilst the average income in Brazil is about 400 dollars, 80 per cent of the total Brazilian population have to be completely excluded from the benefits of increases in labour productivity. This impinges on the process of industrialization, causing an industrial structure not only different from what can be found in the developed countries today, but still more different from what existed in such countries when they had reached the level of capital accumulation now prevailing in the peripheral countries. In effect, there is evidence that income is much more concentrated now in countries like Brazil and Mexico than it was in the developed countries during the first phase of their industrialization. Furthermore, concentration of income is apparently accelerating in those peripheral countries getting into a more advanced phase of industrialization. For example: during the decade of the 60s average productivity, that is income per head, increased one third in Brazil, but all the benefits accrued exclusively to one person out of five, and the income of the rich minority (5 per cent of the population) increased three times more rapidly than the average.

To speak of trends in the world economy it would be necessary firstly to define the nature of the international economic relations we think will prevail. How will the prices of the commodities traded in the international markets be formed? Will the old forms of international domination, now under the guise of technical and financial cooperation of the multinational corporations, survive? What other forms of market power will emerge in the international scene? Secondly, we need some hypothesis on the degree of international mobility of labour. In some European countries the share of the labour force not integrated in the local society, that is supposed to belong in a permanent way to another country, is approaching 10 per cent. Nobody knows how far this process can go, but it seems unlikely that international mobility of labour will increase much more. Therefore, demographic pressure on local natural resources is not bound to provoke important international movements of population.

However, rather than focusing on the present changes in the economic international relations or on the evolution of the world demographic structure – matters to which I will refer later – I intend to approach a more neglected but not less fundamental problem, namely: the qualitative difference between central and peripheral capitalism, and its implications from the viewpoint of the present and future structure of the world economy. I have stressed the fact that the dynamism of central capitalism stems from the flow of new products being introduced and from the permanent expansion of mass consumption. Quite differently, peripheral capitalism is based on cultural imitation and depends on concentration of income to grow. Disregard for the existence of such a fundamental disparity between the two parts of world capitalism is the most important single factor responsible for the lack of realism of the models featuring the structure of the world economy. Indeed, if we take into account that the enormous demographic expansion expected to proceed up to the middle of the next century is in practice confined to the peripheral countries, we immediately realise the importance of such a disparity in any attempt to project the behaviour of the world economy in the long run.

Once the existence of a world capitalist economy with a homogeneous structure is postulated, catastrophic conclusions show up almost necessarily. This shortcoming distorts the only thing we know for sure about the industrialization in the periphery of the capitalist system, namely: that the masses of the population have no access to the fruit of the increment in labour productivity. A model assuming that no more than 5 per cent of the thousands of millions of human beings living in the peripheral countries will indeed have access to the American Way of life, while 95 per cent stay near to a subsistence level, would certainly produce quite a different set of conclusions.

Demographic expansion is bound to proceed in the peripheral countries as long as there exists an open frontier of farm land – a situation that prevails, as a general rule, in most of Latin America, tropical Africa and certain regions of southeast Asia – or as far as intensification in land use can be secured with small increases in cost of production in terms of hours of unskilled labour. The glaring ignorance of such institutional factors commanding the use of farm land is evident in statements like this, that can be read in the above-mentioned study: 'If good fertile land were still easily reached and brought under cultivation, there would be no economic barrier to feeding the hungry and no difficult social choice to make' (p. 52). Now, in Brazil, in spite of the fact that fertile land still not used could be easily reached, a sizable part of the rural population presents all the symptoms of undernutrition. In fact, in Brazil as well as in other Latin American countries it is usual to find side-by-side people piled up in tiny plots of land, too small to absorb the labour force of a family, and big latifundia farming less than one tenth of the arable land they have. Actually, since the bulk of the peripheral countries population lives near a subsistence level and no important change in this situation can be reasonably anticipated, one can assume that demographic evolution on in this part of the world will continue to depend basically on the supply of farm land inside the frontiers of each country. Therefore, abundance of unused farm land in a country does not preclude the existence of a Malthusian situation on the other side of the front and yet occasional catastrophes such as the one now striking a group of countries in West Africa. There is no ground to expect that catastrophes of this type have more than a local impact.

As regards the group of countries of central capitalism it is misleading to speak of an exponential increase in the demand for raw materials independent of demographic increase. The problem here is much more of depletion of domestic resources and increasing dependence vis-à-vis external sources, as we have said. A low rate of demographic expansion combined with a very high level of per capita income produces sluggish demand for raw materials, particularly raw food, while the possibility of recycling basic metals is stepped up. For example: consumption of copper per inhabitant in the United States increased more than three times from 1900 to 1950, but remained stable from 1950 to 1970. On the other hand, consumption of basic metals per inhabitant presents a similar level in a group of highly industrialized capitalist countries (a group including the United States, Occidental Germany, Japan, Sweden, Switzerland) in spite of the fact that between such countries the difference of per capita income is as big as 1–2. No doubt, demand for most of the raw materials increased in the international markets at a rather high rate during the last three decades. But this fact is linked to the depletion of domestic resources in the industrialized countries, particularly the United States, and to the fact that the process of industrialization in West Europe and Japan had been considerably delayed during the first half of the century, vis-à-vis the United States. However, once this gap closed, one must expect that an asymptotic curve of demand similar to that prevailing in the US economy during the last quarter of a century, will show up.

Had I the necessary means to project separately the present trends of the two main parts of the world capitalist economy, taking into account the specificities of each one, results much more realistic than those of the study we are considering would certainly show up. The collapse of the global system in a few decades is a spin-off of the implicit adoption of the hypothesis of a progressive generalization at a world scale of the present forms of living (and the consequent pattern of resources waste) of the central capitalist countries. But a more detailed analysis of the behaviour of the world capitalist economy during the last quarter of a century points out quite a different set of trends: first, towards concentration of income and wealth benefiting the central economies, at a planetary scale, and second a still more accentuated concentration of income and wealth inside the peripheral countries benefiting the very small minorities which reproduce the patterns of living of the rich countries.

Let us approach the problem from its most alarming aspect: the demographic explosion. Population in the capitalist world is today roughly 2.5 billion (that is 25 hundred million). About 800 million live in the capitalist developed countries and 1.7 billion in the underdeveloped countries of the capitalist world. We know that the rate of growth of population in the first group of countries is tapering off and if we exclude the hypothesis of important migratory inflow, we can expect that such population will approach 1.2 billion a century hence. The picture of the other group of countries is much more complex. Nobody knows how more effective will be the Malthusian check of famine, disease, and the like, if the present trends of increasing population and income concentration proceed. But if we take into account the present-age distribution in which almost half the population is below child-bearing age, it becomes evident that high rates of growth will proceed during at least two generations. Personally, I believe that the Malthusian check is bound to be much more drastic in two generations, but I shall assume the rather alarming hypothesis that the population of the present capitalist underdeveloped world will keep doubling every thirty-three years for a century; namely, will increase from 1.7 billion to 13.6 billion. In other words: the population of the rich countries would be multiplied by 1.5 and that of the poor countries by 8. The total population of the capitalist world would increase from 2.5–14.8 billion, that is would multiply by 5.9.

I will distinguish two forms of pressure on the resources. I call the first Malthusian check: it refers to the availability of farm land to be used in the context of subsistence agriculture. The scarcity of this type of land can be aggravated by a rapid expansion of cash-crops which reduce the real income of the peasants. The second type of pressure is caused by the increase in the level of consumption, and is basically the result of the adoption of the patterns of consumption of the rich countries. It is this second type of pressure that is behind the alarming results of projections such as those we have mentioned. But if this pressure is a function of the increase in real income (more precisely of the real income of people reproducing the patterns of consumption of the rich countries), to measure its increase we must limit our observation to the minority that is really integrated in the American way of life. If the present structure of the system is to remain, this minority would pass from 85 million to 680 million. Therefore, the ensemble of the population with access to the advanced forms of consumption would increase from 885 million to 1,880 million, that is it would little more than double. In sum: the population of the capitalist world is bound to increase almost 6 times a century hence, but the part of this population causing pressure of the second type on limited resources, would only double.

The proportion of the privileged minority in the capitalist world as a whole is shrinking. In the period we are considering, it is bound to decline from 35 to 13 per cent, if we assume the hypothesis that the structure of the system will remain stable.

The inevitable conclusion that emerges from these considerations is that the style of life created by industrial capitalism will always be a preserve, accessible only to a minority. Any attempt to generalize such a style of life would precipitate a collapse of the system as a whole. The implications of this conclusion are of a far-reaching kind. In effect, it is now apparent that what we have been calling *economic development* – namely a policy aiming at bridging the gap between the standards of living of the poor and rich countries – is nothing more than a myth. It has now been clearly established that the countries of the Third World will never be developed, if we mean by this to have access to the standard of living of the developed countries of today. Any attempt to fill the gap between the poor and the rich countries within the framework of the present system does add pressure in a dramatic way on non-renewable resources. There-fore, the present form of development tending to exclude the big majority of the popu-lation of the Third World of the fruits of labour productivity increase, is much more than a simple accident. It can be interpreted as an inherent feature of the system, since it is a necessary condition to cope with the increasing inelasticity in the supply of non-renew-able resources.

Yet to identify the structural tendencies of a social system alone is far from being sufficient in order to forecast its future. History is a process open to human intervention. No one can a-priori exclude far-reaching changes in the present structure of the world capitalist system and, in particular, mutations in the internal structures of some of the underdeveloped countries. The recent events concerning the relative prices of raw mate-rials and manufactured products in the international economy may be one of these changes with far-reaching repercussions in the allocation of resources on a planetary scale. However, this particular change by itself is not bound to affect the present trends of the world capitalist economy. The fact that some oil countries are going to receive a bigger part in the net product of the world economy does not imply necessarily basic modifications in the way resources are used now. Doubtless, such change will most probably allow the incorporation of a bigger share of the population of the benefited countries into the minority with access to the American way of life. This will entail a change, indeed a slight change, in the distribution of income inside the privileged minor-ity. Equally irrelevant, from the point of view of the structural tendencies of the system, is the present process of transfer of industries from the centre to certain segments of the periphery of the capitalist world economy. Such a decentralization helps to cope with the problems of pollution and shortage of labour in the centre of the system. But because it is basically grounded on the exploitation of cheap labour by branches of cor-porations geared to the centre of the system its impact on the world distribution of income is bound to be rather limited.

But there is another kind of change which can become increasingly important in the peripheral countries. I am referring to deep structural changes caused by the awareness of the increasing social inequalities emerging between countries and, still more important, inside the underdeveloped countries. In a recent article Robert L. Heilbroner hinted that

> Even the most corrupt governments of the underdeveloped world are aware of the ghastly resemblance of the world's present economic condition to an immense train, in which a few passengers, mainly in the advanced capitalist world, ride in the first-class coaches, in con-ditions of comfort unimaginable to the enormously greater number crammed into the cattle cars that make up the rest of the train's carriages.[3]

---

[3]Robert H. Heilbroner, *The Human Prospect*. The New York Review of Books, January 24, 1974.

All the evidence points to the aggravation of this situation, as patterns of consumption of the privileged minorities go on diversifying and the population in the periphery of the system goes on expanding.

We do not have a theory of history and such a theory may even be a logical impossibility. But I shall submit that the most probable outcome of the present trends, in the peripheral countries, is eruption of a series of political upsurges aiming to cope with the alarming rise in social inequality. The question I want to raise is that: will such changes unleash an increased pressure on non-renewable resources, therefore contributing to the above-mentioned collapse of the world economy? If the objective of such changes is to enlarge the relative number of those sharing in the American way of life, it is evident that pressure on resources is bound to augment. But this could only be feasible if the underdeveloped countries concerned succeeded in catching up with the presently developed countries, which is only conceivable in the case of rather small countries drawing heavily on non-renewable natural resources, such as the oil economies. In the case of the big peripheral countries such a catching-up would require so enormous a process of capital accumulation that no one can imagine to be possible. And, as the socialist countries have learned in the last fifty years, to catch up in this case does not mean to reach a certain level of living; it means to reach simultaneously a certain level of consumption and a certain rate of growth.

It seems more likely that the social mutations that are bound to emerge in the underdeveloped countries will provoke significative changes in the general orientation of the process of development. In a country like Brazil, where 1 per cent of the population appropriates a part of the national product as big as that shared by half of the population, any effort to reduce social inequality would imply cutting the consumption of the rich minority, which would have far-reaching implications. Indeed, it is difficult to imagine relevant social changes in the underdeveloped countries, without changing the global vision of economic development.

But it would be naïve to assume that a change in the vision of economic development is sufficient to exempt an economy from predatory tendencies in relation to the environment. What social group will have the responsibility of defining the social welfare function? On what ground will the immediate advantages be compared with future advantage, the interests of this generation with those of people not yet born? On decisions like these depend the conservation of non-renewable resources and the accumulation of pollutants. Doubtless capitalism stirs up predatory behaviour in social life, but by no means is it the ultimate source of such forms of behaviour.

It seems likely that the underdeveloped countries under the social tension created by increasing economic inequality and trying to cope with the problem of scarcity of resources will be forced into a process of thorough social reconstruction, from which one may expect that societies will emerge much more egalitarian than those now existing in the centre of the capitalist system, having been created by capitalism from the inception of the industrial revolution. This is a point of far-reaching importance, and nothing is more peculiar to capitalism than its tendency towards rapid diversification of consumption which requires an income which is highly concentrated.

A point that can hardly be overemphasized is that a system based on permanent diversification of consumption and rapid obsolescence is inadequate to cope with the problem of misery in the periphery of the capitalist world. As long as the patterns of consumption orienting the allocation of resources are dictated by rich minorities conditioned from outside, no possibility exists of simplifying consumption to attend the needs of the whole of the population. But if allocation of resources is geared to social criteria, technical progress can be focused on the economy of resources so as to prolong the life of all kinds of commodities. It is in this particular sense that we can expect a reduction in the present squandering of non-renewable natural resources from social changes in the peripheral countries. But this does not mean necessarily that pressure on non-renewable resources will be smaller, hence the increase in the consumption of the masses is bound to make up for the reduction in the consumption of the elite. All we can say is that such a pressure would be much less than would be the case if the present patterns of consumption of the developed countries had to be generalized in the periphery of the capitalist system.

Furthermore, it is unlikely that a reorientation of the process of development would take place without other important structural changes. For example: a great reduction in the present degree of external dependency is likely to be expected. Once the local sources of natural resources (including farming soils and irrigation water) come to be locally controlled and geared to the new objectives of development, one must expect significant changes in the international prices of the basic products on the lines of those now occurring.

On the other hand, an international minimum price of labour – defined in terms of a basket of goods internationally traded – will most probably emerge from agreements between the peripheral countries where exporting industries are developing under the control of multinational corporations. In sum: the old fiction of an international economy, ruled by economic mechanisms, is bound to give to a new conception in which the political factors conditioning the appropriation of resources in a world scale will come to the fore.

From all this one must expect changes in the world distribution of income in favour of the peripheral countries, and modifications in the overall pattern of development entailing reduction in the process of accumulation in the rich countries and a concomitant speeding-up of the same process in the peripheral economies. If we admit that development in this second group of countries tend to be reoriented to economize resources and extend the life of all commodities, the outcome of the transfer of income has to be positive from the point of view of pressure on resources.

In synthesis: a more accurate analysis of the structure of the world capitalist system brings out that the vast majority of the population in the peripheral countries are and tend to remain excluded from the fruits of technical progress and capital accumulation. On the other hand, to envisage important social changes in the peripheral countries is to expect a full reorientation in the process of development; more precisely, a progressive reshaping of the system of priorities, aiming to satisfy those necessities that are common to the great majority of the population. In both cases – persistency of the present trend towards increasing inequality or emergence of important social changes entailing reduction of inequality – pressure on non-renewable resources is bound to be much smaller than comes out from the projections of *Limits to Growth*. For the masses of the Third World the predicament is to stay where they are, while small minorities in their respective countries share *les douceurs* of the modern way of life, as long as they are not prepared to build for themselves a different destiny.

Trying to decipher in the present trends of the world capitalist economies a scenario that allows the masses of population in the peripheral countries to reach the level of consumption of the rich countries, immediately afterwards to face a doomsday, is a fantasy; as brilliant as one born in an electronic mind can be, but yet a simple fantasy.

Cambridge, 1974

Celso Furtado and the Myth of Economic Development: Rethinking Development from Exile

Pedro Loureiro ⓘ, Fernando Rugitsky ⓘ and Alfredo Saad-Filho ⓘ

ABSTRACT
This article introduces two previously unpublished working papers by the Brazilian economist Celso Furtado (1920–2004). Following a brief outline of his life and ideas, the arguments in the two papers are examined, taking into account their context and place in Furtado's evolving body of work. These two papers represent a crucial turning point in Furtado's thinking, highlighting his critical perspective on (under)development and laying the basis for four books that he would publish in rapid sequence. We stress Furtado's growing scepticism with the prospects for international development and global convergence, and his attempt to reimagine the meaning of development and the potential paths to development by peripheral countries. Furtado's approach to global capitalism in these two papers shed an even more critical light on its structure and evolution than his better-known works from the 1950s. Finally, the contemporary relevance of his ideas is illustrated by reference to their relationship with the current heterodox literature.

1. Introduction

Celso Furtado (1920–2004) was one of the most remarkable Latin American economists of his generation, and his thought has influenced policymakers and social movements in the region since the 1950s. It is, however, the fate of ideas emerging in the periphery that they tend to remain outside the dominant academic circuits; Furtado would have been a household name if he had written exactly the same books from the comfort of a wealthy English-speaking country. Since he came from Paraíba, one of the poorest states in Brazil, and led a nomadic existence including many years in exile, his ideas have remained unjustly neglected. By making available for the first time two working papers (WPs) written by Furtado, this issue of ROPE celebrates the centenary of his birth and the originality of his thought, and offers a small contribution to the decolonisation of political economy.

Most introductions to Furtado's thought begin with his best-known book, *The Economic Growth of Brazil* (*Formação Econômica do Brasil*, originally published in 1959).[1] The two papers published in this issue of ROPE offer an alternative entry point for two closely related reasons. First, they represent a crucial step in Furtado's career. They came out of his reconsideration of the prospects for development in the periphery in the light of the setbacks imposed by the military coups of 1964 in Brazil, and 1973 in Chile; they also prepared the ground for a series of works published between the late 1970s and the early 1980s, when Furtado returned to Brazil after years in exile. Second, the critical perspective in these two WPs has withstood the test of time even better than his earlier writings. This article introduces both papers to the readers of ROPE, locates them within Furtado's thought, and places them in the context of key debates in development then and now. In the following section, Furtado's life and ideas are briefly summarized. Section Three examines the main arguments in the two papers. Section Four assesses their contemporary relevance, and section Five concludes.

2. Furtado: Ideas and Significance of his Work

Celso Furtado played a key role in the rise of Latin American political economy in the 1950s. His work examines, from an interdisciplinary perspective, different aspects of the economy, society and politics in Latin America, with particular focus on Brazil.

Furtado originally trained as a lawyer, and he found employment in Brazil's rapidly expanding civil service. His interests gradually shifted towards economics and, following his military service during World War II, he obtained a PhD at the Sorbonne, in 1948.[2] Furtado spent the next decade in Chile, at the newly-formed United Nations Economic Commission for Latin America (ECLA, later ECLAC, with the inclusion of the Caribbean), working closely together with the Argentine economist Raúl Prebisch, who led the organization from 1950 to 1963. Throughout his professional life, Furtado remained strongly committed to a national democratic project for Brazil and other peripheral countries, including industrialization, national autonomy, distribution of income and wealth (especially land), and regional development. He welcomed the emergence of trade unions and strongly supported progressive movements led by workers, the emerging middle classes, the youth, the Church, and in the Armed Forces. He would pay a heavy price for his ideals.

Furtado believed that the economic development of the periphery had been traditionally driven by external demand for primary commodities, but this modality of growth had adverse implications for their balance-of-payments constraint, long-term economic performance and political independence. The only way to tackle these limitations was through industrialization, which would turn the domestic market into the main driver of growth and, eventually, help to consolidate the nation itself. From this perspective, Furtado examined the economic history of Latin America, the accomplishments of import-substituting industrialization (ISI) since the late 19th Century, and the bottlenecks that limited the development of the region and that tended to channel the gains

---

[1]For a recent assessment of the book, see Saes and Barbosa (2020).
[2]For details about his life, see d'Aguiar (2015), Bianconi (2014) and Furtado (1985, 1991, 2019). See also the chronology available in Tavares (2000, pp. 155–160), and the entry on him in *The New Palgrave Dictionary of Economics* (Boianovsky 2008).

from industrialization towards the rich – in his own words, 'industrialization based on import substitution to the benefit of small minorities and [based] on the exploitation of cheap labour in exporting industries' (Furtado, 2020b, p. 19).

His view of development lies at the cusp of two traditions. On the one hand, Brazilian modernism, a tendency emerging in the 1920s and affirming the value of national culture and the promise of progress, as opposed to the racist, colonial and agrarian mentality that had dominated the country since the 16th Century. On the other hand, structuralism, the ground-breaking strand of development economics that Furtado helped to elaborate at ECLA. Methodologically, Furtado's work draws upon historical analysis, observation, and the identification of empirical regularities. For him, this approach could offer both the key to an original interpretation of Brazilian society and the policy tools to enable its autonomous development.

Furtado's work was an integral part of the rise of development economics in the postwar era. He was influenced by the work of Lewis (1954), for whom developing countries have a large surplus of labour that can be attracted to high productivity urban sectors at the prevailing low wages. Structuralists claim that the surplus agricultural labour cannot be fully absorbed by the urban sector, which depresses wages both in urban areas and in agriculture itself. In order to address these limitations, structuralists argued that it was essential to lift productivity and wages. In addition to these internal blockages to development, the periphery also suffered from a long-term tendency of deterioration of its terms of trade vis-à-vis the centre, which transferred its productivity gains to the industrialized countries (see Boianovsky and Solís 2014; Saad-Filho 2005). To escape from this dilemma, developing countries should adopt bold state-driven policies to distribute income and wealth, industrialize, reduce regional inequalities, pursue national autonomy, and achieve self-sustaining growth.

Drawing upon this emerging approach, Furtado was the first economist to respond to Nurkse's (1953) lectures on development (Boianovsky 2010). Furtado (1952, pp. 24–25) welcomed Nurkse's extension of Duesenberry's demonstration effect to international economic relations, referred to its affinities with the work of US economic sociologist Thorstein Veblen, and outlined one of his own key contributions: the study of the relationships between aggregate supply and demand in the process of development. In these debates, Furtado attempted to historicize what appeared to him as abstract formulations (Boianovsky 2015, p. 429). That is the tone, for example, of his debate with Rosenstein-Rodan's (1963) notion of the 'Big Push' (Furtado 1963). In a textbook that he wrote for his development economics course at the Sorbonne, in the 1970s, Furtado (1975, pp. 279–280) claimed that the controversy about balanced versus unbalanced growth was misplaced, since each side was focusing on different phases of the trajectory of underdeveloped countries.

In 1957, Furtado accepted Kaldor's invitation to spend a year at the University of Cambridge – an invitation made after he told Kaldor that 'economic theory will not escape its current dead-end if there is no genuine breakthrough in the field of distribution' (Furtado 1985, p. 196). There, Furtado wrote his most famous book, *The Economic Growth of Brazil*, which remains a key textbook in Brazilian universities.

On his return to Brazil, Furtado was invited to chair SUDENE, a government agency created in 1959 to promote the development of the country's poor Northeastern region, which included Furtado's birthplace. Between 1962 and 1963 he served as Minister of

Planning in the government of President João Goulart (1961–1964), when he strongly advocated for democratic economic reforms. Goulart's government was overthrown by a military coup, and Furtado was on the first group of public figures to be persecuted. He left the country, and would spend several years in exile in Chile, the USA and, finally, in France.

The experience of defeat and exile drove Furtado to reformulate his views. In doing this, he was part of a larger trend noticed by Hirschman (1981, p. 20), for whom the 'political disasters that struck a number of Third World countries from the sixties on' led many progressive development economists to reconsider their theories:

> Experiencing a double frustration, one over the appalling political events as such, and the other over their inability to comprehend them, a number of analysts and practitioners of economic development were moved to look at the economic performance itself with a more critical eye than before. (Hirschman 1981, p. 21)

Across Latin America, this reformulation involved a close engagement with Marxism, that would lead to different strands of dependency theory (Saad-Filho 2005). In Brazil, the mid-1960 were a period of economic instability, high inflation, low growth rates and worsening political repression. In these adverse circumstances Furtado lost his earlier optimism, and his work increasingly stressed the stagnation tendencies in the economy (for an assessment, see Coutinho 2015, 2019). He also argued that ISI had been unable to address the economy's bottlenecks and that it had worsened Brazil's social problems. This led him to highlight the need for social policy and the distribution of income and land, both as necessary conditions for social justice and to permit a self-sustaining process of economic growth (Furtado 1965; see also Medeiros Filho 2020; Vieira 2020).

Furtado's stagnationism was misplaced: between 1968 and 1973 Brazil experienced an unprecedented economic boom, the so-called 'Brazilian miracle'. The boom was driven by abundant external loans, the explosive growth of domestic credit and the concentration of income enforced by the military regime, which dramatically expanded consumption among the privileged strata of the population. Furtado reassessed his views again, famously clashed with other dissident economists,[3] and shifted his critique of Brazilian development away from narrow economic notions of stagnation driven by underinvestment and underconsumption and, increasingly, towards an interdisciplinary approach encompassing economic theory, politics, sociology and culture; he also stressed the imperative of distribution to achieve social integration and national autonomy.[4]

This was more than a symptom of Furtado's growing scepticism that industrialization might deliver the economic development of the periphery: it represented a break with mainstream notions of 'modernization' that drove the privileged in the periphery to replicate the culture and patterns of consumption prevailing in the centre. Furtado claimed that this was untenable, and that even the attempt to do so would bring potentially devastating social, economic, environmental, and cultural consequences.

---

[3]The most famous debate on the 'Miracle' was initiated by Tavares and Serra's (1976) critique of Furtado stagnationist view. For a recent assessment, see Coutinho (2019); see also Cardoso and Faletto (1979) and Oliveira (1972).

[4]For example, in a debate in the late 1980s attended by one of the authors (ASF), Furtado argued strongly for interdisciplinary approaches in the social sciences, but cautioned that true interdisciplinarity cannot be achieved by working in large committees, but only through *individual* learning from different views, approaches, traditions and disciplines.

Furtado's commitment to a national development project and to a socially integrated and autonomous nation became increasingly prominent as he aged. He returned to Brazil in the early 1980s, and immediately joined the national campaign for democracy, which finally succeeded in 1985. He served as Minister of Culture in the first democratic administration, held other prominent positions in government, and would continue to debate economic and development policy until his death in 2004. His reputation remains extremely strong across Latin America, where his work and his life continue to inspire heterodox economists of all ages.

3. The Two Working Papers

Furtado's two stints in Cambridge were major milestones in his career. In his words, 'the University of Cambridge … has been for me, since the 1950s, a fundamental point of reference' (Furtado 1991, p. 190). In his first visit, in the late 1950s, Furtado had the goal of 'studying economic dynamics, with special emphasis on the theory of underdevelopment … revisiting the classical, neoclassical and Keynesian approaches to production, distribution and international trade' (Furtado 1985, p. 197). At Cambridge, Furtado studied the economic development of Asia and the Americas, and contributed to debates with Joan Robinson, Nicholas Kaldor, Piero Sraffa, Amartya Sen and others. In his memoirs, Furtado noted that these exchanges 'helped to shield me from the insidious forms of monetarism that sterilize contemporary economic thought, draining it of all concern with social issues' (Furtado 1991, p. 190). Feeling enriched after his engagement with high theory, Furtado would come full circle. As he completed *The Economic Growth of Brazil*, he concluded that economic development would require completing the process of industrialization and addressing the disparities within the country. His own priorities were clear, and he stated that 'this time, I returned to Brazil with a definite task' (Furtado 1985, p. 227): he would dedicate himself to the practical work of reducing regional inequalities. This was the prelude to his engagement with SUDENE, highlighting how Furtado was both a cosmopolitan intellectual and someone acutely aware of, and active upon, local issues (see Paula 2019).

Furtado returned to Cambridge under very different circumstances in 1973–1974. The limitations of ISI in Latin America had become strikingly clear, and a cloud hung over him after the military coup that deposed Chilean President Salvador Allende, on 11 September 1973. During this stay, Furtado was the Simón Bolivar Professor at the Centre of Latin American Studies, the sixth person to occupy this chair that has been held by Guillermo O'Donnell and two Nobel laureates, Octavio Paz and Mario Vargas Llosa. The two WPs included in this issue of ROPE were written during this period, that Furtado generally called his 'rambling years' of exile. They are marked by a heavy pessimism, illustrated by the lament in his diary entry for 31 May 1974: 'All the myths in which I believed! Can one believe in anything beyond myths? And are they myths, once we believe them?' (Furtado 2019, p. 233).

Furtado was never was a narrow-minded economist, but the two WPs written at Cambridge became milestones in his intellectual development, and they laid the basis for his work during the following decade. The WPs were originally published by the Centre of Latin American Studies, in a series that had a small print-only circulation, and was discontinued in the 1990s. They circulated only in a limited way, but strongly impacted those who read them. For example, Lall (1975, p. 805) based his critique of the concept of dependence on WP-17 (Furtado, 2020a), writing that 'The best statement of the consumption-distorted pattern of dependent development is by Furtado [in Furtado (2020a)]'. In turn, WP-16 (Furtado, 2020b) was probably read in Mexico, since it is mentioned in Combe (1977). There are a few other references to the WPs (e.g., Cunha and Britto 2018), but they are rare. This is the first time that these important works of Celso Furtado are made available to a wider audience, making it possible to examine this key moment in the evolution of his thought.

Furtado's writings in the decade following his stint at Cambridge include four books that, while remaining anchored in political economy, sought to build a transdisciplinary approach to development incorporating – most innovatively – the cultural and environmental dimensions of (under)development (see his autobiographical note in Furtado 1991, p. 190). The book *The Myth of Economic Development* (*O Mito do Desenvolvimento Econômico*), completed in 1974, is heavily indebted to the WPs. WP-16, which shares a similar title with the book, was substantially edited and spread throughout sections One, Two and Five of chapter I (called 'Structural tendencies of the capitalist system in the stage of the predominance of large corporations'). Compare, for example, these two formulations:

> Underdevelopment is certainly a very complex problem. But it has nothing to do with the fact that a country or a society is old or young. It can better be described as a series of imbalances caused by technological heterogeneity introduced by a certain type of external relation which always involves dependency. (Furtado, 2020b, p. 19)

> Capturing the nature of underdevelopment is not an easy task: many are its dimensions and the most easily noticeable are not always the most relevant ones. But if we know something for sure it is that underdevelopment has got nothing to do with the age of a society or country. And we also know that the parameter to measure it is the degree of capital accumulation applied to productive processes and the access to the panoply of final consumption goods that characterises what came to be known as the modern lifestyle. (Furtado 1974, p. 20)

WP-17 was re-worked into chapter II, which kept the original title. The book includes two further chapters, 'The Brazilian model of underdevelopment' and 'Objectivity and illusionism in economics'. An abridged version of this book was published in Portuguese, including only chapter I (and, hence, having little connection with WP-17). This abridged version has been translated into English and published by Polity Press (Furtado 2020c). The *Preface to a New Political Economy* (*Prefácio à Nova Economia Política*), published in 1976, and the *Brief Introduction to Development* (*Pequena Introdução ao Desenvolvimento*), from 1980, developed arguments advanced in the WPs. Finally, the cultural dynamics of reproduction and contestation of underdevelopment, which were also evident in the WPs, would flourish in his 1978 book, *Criatividade e Dependência na Civilização Industrial* (published in English as *Accumulation and Development: The Logic of Industrial Civilization*, although the closest translation would be *Creativity and Dependence in Industrial Civilization*).

Furtado stated in WP-17 that, in order to understand underdevelopment, one must focus on production as well as circulation, with the latter including the 'adoption of new patterns of consumption copied from countries at higher levels of capital accumulation, which in its turn generates cultural dependence' (Furtado, 2020a, p. 8). Furtado's focus on consumption and exchange would extend to his understanding of inequality, the definition of underdevelopment and the obstacles to development, which he revisited in the light of his earlier work. In doing this, Furtado vastly expanded the scope of his reflections, indicating that 'my objective was to develop a common language for the several branches of the social sciences, allowing development to be apprehended as the fulfilment of human potentialities' (Furtado 1991, p. 192) – which invites a (so far under-examined) dialogue with Amartya Sen's capabilities approach (see, e.g., Sen 1999).

In turn, Furtado welcomed the publication of the 1972 report to the Club of Rome, *The Limits to Growth*, and reproached the economic development literature for disregarding 'the long-term impact of economic decisions geared to private interest on the physical environment' (Furtado, 2020b, p. 16). He stressed that the 'acceleration of technical progress by itself will not make our civilization less predatory; indeed it could accelerate the tapping of non-renewable resources and the flow of polluting waste' (Furtado, 2020b, p. 18). However, Furtado also stated that the projections of resource use in *The Limits to Growth* were vastly over-estimated, because of the study's mistaken reliance on the hypothesis of convergence, that is, that the underdeveloped countries will catch-up with the level of income, the structure of distribution, and the pattern of consumption in the USA. For Furtado, this hypothesis 'reveals an absolute ignorance of what has been specific to the underdeveloped countries from the inception of the industrial revolution' (Furtado, 2020b, p. 19).

The WPs reveal Furtado's growing scepticism about the possibility of overcoming underdevelopment, even though he did not completely jettison his earlier ambition to find pathways to development. To be sure, in his previous works Furtado had always highlighted the specificity of underdevelopment, which – along the lines of dependency theory, and in contrast with the mainstream – he did not consider a 'stage' prior to development. Instead, he underscored the interdependence between development and underdevelopment and the challenges that this relationship posed to attempts to escape underdevelopment. Nevertheless, Furtado had previously understood that development was *possible*, at least in principle, through industrialization, structural reforms and other socioeconomic policies and processes. His change in perspective, beginning with the WPs, and developed in the coming decades, is encapsulated in the title of WP-16, which suggests that economic development is a *myth*. In his words, the 'myth' refers to

> the implicit idea that economic development, *such as has been practiced in the countries that led the industrial revolution*, can be universalized; more precisely: that the standards of consumption presently enjoyed by the population of the industrialized countries could be shared by the masses of population living and rapidly expanding in the Third World, *provided that they work hard and behave well* (Furtado, 2020b, p. 16, emphases added).[5]

The notion of linear progress and the closely related myth of economic development provided a meta-narrative holding the capitalist system together ideologically, and anchoring economic thought. However, the idea that continuing progress might be achieved is fallacious, since it 'has now been clearly established that the countries of the Third World will never be developed, *if we mean by this to have access to the standard of living of the*

---

[5] The striking sentence 'provided that they work hard and behave well' does not appear in the book.

developed countries of today' (Furtado, 2020b, p. 23, emphasis added).[6] This does not mean that Furtado had abandoned the notion of development; instead, he had concluded that development had to be rethought *from the periphery* in order to become achievable. In this sense, the periphery had a historical role driving human emancipation since, through creativity and the struggle against underdevelopment, 'one may expect that societies will emerge [in underdeveloped countries, that are] much more egalitarian than those now existing in the centre of the capitalist system' (Furtado, 2020b, p. 24).

By stressing in the WPs the agency of 'the masses of the Third World', Furtado counterbalanced his growing pessimism with an increasingly radical commitment to emancipation. He wrote in his diary on 31 May 1974: 'How sick am I with politics, after all I have come to know about Chile ... To what extent did vanity play a role in all that Allende did?' (Furtado 2019, pp. 233–234). In turn, he stated in WP-16 (Furtado, 2020a, p. 14): 'For the masses of the Third World the predicament is to stay where they are, while small minorities in their respective countries share *les douceurs* of the modern way of life, *as long as they are not prepared to build for themselves a different destiny*' (emphasis added).[7] Furtado thus recognized the mounting challenges faced by underdeveloped societies, but he did not surrender: instead; he changed his notion of development and identified the social agent – no longer the state or the investors – that could address that historical task.

This new perspective feeds a related set of changes in Furtado's thought: it is well-known that Latin American structuralism eschews the critique of capitalism in the centre, except for the argument that the economic relations with the centre prevent the development of the periphery (see, for example, Oliveira 1972, p. 9). This implies, somewhat paradoxically, that the structuralists criticize the global capitalist system because it produces a centre and a periphery but, implicitly, they assume that this polarization would be eliminated if the periphery became 'developed'. In his innovative critique of capitalism in the centre Furtado went a step beyond structuralism, and showed how the viewpoint *of the periphery* could expose the impossibility of development *for the entire system* – while, simultaneously, showing a way forward for the world (see also Albuquerque 2013).

This dramatic inversion of the terms of the development debate reveals the growing relevance of culture in Furtado's work. Culture and cultural change have always played a role in development studies, ranging from crudely racist, orientalist and paternalistic views to more sophisticated examinations of the richness of the traditions from the periphery; however, Furtado adopted a different perspective (Cunha and Britto 2018; Lins 2014; Paula 2019). First, he argued that underdevelopment was underpinned by, and reproduced through, cultural dependence, expressed in the mimicking of the consumption patterns of developed countries in the periphery, and the latter's growing technological dependence. Second, he explored how the process of development established new forms of rationality, not only the instrumental rationality focusing on efficiency and

---

[6]Arrighi (1990) would reach a similar conclusion. It is worth mentioning that in an unpublished early draft called 'The Limits to Economic Growth' (*Os Limites do Crescimento Econômico*), Furtado uses the term 'myth' only three times, all of which in the penultimate page. This suggests that, as Furtado deepened his critique of *The Limits to Growth*, he increasingly focused on the possibility of development and the corresponding challenges for underdeveloped countries, and came to the view that commonly-held notions of development were merely myths.

[7]This sentence in WP-16 is not present in the book.

accumulation but, also, the diffusion of new values. Third, and this is where the notion of 'creativity' operates as a counterpoint to the pessimistic turn in his analysis, the answer to economic, technological and cultural dependence should come through creative efforts taking place in the periphery. This implies that, for Furtado, the periphery must develop new forms of rationality, re-imagine social organization and define its own goals in order to foster innovation, stimulate technological change and overcome under-development. This conclusion illustrates the depth of Furtado's mature work, in which development is inseparable from the realization of human potentialities and, in order to become more than a myth, it must be creatively reimagined from the periphery.

One aspect of the WPs that cannot be reviewed in detail here for reasons of space is Furtado's critique of the impact of multinational corporations (MNCs) on development. He examined this issue for the first time in the 1960s, after his spell in the USA, and wrote about it in his 1966 book Underdevelopment and Stagnation (*Subdesenvolvimento e Estagnação*; see Boianovsky 2010; Coutinho 2015, 2019). He returned to this issue in the WPs and, even more strongly, in the 1974 book. They show Furtado's concern with the changing institutional configuration of global capitalism and the closely related (re)distribution of power, leading him to point out, long before this became fashionable, that intra-firm transactions were driving international trade:

> Transactions between branches and the headquarters of the multinational corporations are replacing or complementing the traditional forms of international trade, which enables the peripheral countries to pay for their increasing requirements of technology with cheap labour. The forms of the new type of underdeveloped economy, growing on the basis of exports of cheap labour embodied in industrial products produced by foreign firms for foreign markets, are still in the making. (Furtado, 2020a, p. 14)

Finally, it is worth pointing out two curious shortcomings of the WPs. First, perhaps as a sign of how much the world has changed in recent decades, Furtado suggested that 'it seems unlikely that international mobility of labour will increase much more. Therefore, demographic pressure on local natural resources is not bound to provoke important international movements of population' (Furtado, 2020b, p. 20). He also overestimated the rigidity of the distribution of income stating, for example, that income had remained 'as concentrated as it was a century ago when average productivity was much lower' (Furtado, 2020b, p. 19). These lapses reveal some pitfalls of generalising from past experience, but they do not compromise Furtado's analytical framework.

What might invite a more substantive debate is the extent to which Furtado's WPs can inform the analysis of the divergences between Latin America, Africa and East Asia. On the one hand, he still seems attached to the general scheme of industrialization in Latin America:

> The recent experience of countries like Brazil and Mexico has demonstrated that such a model of industrialization is far from being reproduced in the periphery of the capitalist world. Adoption of the life style of the rich countries by the ruling minorities of the peripheral countries requires so acute a concentration of income that the process of industrialization tends to be basically different. It takes the form of "import substitution". (Furtado, 2020b, p. 20)

On the other hand, he also offers pointers to a better understanding of the diversity of experiences in the periphery. His analysis of the implications of MNCs for the possibility of development, his focus on technological dependence and the role of creativity in overcoming it, and, as discussed below, his attention to the complex interactions between the productive structure, growth and distribution, can help to inform a sophisticated examination of the dynamics of development in the periphery.

4. Contemporary Relevance

Almost half a century after they were written, how relevant are these two WPs for our understanding of capitalism, both then and now? And, separately, how significant are they for our understanding of Celso Furtado's thought? In both senses, the WPs are the culmination of reflections that began in the mid-1960s (see, especially, Furtado 1965). At that time, focusing on what he called the tendency towards stagnation in the periphery, Furtado argued that the conventional models of development, for example Lewis (1954), disregarded the role of the patterns of consumption. For Lewis, development was mechanically reached through the transfer of labour from the subsistence sector to the urban capitalist sector, raising productivity and (given constant real wages) generating surpluses that would accelerate capital accumulation. Say's law is assumed to hold: whatever is produced in the capitalist sector will be sold. Furtado was not the first to question this claim; for example, Rosenstein-Rodan (1943) and Nurkse (1953) had already argued that, in the absence of a coordinated effort (the 'Big Push') to create a series of industries that would generate demand for each other's output, the growth of manufacturing production could be limited by the lack of demand.[8]

Furtado's approach was different. For him, it was essential to consider the dynamics of sectoral heterogeneity, since it played a key role in the reproduction of underdevelopment. Concretely, capital accumulation expanded the capitalist sector, altering its sectoral composition to reflect the pattern of consumption of the underdeveloped society. In the 1960s, a dualist market for consumption goods, characterized by the stagnant demand of the majority of the population and the rapidly diversifying and expanding demand of the rich minority, created incentives for the production of luxuries. Given the prevailing technologies this implied an increase in the economy's capital-output ratio which, in turn, would slow down the absorption of labour by the capitalist sector and reduce profitability. That is, in attempting to explain the tendency towards stagnation, Furtado ended up suggesting a more general cumulative process: cultural dependence and the prevailing distribution of income determined the pattern of consumption, which impacted the sectoral composition of output and employment, which fed back into the distribution of income and the patterns of consumption; in other words, the structures of demand and supply are mutually determining. Furtado states that:

> To grasp the origins of underdevelopment and to comprehend the process of reproduction of its structure, it is necessary to focus simultaneously on the process of production

---

[8]For them, the obstacle concerned the sectoral balances in the short-term, since they assumed that Say's law would hold in the aggregate:

> Although in backward areas Say's Law may be valid in the sense that there is generally no deflationary gap, it never is valid in the sense that the output of any single industry, newly set up with capital equipment, can create its own demand. (Nurkse 1952, p. 571)

(reallocation of resources producing an additional surplus and the appropriation of such a surplus) and on the process of circulation (adoption of new patterns of consumption copied from countries at higher levels of capital accumulation, which in its turn generates cultural dependence). (Furtado, 2020a, p. 8)

The implications of this argument should not be underestimated. The Lewis model indicated that the increase in inequality that accompanied development was temporary and would be reversed once the pool of surplus labour had been exhausted. Kuznets' (1955) description of the trajectory of inequality in the process of development of the centre – first increasing, then declining – was expected to hold in the periphery (even though Kuznets himself cautioned against this analogy). Furtado's approach offered an interpretation for the evident failure of this prediction: the interaction of the structures of supply and demand reproduced the pool of surplus labour and kept wages low, indefinitely postponing Lewis' turning point. A similar argument was made by Marxist critics of the Lewis model, which read Lewis' notion of unlimited supply of labour in the light of Marx's concept of the industrial reserve army (Arrighi 1970; Nun 1969; Oliveira 1972; Rugitsky 2020).

Interestingly, the cumulative process identified by Furtado was even more general than he had suggested. First, the Brazilian 'miracle' had shown that the stagnationist implications of Furtado's analysis were not necessary, which suggested a more complex relationship between sectoral dynamics and economic growth. For example, Taylor and Bacha (1976) formulated a model incorporating Furtado's cumulative process but leading to accelerating growth and rising inequality, which they called an 'unequalizing spiral'. Second, De Janvry and Sadoulet (1983) proposed a model suggesting that the cumulative process could either increase or decrease inequality depending on the features of the economy; in their words, the model could lead either to 'social articulation' or 'social disarticulation'.

Furtado reviewed the case for the cumulative process in WP-17 in the light of the Brazilian 'miracle' and the critiques to his stagnationist views. In this new formulation, the impact of the cumulative process on the rate of economic growth is replaced by its impact on inequality. The growth spurt that took place in Brazil in the late 1960s had taught Furtado that the cumulative process may not block economic growth, but it would make it reliant on ever-increasing inequality in order to maintain the growth of the market for luxury goods: 'Higher rates of economic growth tend to imply aggravation of both external dependence and internal exploitation. Therefore, higher rates of growth, far from reducing underdevelopment, tend to make it more acute, as it entails increasing social inequalities' (Furtado, 2020a, p. 15). His argument about the myth of economic development could be, at least partly, informed by this shift in his position.

Current heterodox macroeconomic thinking can benefit from Furtado's insights on the cumulative process between the structures of supply and demand, for example by extending its models of growth and distribution to incorporate sectoral heterogeneity as an endogenous variable mediating the relationships between aggregate demand, capital accumulation, and income distribution (Rugitsky 2016; for a recent modelling attempt, see Brenck and Carvalho 2020). If demand regimes (that is, the causal structures between distribution and demand) are independent of sectoral dynamics, then distribution and productivity regimes (the causal structures between demand and distribution) depend on the sectoral features of the economy. Taylor and Ömer's (2020) work can be read as an attempt to bring sectoral heterogeneity back to the core of the theories of growth and distribution, for which Furtado's contribution was seminal.[9]

Interestingly, the cumulative process between supply and demand suggested by Furtado was influential not only within Latin American structuralism (e.g., through Pinto's (1976) notion of 'styles of development') but, also, on early heterodox models of growth and distribution; for example, Taylor (1983, 1989) attempted to recast that process in a Kaleckian model of growth and distribution. Nevertheless, this line of work has remained at the margins of the heterodox literature, perhaps because the rich economies tend to be sectorally more homogeneous, rendering single-commodity models intuitively plausible. Still, there is a growing recognition that the productive structure of the US economy is becoming increasingly dualistic, supporting research work at a more disaggregated level (Storm 2017; Taylor and Ömer 2020; see also Temin 2017). The centrality of sectoral dynamics, which is always evident in the periphery and was strongly emphasized by Furtado, also seems to be gaining recognition as it becomes more and more relevant for the centre. This is another instance in which analyses centred on the periphery can better explain the shortcomings of global capitalism.

Another topic that makes Furtado's thinking from the mid-1970s relevant for the present is his reconceptualization of development. By distinguishing 'development' from 'catching up with the standards of consumption in the centre', and reframing 'development' as the autonomous construction of their destiny by the masses in the Third World, Furtado broke away from the eurocentric and technocratic character of early development economics, and anticipated in important ways arguments that would be brought forward by the post-development literature two decades later.

In a recent assessment, Ziai (2017, pp. 2547–2548) argues that the post-development literature articulated five criticisms of development: (i) that it is a Western ideology deployed in the Cold War to prevent countries from aligning with the USSR; (ii) that it is a failed project of universalizing the way of life of the 'developed countries'; (iii) that it defines non-Western ways of life as 'inferior' and 'in need of development'; (iv) that it privileges activities earning money through the market at the expense of other forms of social existence; and (v) that it legitimates interventions in the periphery in the name of goals decided by people claiming 'expert knowledge'. These criticisms played a crucial role in pointing out the power struggles involved in the process of development, and the narrowness of the horizon of development economics. As Ziai (2017, pp. 2548–2549) points out, however, if part of this literature adopts a 'constructivist concept of culture' leading to a 'radical democratic position', another part has 'reactionary consequences' due to its one-sided rejection of development, essentialist affirmation of traditional cultures and paternalistic approach to the poor.

Read in the light of the recent literature, Furtado's formulation of the myth of development is striking both because it anticipates contemporary criticisms of the development discourse, and because it avoids common pitfalls. Furtado rejects the notion that development means the universalization of the patterns of consumption of the centre on the grounds of viability and desirability, bringing to the fore the ideological nature

---

[9]A similar reasoning has been applied to Argentina's and Brazil's recent combination of accelerating growth, structural regression, and falling inequality; see Rugitsky (2017, 2019) and Loureiro (2018, 2020).

of the literature that he had helped to establish. At the same time, Furtado refuses to replace the much-criticised concept of development with a new one; instead, he devolves its definition to the masses in the periphery. That is, instead of playing the vacuous role of opposition technocrat, Furtado chooses a deep notion of democracy as the starting point for the reorientation of the debate about development. He envisaged this shift as a consequence of the 'probable … eruption [in the periphery] of a series of political upsurges aiming to cope with the alarming rise in social inequality'.

Large areas in the periphery would go through processes of democratization some years later, and these processes would push towards the redistribution of income and wealth. However, these processes coincided with the rise of neoliberalism, which would not only halt the reduction of inequalities but also hinder a democratic redefinition of development and lead to a deep crisis of democracy (the case of Brazil is reviewed in Saad-Filho and Morais 2018). Decades into neoliberalism, economic policy has become increasingly insulated, entrenching the power of technocrats and blocking public debate on the economy. In addition, despite growing criticism, GDP growth remains the dominant measure of prosperity. A concept of development focusing on the autonomy of the masses rather than on technocratically-imposed aims seems even more relevant than it was half a century ago.

A concept of development inspired by the work of Celso Furtado and other heterodox economists could help to inspire policy alternatives in Latin America and elsewhere. This task is urgent since, faced with the hegemony of neoliberalism, it has become common for heterodox economists to criticize the dominant policies and suggest alternatives without questioning the underlying narrowing of the terms of the debate. For example, although a critical standpoint about inequality is generally taken for granted by the heterodoxy, the cultural and environmental consequences of economic growth are rarely acknowledged, despite the excellent work of other social scientists (see, e.g., Gudynas 2016; Svampa 2015). Further, for most economists, it seems that there are only economic lessons to be learned from the shortcomings of ISI and the decline of structuralism. Furtado's work suggests otherwise: the limits of ECLA thought were closely related to its disregard for the social and political dynamics unleashed by the process of development in the region.

5. Conclusion

Critical thinking has much to gain from a closer engagement with Celso Furtado's contributions from the 1970s. This critical moment in the evolution of his thought allowed him to offer a deep and profoundly original interpretation of the accumulation of capital with, at its core, the hierarchical structure of the world economy and the sectoral dynamics that relate accumulation to the social structure and the distribution of income. This approach can contribute to the examination of the relationships between economic and political processes in development, through the interactions between capital accumulation and social structure. The political economy that Furtado developed in the 1970s offered a critique of capitalism from the vantage point of the periphery, which he combined with a reconceptualization of development grounded on his lifelong commitment to democracy. In an age when there is a search for new paradigms of development and alternatives to neoliberalism taking into account urgent concerns with national and global inequalities, racism and environmental and other concerns, these seminal works by Celso Furtado offer a refreshing contribution and illuminating insights.

Acknowledgements

The authors thank Julie Coimbra, Maria Lúcia Pallares-Burke and Rosa Freire d'Aguiar for their generous assistance preparing this article, and Louis-Philippe Rochon for his suport to the publication of the Working Papers by Celso Furtado. Fernando Rugitsky is grateful for the funding support from the Brazilian Coordination for the Improvement of Higher Education Personnel (CAPES). The usual disclaimers apply.

Disclosure Statement

No potential conflict of interest was reported by the author(s).

ORCID

Pedro Loureiro ⓘ http://orcid.org/0000-0001-7517-7351
Fernando Rugitsky ⓘ http://orcid.org/0000-0002-4803-7270
Alfredo Saad-Filho ⓘ http://orcid.org/0000-0002-6625-2273

References

Albuquerque, E. M. 2013. 'Inovação em Celso Furtado: criatividade humana e crítica ao capitalismo.' *Textos para Discussão do CEDEPLAR* 470: 1–15.
Arrighi, G. 1970. 'Labour Supplies in Historical Perspective: A Study of the Proletarianization of the African Peasantry in Rhodesia.' *Journal of Development Studies* 6 (3): 197–234.
Arrighi, G. 1990. 'The Developmentalist Illusion: A Reconceptualization of the Semiperiphery.' In *Semiperipheral States in the World-economy*, edited by W. G. Martin. Westport: Greenwood Press.
Bianconi, R. 2014. 'L'œuvre de Celso Furtado à Paris: le parcours d'un intellectuel et homme d'Etat.' PhD Thesis. Université Paris-Sorbonne, Paris.
Boianovsky, M. 2008. 'Celso Furtado (1920–2004).' In *The New Palgrave Dictionary of Economics*, 2nd ed., edited by S. Durlauf, and L. Blume. London: Palgrave Macmillan.
Boianovsky, M. 2010. 'A View from the Tropics: Celso Furtado and the Theory of Economic Development in the 1950s.' *History of Political Economy* 42 (2): 221–266.
Boianovsky, M. 2015. 'Between Lévi-Strauss and Braudel: Furtado and the Historical-structural Method in Latin American Political Economy.' *Journal of Economic Methodology* 22 (4): 413–438.
Boianovsky, M., and R. Solís. 2014. 'The Origins and Development of the Latin American Structuralist Approach to the Balance of Payments.' *Review of Political Economy* 26 (1): 23–59.
Brenck, C., and L. Carvalho. 2020. 'The Equalizing Spiral in Early 21st Century Brazil: A Kaleckian Model with Sectoral Heterogeneity.' *Structural Change and Economic Dynamics* 55: 298–310.
Cardoso, F. H., and E. Faletto. 1979. *Dependency and Development in Latin America*. Berkeley: University of California Press.
Combe, M. S. 1977. 'Bibliografía seleccionada de obras recientes sobre nuevo orden internacional y diálogo norte-sur.' *Foro Internacional* 18 (2-70): 373–384.
Coutinho, M. C. 2015. 'Subdesenvolvimento e Estagnação na América Latina, de Celso Furtado.' *Revista de Economia Contemporânea* 19: 448–474.
Coutinho, M. C. 2019. 'Furtado e seus críticos: da estagnação à retomada do crescimento econômico.' *Economia e Sociedade* 28: 741–759.

Cunha, A. M., and G. Britto. 2018. 'When Development Meets Culture: The Contribution of Celso Furtado in the 1970s.' *Cambridge Journal of Economics* 42 (1): 177–198.

d'Aguiar, R. F. 2015. 'Celso Furtado — um retrato intelectual.' *Cadernos do desenvolvimento* 10 (17): 122–127.

De Janvry, A., and E. Sadoulet. 1983. 'Social Articulation as a Condition for Equitable Growth.' *Journal of Development Economics* 13 (3): 275–303.

Furtado, C. 1952. 'Formação de capital e desenvolvimento econômico.' *Revista de Economia Brasileira* 6 (3): 7–35.

Furtado, C. 1959. *Formação econômica do Brasil.* Rio de Janeiro: Fundo de Cultura.

Furtado, C. 1963. 'Comments on Professor Rosenstein-Rodan's Paper.' In *Economic Development for Latin America*, edited by H. S. Ellis, and H. C. Wallich. London: Macmillan.

Furtado, C. 1965. 'Development and Stagnation in Latin America: A Structuralist Approach.' *Studies in Comparative International Development* 1 (11): 159–175.

Furtado, C. 1966. *Subdesenvolvimento e estagnação na América Latina.* Rio de Janeiro: Civilização Brasileira.

Furtado, C. 1974. *O mito do desenvolvimento econômico.* Rio de Janeiro: Paz e Terra.

Furtado, C. 1975. *Teoria e Política do Desenvolvimento Econômico.* São Paulo: Companhia Editora Nacional.

Furtado, C. 1976. *Prefácio a Nova Economia Política.* Rio de Janeiro: Paz e Terra.

Furtado, C. 1978. *Criatividade e dependência na civilização industrial.* Rio de Janeiro: Paz e Terra.

Furtado, C. 1980. *Pequena introdução ao desenvolvimento econômico: enfoque interdisciplinar.* São Paulo: Editora Nacional.

Furtado, C. 1985. *A fantasia organizada.* Rio de Janeiro: Paz e Terra.

Furtado, C. 1991. *Os ares do mundo.* Rio de Janeiro: Paz e Terra.

Furtado, C. 2019. *Diários intermitentes.* São Paulo: Companhia das Letras.

Furtado, C. 2020a. 'Underdevelopment and Dependence: the Fundamental Connections.' *Review of Political Economy* 33 (1): 7–15.

Furtado, C. 2020b. 'The Myth of Economic Development and the Future of the Third World.' *Review of Political Economy* 33 (1): 16–27.

Furtado, C. 2020c. *The Myth of Economic Development.* Cambridge: Polity Press.

Gudynas, E. 2016. 'Natural Resource Nationalisms and the Compensatory State in Progressive South America.' In *The Political Economy of Resources and Development: From Neoliberalism to Resource Nationalism*, edited by P. A. Haslam, and P. Heidrich. London: Routledge.

Hirschman, A. O. 1981. 'The Rise and Decline of Development Economics.' In *Essays in Trespassing: Economics to Politics and Beyond*, edited by A. O. Hirschman. Cambridge: Cambridge University Press.

Kuznets, S. 1955. 'Economic Growth and Income Inequality.' *American Economic Review* 45 (1): 1–28.

Lall, S. 1975. 'Is 'Dependence' a Useful Concept in Analysing Underdevelopment?' *World Development* 3 (11): 799–810.

Lewis, W. A. 1954. 'Economic Development with Unlimited Supplies of Labour.' *Manchester School of Economic and Social Studies* 22 (2): 139–191.

Lins, L. M. 2014. 'Racionalidade, criatividade e inovação na endogeneidade do desenvolvimento.' *Cadernos do desenvolvimento* 9 (15): 81–102.

Loureiro, P. M. 2018. 'The Ebb and Flow of the Pink Tide: Reformist Development Strategies in Brazil and Argentina.' PhD Thesis, SOAS, University of London.

Loureiro, P. M. 2020. 'Class Inequality and Capital Accumulation in Brazil, 1992–2013.' *Cambridge Journal of Economics* 44 (1): 181–206.

Medeiros Filho, J. T. 2020. *O Sonho de Celso Furtado.* https://aterraeredonda.com.br/o-sonho-de-celso-furtado/?utm_source=rss&utm_medium=rss&utm_campaign=o-sonho-de-celso-furtado&utm_term=2020-09-05.

Nun, J. 1969. 'La teoria de la masa marginal.' In *Marginalidad y exclusión social*, edited by J. Nun. Buenos Aires: Fondo de Cultura Económica.

Nurkse, R. 1952. 'Some International Aspects of the Problem of Economic Development.' *American Economic Review* 42 (2): 571–583.

Nurkse, R. 1953. *Problems of Capital Formation in Underdeveloped Countries*. New York: Oxford University Press.

Oliveira, F. 1972. 'A economia brasileira: crítica à razão dualista.' *Estudos Cebrap* 2: 4–82.

Paula, J. A. 2019. 'Cultura e Desenvolvimento: 100 anos de Celso Furtado, um intelectual cosmopolita.' *Nova Economia* 29: 1075–1089.

Pinto, A. 1976. 'Notas sobre estilos de desarrollo en América Latina.' *Revista de la Cepal* 1976 (1): 97–128.

Rosenstein-Rodan, P. N. 1943. 'Problems of Industrialization of Eastern and South-Eastern Europe.' *Economic Journal* 53 (210/211): 202–211.

Rosenstein-Rodan, P. N. 1963. 'Notes on the Theory of the "Big Push".' In *Economic Development for Latin America*, edited by H. S. Ellis, and H. C. Wallich. London: Macmillan.

Rugitsky, F. 2016. 'Growth, Distribution, and Sectoral Heterogeneity: Reading the Kaleckians in Latin America.' *EconomiA* 17 (3): 265–278.

Rugitsky, F. 2017. 'The Rise and Fall of the Brazilian Economy (2004–2015): The Economic Antimiracle.' Department of Economics FEA/USP Working Paper Series, 2017-29.

Rugitsky, F. 2019. 'Questão de estilo: a mudança estrutural para a igualdade e seus desafios.' In *Alternativas para o Desenvolvimento Brasileiro: novos horizontes para a mudança estrutural com igualdade*, edited by M. V. Chiliatto-Leite. Santiago: CEPAL.

Rugitsky, F. 2020. 'Luta de classes inibida? Furtado e a especificidade da estrutural social brasileira.' In *Celso Furtado e os 60 anos de Formação Econômica do Brasil*, edited by A. Saes, and A. Barbosa. São Paulo: BBM/Sesc.

Saad-Filho, A. 2005. 'The Rise and Decline of Latin American Structuralism and Dependency Theory.' In *The Origins of Development Economics: How Schools of Economic Thought Have Addressed Development*, edited by E. S. Jomo, K. S. Reinert. London: Zed Books and New Delhi: Tulika Books.

Saad-Filho, A., and L. Morais. 2018. *Brazil: Neoliberalism versus Democracy*. London: Pluto Press.

Saes, A., and A. Barbosa, eds. 2020. *Celso Furtado e os 60 anos de Formação Econômica do Brasil*. São Paulo: BBM/Sesc.

Sen, A. 1999. *Commodities and Capabilities*. Oxford: Oxford University Press.

Storm, S. 2017. 'The New Normal: Demand, Secular Stagnation, and the Vanishing Middle Class.' *International Journal of Political Economy* 46: 169–210.

Svampa, M. 2015. 'Commodities Consensus: Neoextractivism and Enclosure of the Commons in Latin America.' *South Atlantic Quarterly* 114 (1): 65–82.

Tavares, M. C. 2000. *Celso Furtado e o Brasil*. São Paulo: Fundação Perseu Abramo.

Tavares, M. C., and J. Serra. 1976. 'Além da estagnação.' In *C. Da Substituição de Importações ao Capitalismo Financeiro: ensaios sobre economia brasileira*, edited by M. Tavares. Rio de Janeiro: Zahar.

Taylor, L. 1983. *Structuralist Macroeconomics: Applicable Models for the Third World*. New York: Basic Books.

Taylor, L. 1989. 'Demand Composition, Income Distribution, and Growth.' In *Joan Robinson and Modern Economic Theory*, edited by G. Feiwel. London: Macmillan Press.

Taylor, L., and E. Bacha. 1976. 'The Unequalizing Spiral: A First Growth Model for Belindia.' *Quarterly Journal of Economics* 90 (2): 197–218.

Taylor, L., and O. Ömer. 2020. *Macroeconomic Inequality from Reagan to Trump: Market, Power, Wage Repression, Asset Price Inflation, and Industrial Decline*. Cambridge: Cambridge University Press.

Temin, P. 2017. *The Vanishing Middle Class: Prejudice and Power in a Dual Economy*. Cambridge, MA: MIT Press.

Vieira, W. 2020. 'Subdesenvolvimento e dependência: uma análise do pensamento de Celso Furtado e sua aproximação com a teoria da dependência.' In *Controvérsias sobre história, desenvolvimento e revolução: pensamento econômico brasileiro em perspectiva crítica*, edited by M. Malta, J. Leon, C. Curty, and B. Borja, unpublished manuscript.

Ziai, A. 2017. 'Post-development 25 Years after *The Development Dictionary*.' *Third World Quarterly* 38 (12): 2547–2558.

Growth, Distribution, and External Constraints: A Post-Kaleckian Model Applied to Brazil

Douglas Alencar (ID), Frederico G. Jayme (ID) and Gustavo Britto (ID)

ABSTRACT
The purpose of this research is to analyze whether the Brazilian economy behaved under a wage-led or profit-led regime between 1960 and 2011, considering a Post-Kaleckian model in a context of external constraints. The time span is limited by data availability (i.e., 2011). To answer the question of whether the Brazilian economy works under a wage-led or profit-led regime, we propose a simple Post-Kaleckian model. The model suggests that a profit-led regime is more probable for Brazil. Moreover, a wage-led regime occurs when a balance of payments constrained growth model is taken into consideration. Likewise, the real exchange rate has a positive impact on economic growth through the export channel. This result is a novelty in the recent literature about the relationship between real exchange rate and economic growth within a Post-Kaleckian model. The Brazilian economy was chosen as it is one of the biggest economies in Latin America.

1. Introduction

The balance of payments constrained growth (BPCG) model, first developed by Thirlwall (1979), explains developing economies (Jayme Jr. 2003; Britto and Mccombie 2009; Alencar and Strachman 2014). However, as indicated by Seguino (2010), Ribeiro, McCombie, and Lima (2016), there is a lack of understanding of the relationship between the Post-Kaleckian approach and BPCG theory. This paper encompasses the Post-Kaleckian and external constraints in a simple model.

The purpose of this research is to analyze whether the Brazilian economy behaved under a wage-led or profit-led regime between 1960 and 2011, considering a model that integrates features of the Post-Kaleckian and external constraints. The time period is limited by the data availability — the series related to unit labor cost, in particular, were collected from the Brazilian Institute of Geography and Statistics (IBGE), which is only available through 2011.

In order to answer the question of whether the Brazilian economy is under a wage-led or profit-led regime, we propose a simple Post-Kaleckian model under external constraints. In line with Naastepad's (2006) approach, our model suggests a profit-led regime in an open model.[1] When a BPCG model is taken into consideration, we can accomplish a wage-led

---

[1]Blecker (1999) shows how a profit-led regime can prevail in open Kaleckian models.

regime. Similarly, the real exchange rate has a positive impact on economic growth through the export channel.[2] This result is a novelty in the recent literature about the relationship between real exchange rate and economic growth within a Post-Kaleckian model. Brazil was chosen as it is one of the biggest economies in Latin America.

This paper is divided as follows: In the second section, we present Thirlwall's model. In the third section, we build a formal model connecting income distribution, real exchange rate and external constraints to growth. An econometric exercise is performed in Section four. Conclusions are discussed in the last section.

2. Thirlwall's Approach

The balance of payments approach was originally developed by Thirlwall (1979). Assuming that net flows of foreign capital are zero and the terms of trade remain constant, Thirlwall concludes that a country's long-term income growth rate is conditioned by the export growth rate in relation to demand income elasticity for imports, and in models that include capital flows, the long-term net balance of the capital account (Thirlwall and Hussain 1982; Moreno-Brid 1998-99, 2003; Barbosa Filho 2004).

Thirlwall's Law can be represented by $y = x/\varphi$, which means that in the long run, the domestic income growth rate corresponds to the export growth rate divided by the income elasticity of demand for imports. This dynamic is equivalent to Harrod's trade multiplier (Harrod 1933), as improved by Kaldor (1966, 1975) and by Kennedy and Thirlwall (1979).

In Thirlwall's original model, the growth rate compatible with the balance of payments equilibrium is a direct relation between the income elasticity of external demand for its exports and the income elasticity of demand for imports. In equilibrium:

$$\frac{Y_d}{Y_w} = \frac{\eta}{\varphi} \tag{1}$$

where Y_d = domestic income growth rate; Y_f = foreign income growth rate; η = income elasticity of demand for exports; and φ = income elasticity of demand for imports. The external equilibrium condition is as follows:

$$P_d X = P_f ME \tag{2}$$

where X is export volume; P_d is the domestic price of exports; M is import volume; P_f is the foreign price of imports; and E is the nominal exchange rate. Equation 2 expressed in terms of growth rates is:

$$p_d + x = p_f + m + e \tag{3}$$

External demand for exports — and likewise internal demand for imports — depends on relative prices, price and income elasticities and domestic and foreign income (Y and Z respectively), and it, therefore, follows that:

$$M = a\left(\frac{P_f E}{P_d}\right)^\vartheta Y^\varphi \tag{4}$$

---

[2]Regarding the several channels by which the real exchange rate affects economic growth, see Missio et al. (2015); Gabriel, Jayme Jr, and Oreiro (2016), Razmi, Rapetti, and Skott (2012); Alencar, Jayme Jr, and Britto (2018), among others.

$$X = b\left(\frac{P_d}{P_f E}\right)^{\eta} Z^{\varepsilon} \tag{5}$$

where 'a' and 'b' are constant; ϑ is the price elasticity of imports; φ is the income elasticity of demand for imports; η is the price elasticity of exports; and ε is the income elasticity of demand for exports. Equations 4 and 5, expressed in terms of growth rates, are as follows:

$$\hat{x} = \eta\,(p_d - e - p_f) + \varepsilon\hat{z} \tag{6}$$

$$\hat{m} = \vartheta\,(p_f + e - p_d) + \varphi\hat{y} \tag{7}$$

Substituting (6) and (7) into (3) and solving for y gives the solution for the economic growth rate consistent with the balance of payments growth:

$$Y_{BP} = \frac{(1 + \eta + \vartheta)\,(p_d - p_f - e) + \varepsilon z}{\varphi} \tag{8}$$

Considering that the real exchange rate is constant ($e = 0$), and assuming that external inflation is equal to domestic inflation ($pd-pf = 0$), then equation 8 is simplified to the expression known as Thirlwall's Law:[3]

$$Y_{BP} = \frac{x}{\varphi} \tag{9}$$

In the long run, the expansion of a country's real domestic income is given by the ratio of export growth to the income elasticity of imports (Moreno-Brid and Pérez 2003; Britto and Mccombie 2009; Alencar and Strachman 2014). Since the basic features of the BPCG model have been presented, we now move on to the discussion of the attempts to integrate the Post-Kaleckian and models with external constraints features.

Seguino (2010) explores the relationship between the BPCG theory and gender inequality, and thus income distribution. The model is based on stylized characteristics of semi-industrialized economies. Such economies produce manufactured goods that require low technological know-how and imported intermediate inputs and capital goods that are used in domestic production, which makes the price elasticity of imports inelastic. The export is based on the Verdoorn-Kaldor approach — the argument that income growth increases productivity growth. In this model, export growth plays an important role in increasing productivity growth, as emphasized by Kaldor (1956). Although the author bases part of his model on export, in the formal model, he normalizes the exchange rate to 1, which means that he ignores changes in the real exchange rate. The gender inequality is considered in the model through the ratio of nominal female-to-male wages, and hence it is possible to differentiate the wage share of females and males in the income, which leads to differences in propensity to save based on gender. In the model, these differences will have an impact on the BPCG through export and investment. Thus, an increase in gender inequality leads to a decrease in investment and export, which can hurt economic growth through BPCG. The impact of gender inequality is unlikely to be transitory, and this inequality can change the long-term economic growth path of the economy.

---

[3] In which $x = \varepsilon z$ by definition.

Ribeiro, McCombie, and Lima (2016) combine BPCG with the Post-Kaleckian approach. In their model, the variable price is substituted by unit labor costs, as suggested in most models based on Kalecki's work. Therefore, the income distribution is incorporated into the BPCG. Furthermore, the authors introduce the unit labor costs in relation to productivity growth, which opens the door for Verdoorn-Kaldor's Law. One supposition that is emphasized by the authors is that in the long run, the wage share converges to labor productivity growth, which is, of course, unlikely for developing economies. In addition, the income elasticity of the export and import ratio (ε/φ) is endogenized. The elasticities ratio depends on the wage share and technological process. In sequence, it is argued that technological progress depends on the technological gap and profit share. Finally, all the model aspects were combined, and the authors argue that a currency devaluation net effect on the long-term economic growth is ambiguous, since it depends on the size of change in the endogenous variables, that is, the technological gap, wage share and technological process regime — or, in other words, whether the regime is wage-led or profit-led. In fact, exchange rate devaluation would have an effect on the income elasticity of export and import, and it would have a positive impact on non-price competitiveness through changes in income distribution and in technological change. This argument is interesting since it would be possible to advise the exchange rate devaluation to improve competitiveness. Furthermore, the authors conclude that the impact of exchange rate devaluation on growth is ambiguous and depends on several previews conditions, as aforementioned.

3. The Model

This section aims at building a Post-Kaleckian model considering external constraints. The aggregate demand can be expressed as follows:

$$y = c + i + x - m \tag{10}$$

where y is the output; c the aggregate consumption; i the aggregate investment; x the exports; and m the import goods. These variables are measured at constant prices. This aggregate demand definition is a standard one. In the Post-Kaleckian model, an important feature is a distinction between the wage share and profit share. The wage share can be defined as

$$\omega = \left(\frac{W}{P}\right)\lambda^{-1} = w\lambda^{-1} \tag{11}$$

where ω stands for real cost of labor per unit of output, the wage share; W the nominal wage; P the price; and finally λ the productivity. Since the wage share has been defined, the profit share is straightforward:

$$\pi = 1 - \omega \tag{12}$$

Taking equation 12 in growth rate, it follows:

$$\hat{\pi} = \frac{\Delta\pi}{\pi} = -\frac{\omega\Delta\omega}{\pi\omega} = -\alpha\hat{\omega} \tag{13}$$

Having defined the wage and profit share, we need to define the propensity to save. Marginal propensity to save, as suggested by Bowles and Boyer (1995), is denoted by σ, which is different for workers (σ_w) and capitalists (σ_π). The workers' propensity to save is lower than that of the capitalists ($\sigma_w < \sigma_\pi$). Naastepad (2006) and Naastepad and Storm (2007) follow Bowles and Boyer (1995). The consumption function is:

$$c = (1 - \sigma_\omega)\omega y + (1 - \sigma_\pi)\pi y = [(1 - \sigma_\omega)\omega + (1 - \sigma_\pi)(1 - \omega)]y; \quad \sigma_\pi > \sigma_\omega \quad (14)$$

Bowles and Boyer (1995), Naastepad (2006) and Naastepad and Storm (2007) specify the marginal propensity to save as follows:

$$\sigma = \frac{s}{y} = \sigma_\pi + (\sigma_\omega - \sigma_\pi)\omega \quad (15)$$

Taking (14) into (10) and rearranging, it follows that:

$$y = \frac{i + x - m}{[1 - (1 - \sigma_\omega)\omega + (1 - \sigma_\pi)(1 - \omega))]} = \mu^{-1}[i + x - m] \quad (16)$$

or:

$$y = \mu^{-1}[i + x - m] \quad (17)$$

Note that

$$\mu^{-1} = \frac{1}{[1 - (1 - \sigma_\omega)\omega + (1 - \sigma_\pi)(1 - \omega))]}$$

is the Keynesian multiplier, as defined by Naastepad (2006). The magnitude of the multiplier depends on ω. Differentiating equation 17, dividing by y and rearranging the terms, we get the expression for demand-led output growth:

$$\hat{y} = -\hat{\mu} + \frac{\mu^{-1}i}{y}\hat{i} + \frac{\mu^{-1}x}{y}\hat{x} - \frac{\mu^{-1}m}{y}\hat{m} = -\hat{\mu} + \psi_i\hat{i} + \psi_x\hat{x} - \psi_m\hat{m} \quad (18)$$

where ψ_i, ψ_x and ψ_m are the (adjusted multiplier) shares of product in investment, exports and imports, respectively. Note that in this model, the multiplier is also adjusted by the import share. The multiplier is endogenous. Any change in the wage share is reflected in μ. Using the following expression for $\mu, [\sigma_\pi + (\sigma_\pi - \sigma_\omega)\omega = \mu]$, it is possible to differentiate the output growth rate as a function of the growth rate of wage share. The outcome is shown below:

$$\hat{\mu} = -\frac{\omega}{\mu}(\sigma_\pi - \sigma_\omega)\omega = -\xi(\sigma_\pi - \sigma_\omega)\hat{\omega} \quad (19)$$

where ξ is a positive fraction of ω/μ. Following Bhaduri and Marglin (1990), the multiplier and the wage share determine the growth rate of investment, wherein i is positively related to the profit share (π), output (y) and real exchange rate (θ).

The real exchange rate can be a distinct variable in the investment function. Several authors made this suggestion, among them Lima and Porcile (2013), Oreiro and Araújo (2013) and Missio and Jayme Jr (2013). Because the relationship between the real exchange rate and investment growth is an important feature in this model, it is necessary to engage in some discussion about this topic.

The role of the competitive real exchange rate as one of the transmission channels in economic growth has already been well treated in the literature (see Rodrik 2008;

Missio et al. 2015; Razmi, Rapetti, and Skott 2012). The first transmission channel is related to the argument that if the real exchange rate is overvalued, there is a tendency toward deficits in the current account such that — in most of the cases — it is difficult to revert for developing countries. As an upshot, it leads to balance of payment crises, thereby hurting growth. There is robust evidence that an overvalued real exchange rate leads to balance of payment crises, especially for developing countries. Authors that demonstrate this relationship include Bresser-Pereira and Gala (2009), and Alencar and Strachman (2014), for instance. Balance of payments crises remain an issue for developing countries; however, such countries have difficulties in maintaining a real exchange rate at a level that would even the current account, since it seems that these countries use the real exchange rate as a tool to control inflation. The other transmission channel is related to exchange rate misalignment.

In relation to the real exchange rate, there are three main methods to consider exchange rate misalignment: (i) the Balassa-Samuelson effect; (ii) purchasing power parity (PPP); and (iii) the industrial disequilibrium effect. There is robust empirical evidence for the exchange rate misalignment. In relation to the exchange rate policy derived from these theories, the exchange rate misalignment correction would lead to economic growth.

Rodrik (2008) argues that the real exchange rate devaluation boosts economic growth. The transmission channel is through the industrial sector, notably, the tradable sector. He proposes a real exchange index to analyze the effect of real exchange rate devaluation on growth. The reason for this is related to the non-tradable and tradable sectors. For Rodrick, there is a trend to decrease prices in the tradable sector, since in this sector, productivity growth is higher. Consequently, the real exchange rate has a tendency to be overvalued. Besides the Balassa-Samuelson effect, as highlighted by Missio et al. (2015), the real exchange rate devaluation can change the relationship between the elasticities of export and import within the BPCG model. Moreover, the real exchange rate devaluation can have a nonlinear relation with economic growth, as pointed out by Rapetti, Skott, and Razmi (2012), Oreiro and Araújo (2013) and Missio et al. (2015). There is also strong empirical evidence for this real exchange rate misalignment, which can be found in the work of Araujo and Gala (2012), Rapetti, Skott, and Razmi (2012), Oreiro and Araújo (2013), Nassif et al (2015) and Missio et al. (2015). Likewise, we can identify the PPP effect, to which we now turn.

Other research has related overvalued currency with low per capita income growth rate. The empirical evidence for this relationship can be found in the work of Cavallo, Cottani, and Kahn (1990), Dollar (1992), Razin and Collins (1997), Benaroya and Janci (1999), and Acemoglu et al. (2002). Since such corrections have not taken place, it is possible to find a negative relationship between the real exchange rate and investment growth. In a similar vein, Gala (2008) considered the relationship between economic growth and a real exchange rate corrected by the Balassa-Samuelson effect and the PPP effect (i.e., another index for the real exchange rate). The PPP takes under consideration several aspects of different economies, such as subsidies applied by the government, costs of transport and customs duties, among others. The author finds robust empirical evidence in favor of the relevance of real exchange levels to explain per capita income growth rates for several countries on different continents. The upshot is that the real exchange rate devaluation boosts economic growth, which means that the correction of the real exchange rate raises per capita income growth rate. Once more, it is confirmed that the exchange rate misalignment hurts growth. These findings are consistent and robust from a theoretical and empirical viewpoint; however, it seems difficult to be implemented as the exchange rate policy.

Barbosa-Filho (2004), Missio and Jayme Jr (2013), Campos, Jayme Jr, and Britto (forthcoming), and Missio et al. (2015) argue that the real exchange rate level can change the ratio relationship between import and export income elasticities within a BPCG model. The main argument is that if the real exchange rate were at the correct level, it would boost the industrial sector, which would be directed toward the sector with higher technological production. Some empirical evidence of this is provided by Campos, Jayme Jr, and Britto (forthcoming) and Missio et al. (2015).

Following Oreiro and Araújo (2013), Missio and Jayme Jr (2013) and Lima and Porcile (2013), the exchange rate should be a separate component in the investment function. This is due to the fact that exchange devaluations increase profits and investment. Following Missio and Jayme Jr, Rapetti, Skott, and Razmi (2012) and Oreiro and Araújo (2013), the relationship between real exchange rate and investment growth can be either positive or negative. On one hand, the real exchange rate devaluation can boost export and trigger investment growth, and thus, the relationship is positive. On the other hand, at a certain point, the real exchange rate devaluation might increase the import cost of imported physical capital, which leads to decreased investment. Including the real exchange rate in the investment function, and differentiating, it follows that[4]:

$$\hat{i} = \phi_0\hat{b} + \phi_1\hat{\pi} + \phi_2\hat{y} + \phi_3\hat{\theta} \tag{20}$$

where the coefficient ϕ_1 is the elasticity of investment in relation to profit share; ϕ_2 is the elasticity of investment in relation to demand (output); and ϕ_3 is the elasticity of investment in relation to real exchange rate.

Substituting equations 6, 7, 13, 19 and 20 into 18, we get the following equation:

$$\hat{y} = \frac{[\psi_i\phi_0\hat{b} + \psi_x\varepsilon\hat{z}]}{[1 + \psi_m\varphi - \psi_i\phi_2]} + \frac{[\xi(\sigma_\pi - \sigma_w) - \psi_i\phi_1\alpha]}{[1 + \psi_m\varphi - \psi_i\phi_2]}\hat{\omega} + \frac{[\psi_i\phi_3 + \psi_x\eta - \psi_m\vartheta]}{[1 + \psi_m\varphi - \psi_i\phi_2]}\hat{\theta} \tag{21}$$

Equation 21 shows that:

(1) In order for the autonomous components to be meaningful, it is required that $[1 + \psi_m\varphi - \psi_i\phi_2] > 0$, and since $(0 < \psi_i < 1)$, the elasticity of investment related to income should fall with: $0 \leq \phi_2 < (1/\psi_i)$; additionally, the elasticity of imports related to income should fall with: $0 \leq \varphi < (1/\psi_m)$.
(2) In relation to the growth rate of wage share $[\hat{\omega} = (\hat{w} - \hat{\lambda})]$, the impact of increased wage share is ambiguous. If the real wage growth exceeds productivity growth $(\hat{w} > \hat{\lambda})$, which means $(\hat{\omega} > 0)$, there will be two effects on output growth. This reduces export and investment growth, and therefore reduces the output. Alternatively, it increases the multiplier, since the marginal propensity to save decreases, distributing income from profits to wages, as argued by Oreiro, Missio, and Jayme (2015). There is a positive (negative) relationship between the level of real exchange

---

[4] i is similar for the rate of growth of capital stock (I/K), as highlighted in Oreiro and Araújo (2013).

rate and the level of the profit (wage)-share, which means that a real exchange rate devaluation is associated with an increase (decrease) in profit (wage)-share.

(3) The relationship between the real exchange rate and output growth can be seen in the numerator $[\psi_i \phi_3 + \psi_x \eta - \psi_m \vartheta]$ of equation 22. The growth rate is positively related to the income elasticity of both investment and exports. On the other hand, growth is inversely related to income elasticity of imports. The effects of the elasticities are influenced by the share of each of the variables on income. Real exchange rate devaluation can have either a positive or negative impact on investments and on export, but it will have a negative impact on imports.

Assuming that $(1 + \psi_m \varphi - \psi_i \phi_2) > 0$ and differentiating equation 21 respected to $\hat{w}$, the demand regime is wage-led if:

$$\frac{d\hat{y}}{d\hat{w}} = (\sigma_\pi - \sigma_w) > \left(\frac{i}{\pi y}\right)\phi_1 \tag{22}$$

If the elasticity demand of investment, based on profit share, is relatively smaller than the propensity to save (supposing that propensity to save by capitalists is greater than the workers' propensity to save), then the demand regime is wage-led. In this scenario, increases in wage share will boost aggregate demand. This model is different from the approach presented by Naastepad (2006) and Storm and Naastepad (2012), since they defined export function as dependent on labor cost and world income. On the other hand, in our model, the export function depends on the real exchange rate and world income. Conversely, if the elasticity demand for investment is higher than the propensity to save, the demand regime is profit-led. This means that an increase in real wages will reduce growth.

Substituting $[\hat{\omega} = (\hat{w} - \hat{\lambda})]$ in equation 21, the interaction between productivity and demand regime in a profit-led economy is represented in the following expression:

$$\frac{d\hat{y}}{d\hat{\lambda}} > 0 \quad \text{if } (\sigma_\pi - \sigma_w) < \left(\frac{i}{\pi x}\right)\phi_1 \tag{23}$$

If the demand regime is wage-led, we get:

$$\frac{d\hat{y}}{d\hat{\lambda}} < 0 \quad \text{if } (\sigma_\pi - \sigma_w) > \left(\frac{i}{\pi x}\right)\phi_1 \tag{24}$$

The negative impact on output growth of income redistribution implies that the growth rate of productivity is greater than the effects of an increase in investments (via profit share).

The derivative of equation 21 taken in relation to $[\hat{\omega} = (\hat{w} - \hat{\lambda})]$ shows the demand-led growth model:

$$\frac{d\hat{y}}{d\hat{w}} = C = \frac{[\xi(\sigma_\pi - \sigma_w) - \psi_i \phi_1 \alpha]}{[1 - \psi_i \phi_2]} \tag{25}$$

Interaction between productivity and aggregate demand

A simple formulation of endogenous productivity growth can be expressed as follows:

$$\hat{\lambda} = \beta_0 + \beta_1 \hat{y} + \beta_2 \hat{w} + \beta_3 \hat{\theta}; \quad \beta_0, \ \beta_1, > 0; 0 < \beta_2 < 1; \ \beta_3 \leq 0 \qquad (26)$$

where $\hat{\lambda}$ is the growth rate of labor productivity; $\hat{y}$ the growth rate of real output; $\hat{w}$ the growth rate of the real wage; and $\hat{\theta}$ the real exchange rate. As pointed out by Missio and Jayme Jr (2013), the real exchange rate can have a nonlinear relation with capital accumulation. Up to a certain level, the real exchange rate devaluation can increase profit share, which increases firm's internal funds, and thus it can increase productivity by higher innovation. The real exchange rate devaluation can increase the imported prices of production components, which has a negative impact on productivity. A similar argument is used by Alencar, Jayme Jr, and Britto (2018).

Substituting equation 25 into equation 19, assuming that $[\hat{\omega} = (\hat{w} - \hat{\lambda})]$, and substituting equations 6, (7), (13) and (20) into (18), we get the interaction between aggregate demand and productivity:

$$\hat{y} = \frac{[-\xi(\sigma_\pi - \sigma_w)\beta_0 + \psi_i \phi_0 \hat{b} + \psi_x \varepsilon \hat{z}]}{1 + \xi(\sigma_\pi - \sigma_w)\beta_1 + \psi_m \varphi + \psi_i \phi_2} + \frac{[\xi(\sigma_\pi - \sigma_w)(1 - \beta_2) - \psi_i \phi_1 \alpha]}{1 + \xi(\sigma_\pi - \sigma_w)\beta_1 + \psi_m \varphi + \psi_i \phi_2} \hat{w}$$

$$+ \frac{[-\xi(\sigma_\pi - \sigma_w)\beta_3 + \psi_i \phi_3 + \psi_x \eta - \psi_m \vartheta]}{[1 + \xi(\sigma_\pi - \sigma_w)\beta_1 + \psi_m \varphi - \psi_i \phi_2]} \hat{\theta} \qquad (27)$$

For the components to be meaningful, it is required that $[1 + \xi(\sigma_\pi - \sigma_w)\beta_1 + \psi_m \varphi - \psi_i \phi_2] > 0$, since, $\xi(\sigma_\pi - \sigma_w)\beta_1 > 0$ because the propensity to save out of profit is bigger than the propensity to save out of wages. In addition, $\beta_1 > 0$, by definition. Moreover, due to the fact that the term ξ is also positive, $(0 < \psi_i < 1)$ is the elasticity of investment related to income, and should fall with: $0 \leq \phi_2 < (1/\psi_i)$. Also, the elasticity of imports related to income should fall with: $0 \leq \varphi < (1/\psi_m)$.

Differentiating equation 27 with respect to $\hat{\omega}$, it follows that:

$$\frac{d\hat{y}}{d\hat{w}} = C = \frac{[\xi(\sigma_\pi - \sigma_w)(1 - \beta_2) - \psi_i \phi_1 \alpha]}{[1 + \xi(\sigma_\pi - \sigma_w)\beta_1 + \psi_m \varphi - \psi_i \phi_2]} \qquad (28)$$

If:

$$\frac{d\hat{y}}{d\hat{w}} = (\sigma_\pi - \sigma_\omega)(1 - \beta_2) > \left(\frac{i}{\pi y}\right)\phi_1 \qquad (29)$$

Considering the above equation, the first term is $(\sigma_\pi - \sigma_\omega)(1 - \beta_2)$. Comparing this term with equation 21, the term $(\sigma_\pi - \sigma_\omega)$ will be smaller, since $0 < \beta_2 < 1$. If the investment elasticity, based on profit share, is relatively smaller than the propensity to save, supposing that saving propensity by capitalists is greater than saving propensity by workers, multiplied by the term $(1 - \beta_2)$, then the demand regime is wage-led. In this scenario, increases in wage share will increase aggregate demand. Conversely, if the investment demand elasticity is higher than the propensity to save, considering the coefficient (β_2), the demand regime will be profit-led. This means that an increase in real wages will reduce economic growth. Differentiating equation 27 with respect to $\hat{\theta}$, we obtain:

$$\frac{d\hat{y}}{d\hat{\theta}} = D = \frac{[-\xi(\sigma_\pi - \sigma_w)\beta_3 + \psi_i \phi_3 + \psi_x \eta - \psi_m \vartheta]}{[1 + \xi(\sigma_\pi - \sigma_w)\beta_1 + \psi_m \varphi - \psi_i \phi_2]} \qquad (30)$$

The numerator in equation 30 can be positive or negative. In the case where it is negative, the valuation of the real exchange rate boosts economic growth. On the other hand, if the numerator is positive, real exchange rate devaluation is recommended to increase economic growth. From equation 30, in the case where the term $-[\xi(\sigma_\pi - \sigma_w)\beta_3]$ is positive, indicating that real exchange rate devaluation has a positive effect on productivity growth, and the sum of this term plus $\psi_i\phi_3 + \psi_x\eta$ is bigger than $\psi_m\vartheta$, a real exchange devaluation growth is achieved, and in this case, the overall numerator will be positive. In other words, if the relationship between real exchange rate and productivity growth plus the elasticity of the real exchange rate and investment, plus the price elasticity to export are (all together) bigger than the price elasticity to import, the real exchange rate devaluation leads to economic growth. Conversely, the overall outcome is negative, and we obtain a real exchange rate valuation-led economic growth.

The autonomous part of equation 30 can also be positive or negative. Since there is no macroeconomic policy related to the autonomous part of equation 30, this part of the equation is not discussed. However, it is possible to consider that the real exchange rate would affect the income elasticity to export, as is discussed in the work of Missio et al. (2015) and Ribeiro, McCombie, and Lima (2016). Even though this could occur, this possibility is not the main focus of this research.

4. Econometric Exercise

In this section, we analyze the interaction between aggregate demand, real exchange rate, productivity and real wages for the Brazilian economy between 1960 and 2011 using the model developed above. The following equations were estimated:

Saving equation:

$$\sigma = \frac{s}{y} = \sigma_\pi + (\sigma_\omega - \sigma_\pi)\omega \tag{15}$$

Investment equation:

$$\hat{i} = \phi_0\hat{b} + \phi_1\hat{\pi} + \phi_2\hat{y} + \phi_3\hat{\theta} + \phi_4\hat{\theta^2} \tag{20'}$$

In relation to the investment equation, we estimate a modified version of equation 20. Besides the real exchange rate parameter ($\phi_3\hat{\theta^2}$), the real exchange rate squared ($\phi_4\hat{\theta^2}$) was introduced in order to test for nonlinearities.

The gross saving data was found on the IPEADATA database, from 1960 to 2011. The gross saving was deflated by Brazilian Index Consumer Prices (IPCA). The gross domestic product (GDP), the GDP per capita (as a proxy to productivity) and the gross capital formation (as a proxy for investment), from 1960 to 2011, were also collected from the World Development Indicators (WDI) (World Bank database) in constant values. For the wage share data from 1960 to 2008, we used the same data presented by Marquetti and Porsse (2014), and from 2009 to 2011, the data for this variable can be found on the National Account System (SCN) from the Brazilian Institute of Geography and Statistics (IBGE).

The data for profit share and wage share from 1960 to 2011 was obtained from Marquetti and Porsse (2014).

The real exchange rate is obtained in the usual manner: $\theta = (P^*/P)E$, where P^* is US producer price base 100 in 2005, the source of which was the IMF; P is Brazil consumer

Table 1. Estimates of saving, investment, and productivity equation.

Equation	$\hat{\lambda}$	σ	$\ln i$
Constant	−0.02 (−1.76)		−0.01 (−0.46)
σ_π		0.42 (2.49)	
$(\sigma_\omega - \sigma_\pi)\omega$		−0.51 (−1.27)	
$\ln \pi(-1)$			−0.83 (−1.43)
$D \ln y(-1)$	0.50 (2.80)		1.63 (3.78)
$D \ln \theta(-1)$	0.08 (1.92)		−0.14 (−1.99)
$D \ln \theta^2(-1)$	−0.05 (−1.63)		0.08 (0.95)
$\hat{z}$			
$\epsilon_1 \hat{x}(-1)$			
$D \ln w(-1)$	0.13 (1.73)		
Dummy	Yes	Yes	No
Adj. R^2	0.15	0.56	28
SE	0.03	0.03	0.09
D.W	1.93	1.70	2.17
F-stat.	2.48	22.76	3.31
prob > F	0.03	0.00	0.00
obs.	51	51	51
Period	1960–2011	1960–2011	1960–2011

Notes: The estimation method was Least Squares corrected by HAC standard errors and covariance (Bartlett kernel, Newey–West fixed for equation all equations). The t-statistics are the numbers in parentheses below each coefficient. SE is the standard error. D.W. is Durbin–Watson statistic. F is the F-statistic and prob > F is the probability associated with observing an F-statistic. For the productivity and saving equation it was applied an AR (1) and for the investment equation it was applied an ARMA (2,2).

price base 100 in 2005 from IPEADA; E is the end-of-period nominal BRL/USD market exchange rate (buy); and θ is the real exchange rate from 1960 to 1979. From 1979 to 2011, the real effective exchange rate from the WDI-World Bank was used (Table 1).

4.1. Productivity Estimation

The productivity equation was estimated using an ordinary least squares (OLS) model corrected by a Heteroskedasticity and Autocorrelation Consistent Covariance (HAC) matrix, and an Autoregressive (AR) (1) was also applied. Hence, issues related to autocorrelation and heteroskedasticity were resolved.[5] The estimated Kaldor-Verdoorn coefficient is 0.50, very close to that found by Britto and Mccombie (2015). The estimate in this paper is close to the results obtained by Hein and Tarassow (2010) in a study for Europe. At the same time, the results found in this study are smaller when compared with those of Naastepad (2006) and Naastepad and Storm (2007), and slightly lower that that estimated by Romero and Britto (2017) for 15 OECD countries.

The real wage coefficient presents a positive sign, and it is significant at the 10 per cent level. Because the parameter is positive, this indicates a wage-led regime. The real exchange rate ($D \ln \theta(-1)$) coefficient is 0.08, and it is significant at the 5 per cent level. The real exchange rate squared ($D \ln \theta^2(-1)$) is negative, and significant at the 10 per cent level. This result can be explained by two factors: first, the possibility that the real exchange rate can be nonlinear in relation to productivity. This idea is similar to the argument of Missio and Jayme Jr (2013), in which the real exchange rate can have a nonlinear relation with capital accumulation. In the case of this study, up to a

---

[5]The more appropriate model is the OLS corrected by the HAC matrix, since this methodology corrects problems related with autocorrelation and heteroskedasticity.

certain level, the real exchange rate devaluation can increase profit share, which increases firm's internal funds, and thus it can increase productivity by higher innovation.

The real exchange rate devaluation can increase imported prices of production components, which has a negative impact on productivity. Recall that, as highlighted in Missio and Jayme Jr (2013), the nonlinear relationship between growth and the real exchange rate shows that, in the medium and long run, real devaluations can lead to negative effects on growth and productivity (inverse U curve). Besides, there may happen to occur, in the medium or long run, a domestic effect in the opposite direction, i.e, a faster economic growth, brought about by real exchange rate devaluation, can imply larger investments (in physical capital and in R&D) and, thus, a positive impact on productivity, a la Kaldor-Verdoorn. Indeed, what effects will be larger may be difficult to figure out *ex-ante*, but possibly this will depend on the time span considered — the larger that span, the larger the positive effects in relation to the negative ones.[6]

4.2. Saving Estimation

In relation to the saving equation, since there is evidence that the series are stationary, we can estimate the equation using the Ordinary Least Squares (OLS) model corrected by the HAC matrix and an AR (1), since there is evidence for serial correlation and autocorrelation.[7] The coefficient σ_π is significant at the 1 per cent level. The capitalist propensity to save is $\sigma_\pi = 0.42$. However, the coefficient $(\sigma_\omega - \sigma_\pi)\omega$ is not significantly different from zero. From these results, it is possible to suggest that workers do not save, as suggested by the classical economic and Kaleckian theory. Naastepad and Storm (2007) estimated a similar saving equation for advanced economies. The parameter σ_w for France is 0.10; Germany 0.09; Italy 0.17; Japan 0.12; and the Netherlands 0.15. The parameter $(\sigma_\pi - \sigma_\pi)\,\pi$ for France is 0.30; Germany 0.39; Italy 0.35; Japan 0.38; and the Netherlands 0.57. These results are in line with the classical economic and Kaleckian theory, in which the propensity to save of capitalists is bigger than that of the workers.

4.3. Investment Estimation

As pointed out by Hamilton (1994), whether the time series are co-integrated or integrated of order one, the OLS method is a superconsistent estimator. Also, the independent variables were taken with lags to avoid simultaneity. The profit share parameter is negative and non-significant, whereas the output growth parameter is positive and significant at the 5 per cent level. The investment appears to respond more on the output growth than profit share, which suggests a demand growth regime of accumulation. The relation between the real exchange rate and investment is negative and significant at the 5 per cent level. Nonlinearity was tested; however, the real exchange rate squared parameter is not significant.

---

[6]This point was highlighted by an anonymous referee, whom we thank. Indeed, as she (he) has pointed out, China modern development, with its quite perennial devalued real exchange rate, may be a real example of this. Moreover, perhaps one can calculate if these effects (which of them, the negative or the positive), in case of the real exchange rate devaluations are more important, in the case of (a) wage-led; or (b) profit-led economies. That may be another important question to be studied in the future — real exchange devaluations and their impacts on wage-led and profit-led economies, in the short, and in the medium-long runs.

[7]The autocorrelation test is shown in the appendix of this study.

The coefficient related to the profit share is −0.83, and it is not significant, which means that an increase in profit share does not raise investment, considering the Brazilian case. In comparison to advanced economies, in the case of France, the parameter is 0.29; Japan 0.60; the Netherlands 0.47; Germany 0.56; Italy 0.50; the U.K. 0.54; and the U.S. (0.48) (Storm and Naastepad 2012).[8] Oreiro and Araújo (2013) estimated a similar equation with quarterly data from 1994 to 2008, but instead of using the income variable to study the relationship between investment and demand, they used capacity utilization. In the present research, the income was used, given that it better fits the theoretical model.

Also, Oreiro and Araújo (2013) studied nonlinearity in the real exchange rate by using the variables in level. The outcome in their work for the profit share coefficient is 0.66, which is quite close to the coefficient estimated in this research. Araujo and Gala (2012) also estimated a similar equation using quarterly data from 2002 to 2008, but instead of using the profit share, the authors used the profit rate, and they also used capacity utilization for aggregate demand. However, the authors estimated the investment equation in levels, whereas in this study, the investment equation was estimated in the first difference. Bhaduri and Marglin (1990) argue that: 'Given the accountants' book value of capital in the short period, the average rate of profit [...] depends [...], on both the profit margin/share and the degree of capacity utilization' (Bhaduri and Marglin 1990, p. 379).

The demand coefficient for Brazil is 0.53. Again, in contrast to advanced economies, considering only the results that were significant: the U.K. 0.30; France −0.11; Spain 0.16; and the U.S. 0.12. In Brazil, the elasticity to invest in relation to aggregate demand is higher than in the advanced economies, meaning that investment responds more effectively to aggregate demand in Brazil then it does in advanced economies.

The real exchange rate coefficient −0.14 is significant. The real exchange rate is negatively related to investment growth. This result, however, does not disagree with Rodrik (2008), Rapetti, Skott, and Razmi (2012) and Missio et al. (2015). In their work, the focus was on the real exchange rate misaligning. In the present research, the focus is on the real exchange rate as such. It is possible that in the case where the real exchange rate policy considers the issue raised by these authors, the real exchange rate would be positively related to investment growth.

4.4. Import and Export Equation

The data for Brazilian exports and world income can be found in the WDI-World Bank database, from 1960 to 2011. To obtain equation 2, or ($\hat{v} = \hat{w} - \hat{\lambda}$), the data for real wage in growth rate is necessary. From 1960 to 2008, the data can be found in Marquetti and Porsse (2014), and from 2009 to 2011, the data for this variable can be found in the National Account System (SCN) from the Brazilian Institute of Geography and Statistics (IBGE).

The data for Brazilian GDP or (y), export (x), import (m) and world income (z) can be found in the WDI-World Bank database from 1960 to 2011. The real exchange rate was calculated in the usual manner: $\theta = (P^*/P)E$, where P^* is the US producer price base 100 in 2005, and the source of which was the IMF. P is the consumer price in the Brazil base

---

[8]In this comparison, we considered only the figure that was significant.

100 in 2005, from 1960 to 1979, the source of which was IPEADA; E is the end-of-period nominal BRL/USD market exchange rate (buy); and θ is the real exchange rate. From 1980 to 2011, the real effective exchange rate was found in the WDI-World Bank database.

The empirical analysis consists of estimating the imports and exports equation:

$$\log M = \text{constant} + \varphi \log Y + \vartheta \log(p_f + e - p_d) \qquad (31)$$

To estimate the exports equation, the same procedure is applied:

$$\log X = \text{constant} + \varepsilon \log z + \eta \log(p_d - e - p_f) \qquad (32)$$

Since both equations are integrated of order (1), by the Kwiatkowski–Phillips–Schmidt–Shin test, it is possible to estimate equations 31 and 32 by applying the cointegration methodology. Based on the criteria for lag selection, we chose a VAR (1), which corresponds to a VEC (0). The maximum eigenvalue trace statistics accept the hypothesis of at least one cointegration vector, which means that the variables involved in the test have a long-term relationship. All these tests can be checked in the appendix of this study.

In order to estimate the equations, many tests were carried out, such as the Breusch–Godfrey Serial Correlation LM test (LM); heteroskedasticity test (ARCH); Bai-Perron multiple breakpoint test; unit roots test (KPSS); and the cointegration test (in the case in which the variable in a particular equation is stationary in the first difference). All tables with these test results are reported in the appendix.

4.5. Exports Estimation

World income elasticity of export and price elasticity are highly significant; although both present the expected sign. Usually, scholars have calculated the growth rate of export in the balance of payments constrained growth model. As a result, there is scarce work involving estimation of the export equation (Tables 2 and 3).

4.6. Imports Estimation

The income elasticity of imports presents the expected sign, and it is significant. The price elasticity of imports presents the expected sign and is also significant. Bértola, Higachi, and Porcile (2002) and Lima, Carvalho and Lima, and Jayme Jr., Silveira, and Romero (2011) found that the real exchange rate is not significant and has the opposite sign to the one expected. Alencar and Strachman (2014) found the price elasticity of import significant,

Table 2. Exports equation — 1960–2011.

Long run equation	Constant	ln x (−1)	ln z (−1)	ln θ (−1)	@TREND(60)
			Vector Error Correction Estimates		
	10.21	1.00000	1.098974	0.009663	−0.031491
			(0.36948)	(0.00287)	
			[2.97438]	[3.37204]	
Short run equation		Dln x (−1)	Dln z (−1)	Dln θ (−1)	
		(0.10958)	−0.006244	0.970290	
		(0.00214)	(0.02025)	(5.77600)	
		[4.16753]	[−0.30843]	[0.16799]	

Note: Standard errors in () and t-statistics in [ ]

Table 3. Imports equation — 1960–2011.

Long run equation	Constant	Vector Error Correction Estimates			
		ln m (−1)	ln y (−1)	ln θ (−1)	@TREND(60)
	26.64	1.00000	1.771369	- 0.110648	−0.084959
			(0.88543)	(0.01949)	
			[2.00058]	[−5.67800]	
Short run equation		D ln m (−1)	D ln y (−1)	D ln θ (−1)	
		0.051750	0.027378	1.906900	
		(0.02687)	(0.00678)	(0.82086)	
		[1.92571]	[4.03793]	[2.32304]	

Note: Standard errors in () and t-statistics in [ ].

but having the opposite sign to the one expected. Besides Brazil, these elasticities have been estimated for several countries, with robust findings.[9]

Given the outcomes for productivity, saving and investment estimation, as well as export and import, it is possible to calculate equation 29:

$$\frac{d\hat{y}}{d\hat{w}} = C = \frac{[\xi(\sigma_\pi - \sigma_w)(1 - \beta_2) - \psi_i\phi_1\alpha]}{[1 + \xi(\sigma_\pi - \sigma_w)\beta_1 + \psi_m\varphi - \psi_i\phi_2]} = 0,22 \qquad (28\prime)$$

In this case, the regime is wage-led, since the outcome of equation 28′ is positive. The result obtained in this work is different from that of Oreiro and Araújo (2013) and Oreiro and Araujo (2013). This could be due to the size of the database and how the model was built. In the present model, the real exchange rate's effect on investment and productivity is taken into consideration. Also, the BPCG aspect is considered in this model — notably, the price and income elasticity of export and import — and as a result, it would be expected to find different outcomes, since a different model is used, with more variables. Again, by using the estimation results, it is possible to calculate equation 31:

$$\frac{d\hat{y}}{d\hat{\theta}} = D = \frac{[-\xi(\sigma_\pi - \sigma_w)\beta_3 + \psi_i\phi_3 + \psi_x\eta - \psi_m\vartheta]}{[1 + \xi(\sigma_\pi - \sigma_w)\beta_1 + \psi_m\varphi - \psi_i\phi_2]} = -0,04 \qquad (30\prime)$$

A negative relation is found between economic growth and the real exchange rate.

In relation to the real exchange rate misalignment discussion, it was argued that there is robust empirical evidence that the real exchange rate index boosts economic growth. It was seen that this index could be the Balassa-Samuelson effect, the PPP effect or the industrial disequilibrium effect. The evidence for the Balassa-Samuelson effect can be found in the work of Rodrik (2008), Rapetti, Skott, and Razmi (2012); Oreiro and Araújo (2013); Nassif, Feijó, and Araújo (2015); and Missio et al. (2015). However, the evidence for the PPP effect can be found in the work of Cavallo, Cottani, and Kahn (1990); Dollar (1992); Razin and Collins (1997); Benaroya and Janci (1999); Acemoglu et al. (2002),

---

[9]Hansen and Kvedaras (2004) analyze the elasticities for the Baltics countries such as Estonia, Latvia and Lithuania; by using times-series econometrics methods the authors estimated the price elasticity of import, which was −0.27, −0.44 and −0.26, respectively, and the income elasticity of import was 0.82, 1.51 and 0.72. Jeon (2009) analyses the import equation to China. The price elasticity of import was −0.58 and income elasticity to import 1.77. Thirlwall (1979) estimated the income elasticity to import to several countries, and the coefficient value is between 0.85 and 2.25. Moreno-Brid and Pérez (1999) estimated the income elasticity of import to countries in Central America, and found the coefficient to be between 1.10 and 3.70, the price elasticity of import between −0.44 and −1.63. Holland, Vilela, and Canuto (2004) estimated the income elasticity of import for several Latin American Countries, among which was Brazil. The mentioned estimated elasticity was 2.16, for the period between 1951 and 2000.

and Gala (2008). It is noteworthy that these authors found a positive relationship between real exchange rate devaluation through a kind of real exchange rate misalignment. In this paper, we obtained the opposite result. Although the real exchange rate devaluation can hurt investment, as well as aggregate demand, it can have a positive impact on productivity growth.

Krugman and Taylor (1978) present arguments to explain the reasons why aggregate demand falls when the exchange rate is undervalued. First, the devaluation raises the prices of exports and imports. If the trade is in balance, and the terms of trade do not change, the price change is compensated. If, however, the increase in import prices overcomes the variation in exports, the net result will be a reduction of the country's income. Second, the depreciation of the real exchange rate redistributes income from wages to profits. This happens for two reasons: (i) The monetary wages in the short term are rigid, and the depreciation of the exchange rate subsequently reduces the real wage; and (ii) exports increase the volume of income of exporters. Third, if the government budget is not in balance, it will have a compatible effect on the income of the trade deficit. If the taxes are progressive, due to the devaluation, there will be a distribution of income from wages to profits, as well as greater participation in the economy of the collection tax. The devaluation transfers income from the private to the public, since, assuming *ad valorem* taxes, depreciation increases the price of imports, causing a positive impact on the collection of the public sector.

5. Conclusion

The aim of this research was to build a Post-Kaleckian model in the context of external constraints. Several authors, including Seguino (2010), Ribeiro, McCombie, and Lima (2016) and Botta, Porcile, and Ribeiro (2018) argue that there is a lack of understanding about the relationship between the balance of payments constrained growth (BPCG) theory and functional income distribution. In this research, we advanced the understanding of this subject.

Some aspects of the model can be highlighted: (i) In the model present in this research, when income distribution is combined with the external constraints, the possibility of a wage-led regime is increased; and (ii) it is possible that even if an economy is profit-led, the real exchange rate can boost economic growth, and, even if an economy is wage-led, real exchange rate devaluation can improve economic growth. The latter is possible because the investment and productivity equations are dependent on the real exchange rate, just as the import and export equations. Therefore, the real exchange rate devaluation can be positively or negatively related to investment and productivity.

An empirical exercise was performed for the Brazilian economy in the period between 1960 and 2011. For this specific case, although the regime is wage-led, when an external constraint is taken into consideration, the real exchange rate has a positive impact on economic growth. In relation to the literature on exchange rate misalignment,[10] the model suggested in this research developed a positive relationship between real exchange rate

---

[10]See: Cavallo, Cottani, and Kahn (1990); Dollar (1992); Razin and Collins (1997); Benaroya and Janci (1999); Acemoglu et al. (2002); Rodrik (2008); Gala (2008); Rapetti et al. (2012); Oreiro and Araújo (2013); Nassif et al. (2015); and Missio et al. (2015).

devaluation and growth. In fact, by using a Post-Kaleckian approach, we obtained a similar result when compared with the literature on exchange rate misalignment. The innovation in this research is that although the real exchange rate devaluation can hurt investment and productivity growth, as can be seen in the estimations provided in this research, the overall outcome suggests that real exchange rate devaluation boosts economic growth through the export channel.

Acknowledgements

We would like to thank two anonymous referees, as well as Malcom Sawyer for helpful comments, with improving the paper. The usual disclaimers apply.

Disclosure Statement

No potential conflict of interest was reported by the author(s).

Funding

We are grateful to the Brazilian National Council of Scientific and Technological Development (CNPq) for financial support.

ORCID

Douglas Alencar ⓘ http://orcid.org/0000-0002-6077-998X
Frederico G. Jayme ⓘ http://orcid.org/0000-0002-4617-0107
Gustavo Britto ⓘ http://orcid.org/0000-0002-5285-3684

References

Acemoglu, D., S. Johnson, Y. Thaicharoen, and J. Robinson. 2002. 'Institutional Causes, Macroeconomic Symptoms: Volatility, Crisis and Growth.' Nber Working Paper 9124.
Alencar, D. A., F. G. Jayme Jr, and G. Britto. 2018. 'Productivity, the Real Exchange Rate and the Aggregate Demand: An Empirical Exercise Applied to Brazil from 1960 to 2011.' *Journal of Post Keynesian Economics* 41 (3): 455–477.
Alencar, D. A., and E. Strachman. 2014. 'Balance of Payments Constrained Growth in Brazil: 1951-2008.' *Journal of Post Keynesian Economics* 36 (4): 673–698.
Araujo, E. C., and P. Gala. 2012. 'Regimes de crescimento econômico no Brasil. Evidências empíricas e implicações de política.' *Estudos Avançados* 26 (75): 424–444.
Barbosa Filho, N. H. 2004. 'Growth, Exchange Rates and Trade in Brazil: A Structuralist Post-Keynesian Approach.' *Nova Economia* 14 (2): 59–86.
Benaroya, F., and D. Janci. 1999. 'Measuring Exchange Rates Misalignments with Purchasing Power Parity Estimates.' In *Exchange Rate Policies in Emerging Asian Countries*, edited by S. Collignon, J. Pisani-Ferry, and Y. C. Park. New York: Routledge.
Bértola, L., H. Higachi, and G. Porcile. 2002. 'Balance-of-Payments-Constrained-Growth in Brazil: A Test of Thirlwall's Law, 1890-1973.' *Journal of Post Keynesian Economics* 25 (1): 123–140.
Bhaduri, A., and S. Marglin. 1990. 'Unemployment and The Real Wage: The Economic Basis for Contesting Political Ideologies.' *Cambridge Journal of Economics* 14: 375–393.
Blecker, R. A. 1999. 'Kaleckian Macro Models for Open Economies.' In *Foundations of International Economics: Post Keynesian Perspectives*, edited by J. Deprez, and J. T. Harvey. London: Routledge.

Botta, A., G. Porcile, and R. S. M. Ribeiro. 2018. 'Economic Development, Technical Change and Income Distribution: A Conversation Between Keynesians, Schumpeterians and Structuralists. Introduction to the Special Issue.' *PSL Quarterly Review* 71: 97–97.

Bowles, S., and R. Boyer. 1995. 'Wages, Aggregate Demand, and Employment in an Open Economy: An Empirical Investigation.' In *Macroeconomics Policy After The Conservative Era*, edited by G. Epstein, and H. Gintis. Cambridge, MA: Cambridge University Press.

Bresser-Pereira, L. C., and P. Gala. 2009. 'Why Foreign Savings Fail to Cause Growth.' *International Journal of Political Economy* 38 (3): 58–76.

Britto, G., and J. S. L. Mccombie. 2009. 'Thirlwall's Law and the Long-Term Equilibrium Growth Rate: An Application to Brazil.' *Journal of Post Keynesian Economics* 32: 115–136.

Britto, G., and J. S. L. Mccombie. 2015. 'Increasing Returns to Scale and Regions: A Multilevel Model for Brazil.' *Brazilian Keynesian Review* 1: 118–134.

Campos, R. S., F. G. Jayme Jr, and G. Britto. Forthcoming. 'Endogeneity of the Elasticities and the Real Exchange Rate in a Balance of Payments Constrained Growth Model: Cross-Country Empirical Evidence.' *Brazilian Keynesian Review*.

Cavallo, D. F., J. A. Cottani, and M. S. Kahn. 1990. 'Real Exchange Rate Behavior and Economic Performance in LDCS.' *Economic Development and Cultural Change* 39: 61–76.

Dollar, D. 1992. 'Outward-Oriented Developing Economies Really Do Grow More Rapidly: Evidence from 95 LDCS, 1976–1985.' *Economic Development and Cultural Change* 40: 523–544.

Gabriel, L., F. Jayme Jr, and J. Oreiro. 2016. 'A North-South Model of Economic Growth, Technological Gap, Structural Change and Real Exchange Rate.' *Structural Change and Economic Dynamics* 38: 83–94.

Gala, P. 2008. 'Real Exchange Rate Levels and Economic Development: Theoretical Analysis and Econometric Evidence.' *Cambridge Journal of Economics* 32: 273–288.

Hamilton, J. 1994. *Time Series Analysis*. Princeton, NJ: Princeton University Press.

Hansen, J. D., and V. Kvedaras. 2004. 'Balance of Payments Constrained Economic Growth in the Baltics.' *Ekonomika* 65: 82–91.

Harrod, R. 1933. *International Economics*. Cambridge: Cambridge University Press.

Hein, E., and A. Tarassow. 2010. 'Distribution, Aggregate Demand and Productivity Growth: Theory and Empirical Results for Six OECD Countries Based on a Post-Kaleckian Model.' *Cambridge Journal of Economics* 34 (4): 727–754.

Holland, M., F. Vilela, and O. Canuto. 2004. 'Economic Growth and Balance of Payments in Latin America.' *Investigación Económica* 63 (247): 45–74.

Jayme Jr., F. G. 2003. 'Balance-of-Payments-Constrained Economic Growth in Brazil.' *Brazilian Journal of Political Economy* 23 (1): 62–84.

Jayme Jr., F. G., F. Silveira, and J. P. Romero. 2011. 'Brazil: Structural Change and Balance-of-Payments Constrained Growth.' *CEPAL Review* 4: 173–195.

Jeon, Y. 2009. 'Balance of Payments Constrained Growth: The Case of China 1979-2002.' *International Review of Applied Economics* 23: 135–146.

Kaldor, N. 1956. 'Alternative Theories of Distribution.' *Review of Economic Studies* 23 (92): 83–100.

Kaldor, N. 1966. *Causes of the Slow Rate of Economic Growth of the United Kingdom: An Inaugural Lecture*. Cambridge: Cambridge University Press.

Kaldor, N. 1975. 'Economic Growth and the Verdoorn Law - A Comment on Mr. Rowthorn's Article.' *Economic Journal* 85: 891–896.

Kennedy, C., and A. P. Thirlwall. 1979. 'Import Penetration, Export Performance and Harrod's Trade Multiplier.' *Oxford Economic Papers* 31 (2): 303–323.

Krugman, P., and L. Taylor. 1978. 'Contractionary Effects of Devaluation.' *Journal of International Economics* 8 (3): 445–456.

Lima, G. T., and G. Porcile. 2013. 'Economic Growth and Income Distribution with Heterogeneous Preferences on the Real Exchange Rate.' *Journal of Post-Keynesian Economics* 35: 651–674.

MacKinnon, J., A. Haug, L. Michelis. 1999. "Numerical Distribution Functions of Likelihood Tests for Cointegration." *Journal of Applied Economics* 14 (5): 563–577.

Marquetti, A. A., and M. C. S. Porsse. 2014. 'Patterns of Technical Progress in the Brazilian Economy 1952-2008.' *Cepal Review* 113: 57–73.

Missio, F. J., F. G. Jayme, G. Britto, and J. Luis Oreiro. 2015. 'Real Exchange Rate and Economic Growth: New Empirical Evidence.' *Metroeconomica* 66: 686–714.

Missio, F., and F. G. Jayme Jr. 2013. 'Restrição Externa, Nível da Taxa Real de Câmbio e Crescimento Em Um Modelo Com Progresso Técnico Endógeno.' *Economia e Sociedade (Unicamp. Impresso)* 22: 367–407.

Moreno-Brid, J. C. 1998-99. 'On Capital Flows and the Balance-of-Payments Constrained Growth Model.' *Journal of Post-Keynesian Economics* 21 (2): 283–298.

Moreno-Brid, J. C., and E. Pérez. 1999. 'Balance-of-Payments-Constrained Growth in Central America: 1950–96.' *Journal of Post Keynesian Economics* 22 (1): 131–147.

Moreno-Brid, J. C., and E. Pérez. 2003. 'Trade Liberalization and Economic Growth in Central America.' *Cepal Review* 81: 151–168.

Naastepad, C. W. M. 2006. 'Technology, Demand and Distribution: Application to the Dutch Productivity Growth Slowdown.' *Cambridge Journal of Economics* 30: 403–434.

Nassif, A., C. Feijó, and E. Araújo. 2015. 'Overvaluation Trend of the Brazilian Currency in the 2000s: Empirical Estimation.' *Revista de Economia Política* 35 (1): 3–27.

Oreiro, J. L., F. Missio, F. G. Jayme Jr. 2015. "Capital Accumulation, Structural Change and Real Exchange Rate in a Keynesian-Structuralist Growth Model." *Panoeconomicus* 62 (2): 237–256.

Oreiro, J. L. C., and E. Araújo. 2013. 'Exchange Rate Misalignment, Capital Accumulation and Income Distribution.' *Panoeconomicus* 3: 381–396.

Rapetti, M., P. Skott, and A. Razmi. 2012. 'The Real Exchange Rate and Economic Growth: Are Developing Countries Special?' *International Review of Applied Economics* 26 (6): 735–753.

Razin, O., and S. Collins. 1997. 'Real Exchange Rate Misalignments and Growth.' Nber Working Paper 6147.

Razmi, A., M. Rapetti, and P. Skott. 2012. 'The Real Exchange Rate and Economic Development.' *Structural Change and Economic Dynamics* 23 (2): 151–169.

Ribeiro, R. S. M., J. S. L. McCombie, and G. T. Lima. 2016. 'Exchange Rate, Income Distribution and Technical Change in a Balance-of-Payments Constrained Growth Model.' *Review of Political Economy* 28: 545–565.

Rodrik, D. 2008. 'Real Exchange Rate and Economic Growth.' *Brooking Papers on Economic Activity* 2: 365–412.

Romero, J. P., and G. Britto. 2017. 'Increasing Returns to Scale, Technological Catch-Up and Research Intensity: Endogenising the Verdoorn Coefficient.' *Cambridge Journal of Economics* 41 (2): 391–412.

Seguino, S. 2010. 'Gender, Distribution and the Balance of Payments: Constrained Growth in Developing Countries.' *Review of Political Economy* 22 (3): 373–404.

Storm, S., and C. W. M. Naastepad. 2012. 'OECD Demand Regimes (1960-2000).' *Journal of Post Keynesian Economics* 29 (2): 211–246.

Thirlwall, A. P. 1979. 'The Balance of Payments Constraint as an Explanation of International Growth Rate Differences.' *Banca Nazionale Del Lavoro Quarterly Review* 128 (1): 45–53.

Thirlwall, A., and M. N. Hussain. 1982. 'The Balance of Payments Constraint, Capital Flows and Growth Rate Differences Between Developing Countries.' *Oxford Economic Papers, New Series* 34 (3): 498–510.

Appendices

Appendix 1

Table A1. The KPSS for the productivity, saving and investment.

Variables	t test	Critical value			H0	Result
		1% level	5% level	10% level		
Productivity equation						
ln λ	0.84	0.74	0.46	0.35	Reject	No stationary
ln y	0.91	0.74	0.46	0.35	Reject	No stationary
ln w	0.82	0.74	0.46	0.35	Reject	No stationary
ln θ	0.79	0.74	0.46	0.35	Reject	no stationary
Dln λ	0.22	0.74	0.46	0.35	no reject	Stationary
Dln y	0.39	0.74	0.46	0.35	no reject	Stationary
Dln w	0.18	0.74	0.46	0.35	no reject	Stationary
Dln θ	0.12	0.74	0.46	0.35	no reject	Stationary
Saving equation						
σ	0.42	0.74	0.46	0.35	No reject	Stationary
ω	0.08	0.74	0.46	0.35	No reject	Stationary
Investment equation						
ln i	0.91	0.74	0.46	0.35	Reject	No stationary
ln π	0.08	0.74	0.46	0.35	No reject	Stationary
ln y	0.92	0.74	0.46	0.35	Reject	No stationary
ln θ	0.79	0.74	0.46	0.35	Reject	no stationary
Dln i	0.10	0.74	0.46	0.35	No reject	Stationary
Dln π	0.08	0.74	0.46	0.35	No reject	Stationary
Dln y	0.39	0.74	0.46	0.35	no reject	Stationary
Dln θ	0.12	0.74	0.46	0.35	no reject	Stationary

Table A2. Breusch-Godfrey serial correlation LM test for the productivity, saving, investment and export equations.

Equation	Productivity	Saving	Investment
$RESID(-1)$	0.60 (5.01)	0.83 (5.75)	0.03 (0.22)
$RESID(-2)$	0.47 (3.77)	−0.02 (−0.12)	−0.15 (−0.98)
F-statistic	38.66149	25.39208	0.514612
Obs*R-squared	32.23819	26.73279	1.165697
Prob. F(2,45)	0.0000		
Prob. F(2,48)		0.0000	
Prob. F(2,44)			0.6013
Prob. F(2,48)			
Prob. Chi-Square(2)	0.0000	0.0000	0.5583
Adj. R	0.59	0.51	−0.11
Durbin-Watson stat	1.24	1.93	1.99
Period	1960–2011	1960–2011	1960–2011

Table A3. Heteroskedasticity test ARCH for productivity, saving, investment and export equations.

Equation	Productivity	Saving	Investment
$RESID^2(-1)$	0.29 (2.40)	−0.01 (−0.13)	−0.05 (−0.41)
F-statistic	5.765265	0.017246	0.170700
Obs*R-squared	5.361514	0.017958	0.177182
Prob. F(1,49)	0.0000		
Prob. F(1,48)		0.8961	
Prob. F(1,48)			0.6813
Prob. F(1,49)			
Prob. Chi-Square(2)	0.0000	0.8934	0.6738
Adj. R	0.08	0.000359	−0.01
Durbin-Watson stat	2.26	2.00	1.97
Period	1960–2011	1960–2011	1960–2011

Table A4. Multiple breakpoint tests for productivity, investment, saving and export equations.

Productivity equation				Investment equation			
Sequential F-statistic determined breaks:			3	Sequential F-statistic determined breaks:			0
Break Test	F-statistic	Scaled F-statistic	Critical Value**	Break Test	F-statistic	Scaled F-statistic	Critical Value**
0 vs. 1 *	43.64199	174.5679	16.19	0 vs. 1 *	2.918635	14.59317	18.23
1 vs. 2 *	13.15916	52.63666	18.11				
2 vs. 3 *	9.493310	37.97324	18.93				
3 vs. 4 *	3.299627	13.19851	19.73	Break dates:			
					Sequential	Repartition	
Break dates:							
	Sequential	Repartition					
1	1988	1969					
2	1969	1989					
3	1999	1999					

Saving equation			
Sequential F-statistic determined breaks:			1
Break Test	F-statistic	Scaled F-statistic	Critical Value**
0 vs. 1 *	2.544078	5.088156	11.47
1 vs. 2	2.306901	4.613.802	12.95
Break dates:			
	Sequential	Repartition	
1	1997	1997	

Notes: Bai-Perron tests of L + 1 vs. L sequentially determined breaks; Sample: 1960–2011; Break test options: Trimming 0.15, Max. breaks 5, Sig. level 0.05; Test statistics employ HAC covariances (Bartlett kernel, Newey–West fixed bandwidth) assuming common data distribution.
* Significant at the 0.05 level.
** Bai-Perron (Econometric Journal, 2003) critical values.

Table A5. Autocorrelation test — saving equation — 1960–2011.

Autocorrelation	Partial Correlation		AC	PAC	Q-Stat	Prob
		1	0.624	0.624	21.460	0.000
		2	0.308	-0.13...	26.792	0.000
		3	0.035	-0.16...	26.863	0.000
		4	0.018	0.175	26.881	0.000
		5	-0.04...	-0.14...	27.025	0.000
		6	-0.04...	0.018	27.133	0.000
		7	-0.01...	0.082	27.149	0.000
		8	0.038	-0.00...	27.243	0.001
		9	0.055	0.020	27.443	0.001
		1...	0.102	0.101	28.141	0.002
		1...	0.127	0.025	29.237	0.002
		1...	0.167	0.084	31.197	0.002
		1...	0.160	0.043	33.045	0.002
		1...	0.128	-0.01...	34.260	0.002
		1...	0.081	0.029	34.756	0.003
		1...	0.072	0.053	35.155	0.004
		1...	0.001	-0.11...	35.155	0.006
		1...	0.029	0.137	35.224	0.009
		1...	0.047	0.022	35.411	0.012
		2...	-0.11...	-0.40...	36.488	0.013
		2...	-0.24...	0.022	41.882	0.004
		2...	-0.30...	-0.08...	50.777	0.000
		2...	-0.18...	-0.03...	53.999	0.000
		2...	-0.14...	-0.05...	55.981	0.000

Table A6. Autocorrelation test — productivity and investment equation — 1960–2011.

Autocorrelation	Partial Correlation		AC	PAC	Q-Stat	Prob	Autocorrelation	Partial Correlation		AC	PAC	Q-Stat	Prob
		1	0.615	0.615	20.468	0.000			1	0.032	0.032	0.0538	0.817
		2	0.544	0.266	36.774	0.000			2	-0.14...	-0.14...	1.1783	0.555
		3	0.492	0.144	50.415	0.000			3	-0.04...	-0.03...	1.2675	0.737
		4	0.427	0.046	60.911	0.000			4	0.164	0.150	2.8205	0.588
		5	0.466	0.181	73.696	0.000			5	-0.04...	-0.07...	2.9485	0.708
		6	0.299	-0.18...	79.077	0.000			6	0.211	0.269	5.6190	0.467
		7	0.282	0.007	83.971	0.000			7	0.057	0.031	5.8160	0.561
		8	0.242	-0.01...	87.654	0.000			8	-0.18...	-0.17...	8.0353	0.430
		9	0.209	0.015	90.464	0.000			9	-0.02...	0.058	8.0758	0.527
		1...	0.186	-0.03...	92.739	0.000			1...	0.046	-0.10...	8.2138	0.608
		1...	0.115	-0.01...	93.638	0.000			1...	-0.09...	-0.11...	8.8336	0.637
		1...	0.127	0.028	94.761	0.000			1...	0.007	0.054	8.8374	0.717
		1...	0.080	-0.03...	95.221	0.000			1...	0.098	0.014	9.5226	0.732
		1...	0.075	0.012	95.636	0.000			1...	-0.06...	0.013	9.8333	0.774
		1...	0.129	0.131	96.879	0.000			1...	-0.19...	-0.12...	12.564	0.636
		1...	0.072	-0.04...	97.275	0.000			1...	0.123	0.110	13.724	0.619
		1...	0.071	-0.02...	97.677	0.000			1...	-0.03...	-0.08...	13.842	0.678
		1...	0.016	-0.07...	97.696	0.000			1...	-0.08...	-0.07...	14.487	0.697
		1...	0.044	0.054	97.864	0.000			1...	0.098	0.141	15.294	0.704
		2...	0.042	-0.04...	98.017	0.000			2...	0.076	-0.02...	15.801	0.729
		2...	-0.02...	-0.07...	98.092	0.000			2...	-0.06...	0.090	16.187	0.759
		2...	-0.05...	-0.07...	98.389	0.000			2...	0.010	0.012	16.196	0.806
		2...	-0.20...	-0.24...	102.31	0.000			2...	0.191	0.133	19.727	0.658
		2...	-0.16...	-0.00...	104.94	0.000			2...	-0.07...	-0.02...	20.329	0.678

Table A7. Cointegration test — productivity equation — 1960–2011.

Data Trend:	None	None	Linear	Linear	Quadratic
Test Type	No Intercept No Trend	Intercept No Trend	Intercept No Trend	Intercept Trend	Intercept Trend
Trace	5	2	2	2	3
Max-Eig	2	0	0	1	1

Note: Selected (0.05 level*) Number of cointegrating relations by model. *Critical values based on MacKinnon, Haug, and Michelis (1999).

Table A8. Cointegration test — productivity equation — 1960–2011.

Data Trend:	None	None	Linear	Linear	Quadratic
Test Type	No Intercept No Trend	Intercept No Trend	Intercept No Trend	Intercept Trend	Intercept Trend
Trace	3	3	4	3	4
Max-Eig	3	2	2	2	4

Note: Selected (0.05 level*) Number of cointegrating relations by model. *Critical values based on MacKinnon, Haug, and Michelis (1999).

Appendix 2. VEC Analyses

Table A9. KPSS test.

	Imports and exports equation					
ln m	0.90	0.74	0.46	0.35	Reject	No stationary
ln y	0.91	0.74	0.46	0.35	Reject	No stationary
ln θ	0.79	0.74	0.46	0.35	Reject	No stationary
ln x	0.79	0.74	0.46	0.35	Reject	No stationary
ln z	0.96	0.74	0.46	0.35	Reject	No stationary
Dln m	0.07	0.74	0.46	0.35	No reject	Stationary
Dln y	0.39	0.74	0.46	0.35	No reject	Stationary
Dln θ	0.12	0.74	0.46	0.35	No reject	Stationary
Dln x	0.15	0.74	0.46	0.35	No reject	Stationary
Dln z	0.68	0.74	0.46	0.35	No reject	Stationary

Table A10. VAR lag order selection criteria — imports equation.

Lag	LogL	LR	FPE	AIC	SC	HQ
0	−2.051.708	NA	1.173.712	8.673.784	8.790.734	8.717.980
1	1.186.866	397.9057*	0.000202*	0.005472*	0.473273*	0.182255*
2	2.044.238	1.464.676	0.000207	0.023234	0.841885	0.332603
3	2.588.044	8.610.268	0.000243	0.171648	1.341.149	0.613604
4	3.491.551	1.317.615	0.000248	0.170187	1.690.538	0.744730

Notes: * indicates lag order selected by the criterion, LR: sequential modified LR test statistic (each test at 5% level), FPE: Final prediction error, AIC: Akaike information criterion, SC: Schwarz information criterion and HQ: Hannan-Quinn information criterion.

Table A11. Cointegration test – imports equation.

Data Trend:	None	None	Linear	Linear	Quadratic
Test Type	No Intercept	Intercept	Intercept	Intercept	Intercept
	No Trend	No Trend	No Trend	Trend	Trend
Trace	1	1	1	1	0
Max-Eig	1	1	1	1	0

Note: Selected (0.05 level*) Number of cointegrating relations by model. *Critical values based on MacKinnon, Haug, and Michelis (1999).

Table A12. VAR lag order selection criteria — exports equation.

Lag	LogL	LR	FPE	AIC	SC	HQ
1	5.953.167	NA	2.45e-05*	−2.105486*	−1.754636*	−1.972900*
2	6.382.511	7.513.512	2.99e-05	−1.909.380	−1.207.679	−1.644.206
3	7.312.042	1.510.487	2.98e-05	−1.921.684	−0.869133	−1.523.924
4	7.455.647	2.154.080	4.16e-05	−1.606.520	−0.203119	−1.076.172

Note: * indicates lag order selected by the criterion, LR: sequential modified LR test statistic (each test at 5% level), FPE: Final prediction error, AIC: Akaike information criterion, SC: Schwarz information criterion and HQ: Hannan-Quinn information criterion.

Table A13. Cointegration test — exports equation.

Data Trend:	None	None	Linear	Linear	Quadratic
Test Type	No Intercept	Intercept	Intercept	Intercept	Intercept
	No Trend	No Trend	No Trend	Trend	Trend
Trace	1	2	1	1	0
Max-Eig	1	2	1	1	0

Note: Selected (0.05 level*) Number of cointegrating relations by model. *Critical values based on MacKinnon, Haug, and Michelis (1999).

The Limitations of International Relations Regarding MNCs and the Digital Economy: Evidence from Brazil

Marcos Vinícius Isaias Mendes ⓘ

ABSTRACT

Multinationals (MNCs) have been considered a relevant research topic for International Relations since the emergence of the field of International Political Economy in the 1970s. Nowadays, MNCs are undergoing deep changes in their business models and global strategies due to the digital economy. This has considerable implications for the international system. For instance, the rise of information and communication technology (ICT) MNCs to the top of market value lists globally. Nonetheless, IR scholars have been slow in grasping the importance of ICT MNCs and the digital economy. In this paper, I justify this statement by evaluating the inclusion of MNCs and ICT MNCs in Brazilian IR scholarship. The method used is a bibliometric mapping of the scientific production of Brazilian IR scholars, supported by a systematic literature review. The results showcase that, in spite of the impact of digitalization on Brazil's economy and politics, IR scholars have conducted few studies on MNCs and practically no studies on ICT MNCs. This case illustrates the emergence of new dynamics in global value chains triggered by digitalization. It also illustrates the challenges for developing countries such as Brazil to engage in global production networks within the highly competitive ICT sector.

Introduction

In April 1970, Susan Strange published *International Economics and International Relations: a case of mutual neglect*, which according to Cohen (2014) constitutes the cornerstone of the field of International Political Economy (IPE). Strange (1970) observed that the international economic system had been scarcely studied by International Relations (IR) scholars. In her critique regarding International Economics research, she noted the prevalence of certain issues (such as international trade and the payment system) over others; the leadership of the U.S. in the production of these studies, inevitably considering its political and economic interests in the choice of research topics; and a kind of political naivety in the excessive optimism about international relations. In her own words, there was a need for a theory to answer 'some key questions at the border between economics and politics', concerning, for instance, 'the implications of the growing European financial markets for governments' fiscal capacity; and the obsolescence of international trade theory vis-à-vis the reorganization of international production in light of the growing expansion of multinational corporations (MNCs)[1]' (Strange 1970, p. 311). Two decades later, the author questioned why MNCs were still not a common research topic in IR (Strange 1991). According to her, at that time most IR scholars defined power exclusively as the ability to create/destroy order in the international system, thus it was natural for them to focus on the state as a central actor. However, when power is conceived of as the ability to create or destroy wealth (and not 'only' order) in the international system, and when the influence of elements such as justice and freedom in the composition of this wealth is considered, MNCs play a central role.

Despite this prevailing neglect, some scholars soon became aware of the importance of MNCs to IR. Nye (1974) emphasized that MNCs played at least three roles in day-to-day world politics: *private foreign policy*, when companies affect government's decisions through economic means (promises of new investments, threats of withdrawal, bargaining); *instruments of influence*, when companies are used by governments as instruments of influence concerning trade, financial or security policies; and *setting the agenda*, i.e., intentional or unintentional roles of MNCs in helping setting the agenda of interstate politics. Jenkins (1987) distinguished four schools of IPE research on multinationals: Marxists and non-Marxists, and within each current those who were critical and those who supportive of MNCs activities. Drawing on a critical Marxist perspective, Tarzi (1999) and Fieldhouse (1999) analyzed the bargaining relationship between Third World host governments and MNCs. Both authors concluded that actual bargaining power of host governments vary according to societal pressures, MNCs strategies, and pressures from MNC's home governments. Levy and Prakash (2003) observed that MNCs play an active role in global governance in order to increase their importance in various arenas, considering the costs of political participation and the benefits for their international competitiveness. More recently, advances have been made concerning MNCs and corporate social responsibility (CSR) issues (Falkner 2009; Jamali 2010; Gamu and Dauvergne 2018), and on developing countries MNCs (Aykut and Goldstein 2007; Cuervo-Cazurra 2012).

As regards ICT MNCs[2] in global affairs, a variety of approaches can be found in the literature. Considering that the world is passing through a substantial transition in its basic mode of production, from an industrial (manufacturing) to a post-industrial (information processing) phase, ICT MNCs are those that are leading this transition. Authors such as Curtis (2009) and Schwab (2016) understand that the basic transformational resource in the 21st century increasingly is based on information and knowledge, programming and algorithms, computer and data transmission. Thus, companies such as Google, Amazon, Facebook, Apple, Alibaba, Tencent and Huawei are examples of ICT MNCs. According to Wolf (2017), in the list of the world 10 largest corporations by market value in 2017, 7 were ICT MNCs (Apple, Alphabet/Google, Microsoft, Amazon,

---

[1]According to UNCTAD (2017b), a company qualifies as a MNC (or MNE, multinational enterprise) if (1) its foreign revenues or foreign assets (or both) are more than 10 per cent of the total, or (2) if it has a significant number of subsidiaries outside the home economy (excluding affiliates in offshore financial centers).

[2]UNCTAD (2017b, 3) distinguished two types of MNEs in the information economy: Digital MNEs and ICT MNEs (IT and Telecom). Despite the validity of such categories, here I consider these two types of companies under the same label 'ICT MNCs' for the sake of simplification.

Facebook, Alibaba, Tencent, and Samsung). In fact, the IR literature concerning ICTs has had a considerable progress in the last decades. Rosenau and Johnson (2002) observed that technology can underlie cooperation or conflict in world politics, while Fritsch (2011) recognized that the transformational power of technology has yet to be integrated into theories of IR/IPE. Others highlight the role of ICTs for international development (Nwagwu 2006; Heeks 2008), the influence of ICT industries on the international political rise of China and India (Franda 2002; Ning 2009; Niosi and Tschang 2009), and the internet global governance and its challenges (Mueller 2010; Klein 2011).

While studies on MNCs underwent considerable progress since the 1990s in the international literature, in Brazilian IR/IPE literature, we can nonetheless argue that 'time has stopped' in that decade. In Brazil, MNCs are a research topic mainly in Economics (Hiratuka 2005; Queiroz and Carvalho 2005; Stal and Campanário 2010), Management and International Business (Amatucci and Bernardes 2008; Ramsey and Almeida 2010; Rocha and Ávila 2015). Very few studies on this topic have been published in the fields of IR/IPE (Becard and Macedo 2014; Silva-Rego and Figueira 2017; Rodrigues 2018). Concerning ICT MNCs, hardly any studies have been published, even though some recent research on the global internet governance can be found (Canabarro and Wagner 2014).

I argue that Brazil is a relevant international case for the study of MNCs and ICT MNCs for several reasons. First, despite the expansion of developing-countries MNCs (Cuervo-Cazurra 2012, 2008), studies focus on Chinese (Wang 2016; Ramamurti and Hillemann 2017) and Indian MNCs (Buckley 2016; Thite 2016), hence the literature is scarce concerning other big developing countries such as Brazil. Second, there is a recent trend for the internationalization of Brazilian MNCs, especially since the 2014 economic and political crises (Sheng and Junior 2017). Third, Brazil is home to subsidiaries and assemblage facilities of the world's leading ICT MNCs, and currently ranks 6th globally regarding investments in the sector (Zylberberg 2016; Agência Brasil 2018). Fourth, Brazil has a Digital Governance Strategy (BRASIL 2018a), policy instruments such as the Internet Civil Regulation (BRASIL 2014), the General Law on Personal Data Protection (BRASIL 2018b), the National Plan on the Internet of Things (BRASIL 2019), and international cooperation agreements (BRASIL 2015) concerning investments in ICT infrastructure and the development of digital industries.

The central question that animates this article is, thus, why MNCs and ICT MNCs are still a neglected research topic amongst Brazilian IR scholars, despite their importance for the country's international profile, the government's strategic perception regarding the digital economy, and the long-standing research tradition on MNCs within IR. In order to address this question, I structure the paper in four sections, besides this introduction. In Section one, I review a body of scientific literature on MNCs produced in Brazil and abroad, emphasizing the importance of these studies to IR. In Section two, I present some reflections on the digital economy, and its implications for MNCs and ICT MNCs. Section three introduces the Brazilian case, highlighting the country's position in ICT global value chains (GVCs) along with its economic and political responses to digitalization. In Section four, I use the Alexandre de Gusmão Foundation (FUNAG)[3]

---

[3]FUNAG is a public foundation, instituted by Law 5.717 of October 26 1971, linked to the Brazilian Ministry of Foreign Affairs, whose basic objective is to organize and to promote cultural and educational activities in the fields of international relations and Brazilian diplomatic history.

database on IR academic works, as well as data from the Sucupira Platform[4], visits to the websites of the 13 Brazilian Graduate Programs in IR, articles published in the last 10 years (2009–2018) in the main international and Brazilian[5] IR/IPE journals, and articles published in the annals of the Brazilian Association of International Relations (ABRI) annual meetings, in order to map the research on MNCs and ICT MNCs produced by Brazilian IR scholars. Finally, a conclusion is presented in order to discuss the main implications of the findings.

Data collection was conducted in the aforementioned sources because they showcase the bulk of the work produced by the Brazilian IR scientific community. Data analysis was performed mainly through the keyword search technique, which made it possible to demonstrate the very limited number of works regarding MNCs and ICT MNCs in Brazilian IR research.

The Relevance of MNCs to IR

Since the 1970s, IR/IPE scholars have studied MNCs through a variety of lenses. Fundamentally, much of the international literature, and a scarce set of studies published in Brazil, analyze the performance of MNCs in international politics in three axes: a) as an extension of the hegemonic influence of great or rising states; b) by studying the relationship between exploitation and production, and the negative socioeconomic and environmental externalities of these companies' operations, especially in developing countries; and c) by investigating state-business relations, lobbying activities, and possible threats to the national sovereignty that these companies may represent to host countries.

In the first set of works, MNCs are understood as tentacles of the global expansion of hegemonic or rising states. Of course, studies about U.S. based MNCs prevail. Vernon's (1971) classic study, *Sovereignty@bay: the multinational spread of U.S. firms*, is perhaps one of the first papers in this sense. When analyzing 187 U.S. MNCs, the author highlighted the conflicts between these companies and the governments of the host countries. Arrighi (1994) underlined that since the 1970s, the U.S. practiced a 'capitalism of corporations.' Through the internalization of transaction costs, U.S. MNCs have spread throughout the globe, and provided the financial and material basis for the North-American hegemony (Arrighi 1994; Mendes 2018). This logic was also used by rising powers. Examples of research in this vein include the analysis of the expansion of Japanese MNCs to Latin America and East Asia in the late 20th century (Kimura and Ando 2003), the geo-economic interests behind the presence of Chinese MNCs in Brazil (Becard and Macedo 2014), the expansion of Brazilian multinationals abroad (Ramsey and Almeida 2010; Rodrigues 2018), and the importance of ICT industries to the geopolitical rise of China and India (Franda 2002; Ning 2009).

The second set of works relates to the exploitation mechanisms used by MNCs in their host countries. Gamu and Dauvergne (2018) observe that discursive practices around the idea of CSR were used by mining MNCs to legitimize their work in areas inhabited by small communities in Peru. While these practices in the short term have curtailed the

---

[4]Sucupira Platform is an online tool created in 2014 by the Brazilian government to collect information, perform analyzes and evaluations, and be a reference base of the National Graduate System.

[5]The Brazilian journals selected were those of higher quality in the fields of IR/IPE, according to the most recent Qualis Capes, 2013–2016: *Revista Brasileira de Política Internacional*, Brazilian Journal of Political Economy, and *Contexto Internacional*.

conflicts between these MNCs and local communities, the authors argue that the rhetoric of CSR was used as a political mechanism for legitimizing predatory practices that degrade the environment through 'slow violence.' Rodriguez et al. (2006) investigated the performance of MNCs under three lenses: politics, corruption, and CSR. In political terms, the International Business literature is extensive in cases of MNCs' political strategies for negotiating with the governments of host countries (Vernon 1971; Dunning 1993; Dunning and Lundan 2008). However, institutional differences between the governments of host countries, and how they affect the political strategies of these MNCs, have not yet received due attention in IR. Also scarce are case studies of corruption involving MNCs and the governments of host countries (Rodriguez et al. 2006). Investigations into local political systems and how they stimulate or hinder lobbying or corruption involving MNCs provide fertile ground for future IR research. CSR practices configure the most scarcely researched topic. In this case, studies on the relationships of MNCs with NGOs and local activists are necessary and relevant to IR.

Research on state-business relations represents the third set of works on MNCs of interest to IR. Murtha and Lenway (1994) verified that host countries' industry-specific policies affect the relationship between these governments and MNCs, and influence their permanence. Levy and Prakash (2003) observed that MNCs affect global economic governance by creating market regimes that favor their performance, through interactions with civil society agents and states in complex negotiations. Kobrin (2009) examined how MNCs impact sovereignty, autonomy, and state control. Although MNCs' activities may involve legal asymmetry, overlapping of rules, and disputes over the control of natural resources and capital, the authors argue that they do not represent threats to state sovereignty. Silva-Rego and Figueira (2017) explored the relationship between Brazilian foreign policy and the internationalization of local firms. The authors verified a close connection between Brazilian civil construction MNCs and the Ministry of Foreign Affairs, in search of technical and diplomatic support, and with the National Bank for Economic and Social Development (BNDES), in search of financial support, throughout the whole process of internationalization of these companies.

Research conducted by IR/IPE scholars on MNCs differs considerably from research performed by Management or International Business scholars. As Strange (1991) pointed out, studies in these latter areas tend to analyze the performance of these firms from an inside-out perspective. Important theories in International Business, such as Dunning's (1993) eclectic paradigm[6], consider the firm as a rational strategic actor, capable of adapting to virtually any intemperance in the international system. Approaches such as the Uppsala School, which consider incremental learning throughout the internationalization process (Johanson and Vahlne 2009) underestimate the complexity of the political systems of host countries. That is, none of these models focus on systemic outside-in analyzes.

---

[6]The eclectic paradigm is an approach developed by Dunning (1993) to explain under what conditions the firm would be most successful in the internationalization process. According to the paradigm, the firm will open a subsidiary abroad if three conditions are satisfied: 1) if it possesses assets superior to those of its local competitors, a condition understood as ownership advantage (Ownership, O); 2) if it can efficiently combine its skills and needs with factors of production of host countries, acquiring location advantage (Localization, L); 3) if it is able to decide correctly which activities should be conducted internally and which should be delegated to third parties on the host countries, a condition understood as internalization advantages (Internalization, I).

It is precisely in this respect that IR scholars can bring significant contributions regarding the agency, the influence and importance of MNCs in international affairs. Analyzes of the political-economic complexity of the international system, for instance, through patterns of recurrence and evolution of financial crises, can shed light on opportunities and threats to the performance of MNCs in host countries (Sauvant, Maschek, and McAllister 2010). In this sense, studies on multinational banks and insurance companies can represent important cases. Moreover, papers that analyze the negotiations of business groups with the political institutions of home and host countries, the complexity of these negotiations, and the results in terms of foreign policy would show the extent of the political power of these MNCs (Oliveira and Onuki 2007; Silva-Rego and Figueira 2017). Another still little explored possibility is research on MNCs headquartered in developing countries. In particular, Brazilian MNCs are practically unexplored in IR research[7], despite their growing level of internationalization (Ramsey and Almeida 2010), and the fact that their stocks are being traded with increasing frequency on global financial markets (Sheng and Junior 2017).

The headline of a recent article published by the World Bank further illustrates the importance of MNCs to IR: *The world's top 100 economies: 31 countries; 69 corporations* (World Bank 2016). The article refers to a list produced by the NGO Global Justice Now, based on data from 2015, which compares the revenues of the Fortune Global 500 firms with the revenues of all countries that year. The list shows that out of the world's 100 largest economies, only 31 are countries, and the rest are large MNCs. In addition, it demonstrates that the 10 largest MNCs have combined revenues exceeding those of the 180 poorest countries in the world (Global Justice Now 2016). Again, considering that wealth and power go hand in hand in world politics, a fundamental principle of IPE, it is naïve to neglect the study of MNCs in IR.

MNCs and the Digital Economy

At the current stage of global capitalism, scholars argue that we have entered a post-industrial epoch (Curtis 2009) or at least a new industrial epoch, Industry 4.0 (Schwab 2016). Industry 4.0 is a set of 'technologies and enhanced capabilities that, when combined, are expected to change the way products and services are created, produced and delivered' (Brun, Gereffi, and Zhan 2019, p. 41). Nine technologies make up the core of this new industrial phase: big data and analytics, autonomous robots, simulation, horizontal and vertical system integration, industrial Internet of Things (IoT), cybersecurity, cloud computing, additive manufacturing and augmented reality (Brun, Gereffi, and Zhan 2019). Other scholars adopt an even broader perspective, stating that the *fourth industrial revolution* represents an 'unprecedented fusion between and across digital, physical and biological technologies' (Maynard 2015, p. 1005). If we consider four digital technology waves (internet in the 2000s, mobile internet in the 2010s, IoT in the 2020s, and Artificial

---

[7]Some exceptions are the works of Fares (2007) and Ferreira (2009), who analyzed the importance of the internationalization of Petrobrás for Brazilian foreign policy; Almeida, Oliveira, and Schneider (2014), that analyzed the role of Brazilian state companies such as Petrobrás and BNDES for Brazilian industrial and international trade policy; Silva-Rego and Figueira (2017), who focused on the internationalization of Brazilian construction firms; and Rodrigues (2018), who found that foreign policy plays an important role in the internationalization of Brazilian MNCs, being a central aspect of the country's internationalization strategy.

Intelligence (AI) and robotics in the 2030s), we have indeed already entered Industry 4.0 (Ono, Lida, and Yamazaki 2017). According to the German Trade and Invest agency, *Industrie 4.0* connects embedded system production technologies and smart production processes aiming to 'radically transform industry, production value chains and business models' (GTAI 2014, p. 6). The concept is closely related with the IoT, Cyber Physical Systems (CPS), ICTs, enterprise architecture and enterprise integration (Lu 2017). What are the implications of this digital revolution for MNCs and ICT MNCs?

Li, Frederick, and Gereffi (2019) observe that global commodity chains (GCCs), GVCs, and global production networks (GPNs) are being substantially revamped by Industry 4.0 and by digital multinationals. The platform economies through which many ICT MNCs operate 'bring together producers and consumers in high-value exchanges by blending products with services' (Li, Frederick, and Gereffi (2019) p. 13). While these two-sided markets disrupt traditional sectors, they open several scenarios by which the internet might impact GVCs. In the case of e-commerce, for instance, two such scenarios are (1) infomediary-driven value chains, where internet companies displace traditional retailers, and (2) more integrated value chains, where the internet allows a certain unification of e-commerce transactions and business practices (Li, Frederick, and Gereffi (2019) p. 5). According to Brun, Gereffi, and Zhan (2019, p. 37), digital MNCs adopt 'competitive strategies valuing more asset-light forms of international production.' In fact, the digital revolution contributes to the increasing presence of such MNCs into the manufacturing and services sector. This is achieved through supply chain digitalization, or 'the use of advanced data analytical tools and physical technologies to improve the digital connectivity and technological capabilities of supply chains' (Li, Frederick, and Gereffi (2019) p. 41). Such process leads to three contemporary trends in GVCs: 'extended disintermediation, servicification, and distributed/flexible production' (Li, Frederick, and Gereffi (2019) p. 45). Wu and Gereffi (2018, p. 331) pinpoint that Internet Platform Companies (IPCs) 'provide infrastructure, information, and technology that enable direct transactions or value creation.' In essence, while in traditional sectors a firm's ability to generate economic returns is determined by its internal resources and its supply-side efficiency, in IPCs profits are mainly driven by network effects, where 'the value to users largely depends on the number of others using the same goods or services' (Wu and Gereffi 2018 p. 332).

ICT MNCs increasingly compete with manufacturing and services companies across different industries. Amazon and Alibaba are cases in point. Even though they are both e-commerce MNCs, Amazon Web Services (AWS) is taking an increasing part of the company's total revenue through the provision of cloud computing platforms, and Alipay competes with PayPal and Apple Pay for the global mobile payment market (Wu and Gereffi 2018 p. 331-341). The concept of business ecosystems illustrates well how GAFA (Google, Amazon, Facebook, and Apple) became so powerful. By connecting content producers, advertisers, sellers, application developers, etc., these firms developed multisided platforms (Miguel and Casado 2016) that benefit from network effects, by matching customers with complementary needs, collecting extensive and real-time usage data (big data), and using multiple ways to lock users in, either by increasing the cost or the effort of switching to a rival product or service – a strategy known as winner-take-all (Barwise and Watkins 2018).

The most updated classification of ICT MNCs was provided by UNCTAD (2017b), which grouped such companies into digital MNCs (internet platforms, digital solutions, e-commerce, and digital content), tech MNCs (hardware and software), and telecom MNCs. For each subgroup, business models, strategies and global footprints vary considerably. Large ICT manufacturers tend to outsource production and other non-core business functions to contract manufacturers, which subsist with 'razor-thin' profit margins and are usually located in developing countries (Zylberberg 2016). Platform leaders can operate either in the hardware (e.g., MediaTek, Chinese company which provides low-cost chipsets) or in the software sector (e.g., Google with its Android; Oracle with their ERP solutions) and usually tend to be based in industrialized countries. Other digital MNCs' characteristics and trends were systematically revealed by UNCTAD (2017a). They concentrate on capital components such as brand, know-how, intellectual property and cash, expressing a structural shift in the sources of corporate value from fixed, tangible assets to intangible and current assets. As a consequence, ICT MNCs 'can reach foreign markets with fewer assets and fewer employees overseas, (...) thus their economic impact on host countries is less directly visible in terms of physical investments and job creation' (UNCTAD 2017a p. 164). Foreign affiliates of ICT MNEs retain a sizeable part of their foreign earnings overseas, in order to minimize the burden of deferring the payment of the tax adjustment upon repatriation of foreign earnings (UNCTAD 2017a p. 172). This practice has been criticized because of its tax implications, and currently countries such as the U.S. (home to a large number of ICT MNCs) are discussing changes in their corporate tax systems. Furthermore, most ICT MNCs are from industrialized economies. Thus, these companies' growth could potentially reverse the global trend in outward FDI verified in the last decade back towards concentration in a few developed countries (UNCTAD 2017a).

These trends have many implications for host-countries. The digitalization of global supply chains will increase the technological requirements imposed on local suppliers. Consequently, local firms may find difficulties to participate in MNCs-coordinated GVCs. Some of the industries most affected by digitalization (e.g. finance and retail) face investment restrictions in several countries (UNCTAD 2017a p. 185). At the same time, as digital technologies spread across all sectors, policymakers need to assess the challenges and opportunities that may arise for their participation in GVCs. In sum, countries now 'face the risk of letting rules become obsolete or of creating an uneven playing field for digital and non-digital firms' (UNCTAD 2017a). As will be demonstrated in the next section, this discussion is important in the case of Brazil because the country is host for affiliates of many ICT MNCs. The section also highlights Brazil's current position in ICT GVCs, as well as some economic and political impacts of digitalization.

Digitalization, ICT MNCs and the Brazilian Case

The ICT sector plays an increasingly prominent role in Brazil's economy and in its political agenda. Since 1991 ICT MNCs were encouraged to set up operations in the country thanks to the Informatics Law (Zylberberg 2016). Nowadays both lead multinationals and contract manufacturers have production facilities in Brazil: all the 10 largest ICT manufacturers according to the Fortune 500 (Samsung, Apple, General Electric, Hewlett-Packard, Siemens, Hitachi, Sony and Panasonic), and 6 out of the 10 largest contract manufacturers (Foxconn, Compal Electronics, Flextronics, Jabil Circuit, Sanmina, Cal-Comp) (Zylberberg 2016). The ICT sector is expected to reach 10.7 per cent of Brazil's GDP by

2020, and currently accounts for 1.5 million jobs.[8] Considering IT, in 2017 the country ranked 9th globally regarding investments (US$ 38 billion), whereas the leading positions were occupied by the U.S. (US$ 751 billion), China (US$ 244 billion) and Japan (US$ 139 billion). In Latin America, Brazil ranked 1st, accounting for 39.1 per cent of the total IT investments. If we add the Telecom sector, the total amount of ICT investments in Brazil in 2017 reached US$ 100 billion, leading the country to occupy the 6th position globally (Agência Brasil 2018). The country exports about four to five times more in software and IT services than in hardware (Malacarne 2018). In this sense, initiatives such as the Strategic Program for Information Technology Software and Services, and recent modifications in the Informatics Law revamped efforts to develop the country's software industry, also encouraging ICT MNCs to set up local R&D (Research and Development) centers. Currently Brazil is home to 7 R&D centers of global ICT MNCs (Microsoft, Intel, EMC2, SAP, Qualcomm, Baidu and Huawei) (Zylberberg 2016).

Despite such scenario, Brazil still remains 'behind the innovation frontier in ICTs' (Zylberberg 2016, p. 4). While the Informatics Law has been effective in attracting foreign ICT MNCs, it has been limited (Deloitte 2019) or even a constraint (Zylberberg 2016) for the development of a local ICT industry. To the lack of adequate policy direction, we can add the slow pace in human capital development in ICT-related fields as plausible causes for this setback. As a consequence, Brazil has only two big ICT MNCs: Stefanini (operating in 41 countries) and TOTVS (operating across Brazil, the U.S. and Latin America). Furthermore, the Brazilian ICT trade balance was negative during the period from 2005 to 2016 (Malacarne 2018).

Industry 4.0 amplifies the challenges of digitalization for Brazil. According to Albuquerque et al. (2019) and Pinto (2019), until 2026 more than 30 million job vacancies could be closed in the country thanks to technology advancements in machine learning, AI, and industry automation processes. The digital economy, citizens' private data usage, and the aggressive M&A (Mergers and Acquisitions) strategies of ICT MNCs all pose challenges to government bodies such as the Administrative Council for Economic Defense (*Conselho Administrativo de Defesa Econômica*, CADE) (Zanatta and Abramovay 2019). In addition, knowledge production and political/economic strategies to adjust the country's production systems to the increasing global technological competition are still very incipient (Pires 2018). Despite these challenges, other studies suggest how digital technologies can enhance: the adoption of blockchain in order to achieve a better integration of the Brazilian economy within global financial and real estate markets (Tapscott and Tapscott 2018; Graglia and Mellon 2019); Brazil's role in global agribusiness and in the energy sector, with increasing application of ICTs within the production processes in these fields (Brainard and Martinez-Diaz 2009); and Brazilian cybercrime and cybersecurity policies that, understood as strategic issues, would alleviate the country's dependency regarding Western technologies (Kshetri 2015).

Consequently, the topic of digitalization receives increasing attention in Brazil's domestic and foreign policy agendas. As direct responses to the challenges of the digital economy, the Brazilian government has approved three bills. The Internet Civil Regulation (BRASIL 2014), a bill passed by the Brazilian Congress in 2014, which 'intends to provide privacy protections for internet users, and limit the amount of metadata that can be gathered on Brazilians' (Kshetri 2015, p. 247). The General Law on Personal Data Protection

---

[8] Available from: http://www.brasilitplus.com/brasilit/Ingles/detGrandesNumeros.php Accessed January 30th 2020.

(BRASIL 2018b), which regulates the processing of personal data by individuals or companies. And the National Plan on the Internet of Things (BRASIL 2019), a project led by the BNDES together with the ministry of Science, Technology, Innovation and Communications (MCTIC) with the aim at establishing a strategic approach regarding IoT in Brazil, from 2018 to 2022. In parallel, institutional initiatives have also been coordinated in order to propel the ICT industry. Brazil IT+ was created in 2009 by the Brazilian Trade and Investment Promotion Agency (Apex-Brasil) in partnership with the Brazilian Association of Information Technology and Communication Companies (BRASSCOM) and the Association for the Promotion of Brazilian Software Excellence (SOFTEX) in order to develop a strategy for Brazil's positioning in the global ICT market, the promotion of exports and internationalization of local ICT firms.[9]

The development of ICT industries is also present in Brazil's international cooperation agreements. The joint action plan between Brazil and China 2015–2021 – under the China-Brazil Global Strategic Partnership – has clear goals as regards the ICT sector: 'promote the sharing of experience of industrial and ICT development, explore the potential of ICT for industrial cooperation' (BRASIL 2015, p. 33). Priority industries include: the internet of things, cloud computing, digital TV, mobile technologies, bank automation, digital and smart cities. Also, the BRICS Working Group on Information and Communication Technologies and High-Performance Computing[10] intends to set in motion joint initiatives in ICTs in these five economies. In Latin America, bilateral cooperation agreements in the field of internet access massification were signed with Argentina and Uruguay (BRASIL 2011).

MNCs and ICT MNCs in Brazilian IR Research

In order to analyze the scientific production on MNCs and ICT MNCs by Brazilian IR scholars, I opted initially to map the adherence of economic themes in all the Brazilian Graduate Programs in IR (PPG-RI). Therefore, the initial objective was to analyze how the subfield of IPE is configured in these programs. The Sucupira platform[11] was consulted on October 8th 2018, and I extracted a database with all the Graduate Programs classified in the area of Political Science and IR.[12] I filtered only the PPG-RI, thus excluding programs from the areas of Political Science, Public Policy, Defense Studies, Military Sciences, Regional Integration, and related.

The outcome of this first stage of research were 13 PPG-RI, with three important notes – the Graduate Programs on Political Science and International Relations (PS and IR) of the UFPB (Federal University of Paraíba), on IPE of UFRJ (Federal University of Rio de Janeiro), and on International Strategic Studies (ISS) of UFRGS (Federal University of Rio Grande do Sul) – that are part of this total. Subsequently, in consultation on the websites of these 13 PPG-RI, held between 6–7 September 2019, I verified if there were research lines in IPE. In addition, on the same websites, I consulted the research areas

[9]Available from: http://www.brasilitplus.com/brasilit/Ingles/detHistorico.php Accessed January 30th, 2020.
[10]Available from: http://brics2019.itamaraty.gov.br/images/documentos/20190514_BRICS_WG_ICTHPC3rd_Meeting_Minutes.pdf Accessed January 30th, 2020.
[11]Available from: https://sucupira.capes.gov.br/sucupira/public/consultas/coleta/programa/listaPrograma.jsf Accessed October 8th 2018.
[12]In Brazil the areas of Political Science and International Relations remain incorporated within the evaluation system of CAPES (Coordination for the Improvement of Higher Education Personnel), the Brazilian government body responsible for the country's graduate school guidelines.

of interest of the faculty.[13] In some cases, this information was present on the website itself, in others I had to consult the lattes curriculum[14] of these professors. I considered as 'IPE Faculty' those who included, in their research lines and/or areas of activity, the subjects: International Political Economy, Political Economy, International Economics, Economic Policy, Foreign/International Trade, International Finance, Multinational/Transnational Corporations, or International Business. The results of this step are shown in Table 1.

Out of the total of 236 IR professors from these 13 PPG-RI, 79 (33.5 per cent) are dedicated to IPE. Also, it is observed that IPE has a slightly majority representation among these PPG-RI, with 7 (53.8 per cent) having research lines in this field, and 6 (46.2 per cent) without this focus. Considering the teachers, there is great variability regarding their identification as working within IPE. At the extremes, 100.0 per cent of the professors from UFRJ work in one of the IPE thematic areas, while in PUC-Minas only 11.5 per cent of the professors conduct research in IPE.

Regarding the inclusion of ICT MNCs as a research topic, I used the FUNAG database on academic works in IR.[15] I applied the keyword search technique in the titles[16] of these documents. The keywords selected for the search were based on the scientific literature reviewed and included, in addition to multinational enterprises (*empresas multinacionais*), their closest synonyms: transnational corporations (*corporações transnacionais*), multinational corporations (*corporações multinacionais*), etc. (all keywords are available in Table 2). I also searched for the main synonyms of the word enterprises (*empresas*), such as firms (*firmas*), corporations (*corporações*), companies (*companhias*). In all these cases, the words were searched for both in the singular and in the plural. However, in Table 2, I preferred to differentiate enterprise (*empresa*) from enterprises (*empresas*), because of the higher number of documents that used these words in the title. In the other cases, I added the quantities obtained in the singular and in the plural. I also carried out the search with the terms international business (*negócios internacionais*) and international trade (*comércio internacional*), which are more comprehensive terms, but that may indicate the presence of analyzes regarding MNCs, despite the omission of references to companies in the titles. In addition, I conducted a search for some of the main words related to the digital economy and ICT MNCs, also present in Table 2.

---

[13]In some institutes/departments, not all professors are registered in the PPG-RI. However, for the purpose of this research, I considered all professors regardless of their registration. In fact, even though some professors are not registered to mentor masters or doctoral candidates, they are nonetheless researchers and part of the academic community.

[14]The Lattes Curriculum is a standard record of teaching activities and research in Brazil hosted on the Lattes platform that, in addition to the database of résumés, also brings together research groups and institutions into a single system. For more information, visit http://lattes.cnpq.br/

[15]The database is an Excel spreadsheet, extracted from FUNAG's website on October 8th 2018, and it includes a total of 4093 scientific documents from 74 Graduate Programs published between 1968 and 2016. In other words, the database includes works of relevance for IR, although many of them come from Graduate Programs of other areas (e.g. Sociology, Economics, Law, etc.). I applied the keyword search technique in the titles of these documents. Although FUNAG's database has a field titled "keywords," 788 out of the 4093 documents were with this field blank, making it impossible to search from there. I also chose not to search for keywords in the abstracts of these documents because 891 of the "abstract" fields were blank. Therefore, the "title" field, fully populated for the 4093 documents, was the most suitable for the search. Available from: http://www.funag.gov.br/ipri/index.php/teses-e-dissertacoes Accessed October 8th 2018.

[16]I understand that, although the title provides a good parameter in order to grasp the content of the documents, performing keyword searches on these titles presents a series of limitations. First, this method may disregard articles about MNCs who made no reference to these companies (or related keywords) in their titles. Second, the list of keywords searched in Table 2 is not exhaustive, thus I may have neglected other less used synonyms for 'companies'. Third, in extreme cases, there may be situations in which the title makes reference to 'companies' (or synonyms), but the content of the documents do not make a thorough analysis of MNCs.

Table 1. IPE Faculty Representation in Brazilian IR Graduate Programs.

Graduate Program	University	Research Line in IPE?	Total Faculty	IPE Faculty	%
IPE	UFRJ Federal University of Rio de Janeiro	X	13	13	100,0%
ISS	UFRGS Federal University of Rio Grande do Sul	X	17	10	58,8%
IR	UFSC Federal University of Santa Catarina	X	16	9	56,3%
IR	USP University of São Paulo	X	33	13	39,4%
IR	UFU Federal University of Uberlândia	X	12	4	33,3%
PS and IR	UFPB Federal University of Paraíba		15	5	33,3%
IR	UNESP – UNICAMP – PUC-SP San Tiago Dantas	X	26	7	26,9%
IR	UFBA Federal University of Bahia		13	3	23,1%
IR	UERJ State University of Rio de Janeiro	X	13	3	23,1%
IR	UnB University of Brasília		21	4	19,0%
IR	UEPB State University of Paraíba		12	2	16,7%
IR	PUC-Rio Pontifical Catholic University of Rio de Janeiro		19	3	15,8%
IR	PUC-Minas Pontifical Catholic University of Minas Gerais		26	3	11,5%

Note: Based on consultations on the PPG-RI websites originally between 8–9 October 2018, and updated between 6–7 September 2019.
Source: Author.

Finally, I searched for the names of the 10 largest ICT MNCs, as listed by the 2018 Fortune 500 list.[17] As the majority of these works were written in Portuguese, I performed the keyword search in this language and also in English.

Table 2 shows the 41 keywords used in the search, and three columns with counts. The works from PPG-RI refers to the number of documents retrieved for each keyword searched, in a total of 1192 theses and dissertations, obtained after the application of two filters: first, I excluded all the monographs from *Instituto Rio Branco* (preparatory school for Brazilian diplomats), leaving only academic works of Graduate Programs; and then I ignored documents from all Graduate Programs other than IR. That is, count 1 refers only to doctoral theses and master dissertations from PPG-RI. The works from all PPG refers to the number of documents retrieved for each keyword searched in a total of 3137 doctoral theses and master dissertations, obtained after the application of only the first filter above. All works in the FUNAG database covers the entire database, without any type of filter. That is, 4093 theses, dissertations, and monographs from *Instituto Rio Branco*.

The results shown in Table 2 are both unexpected and worrying. In a universe of 4093 scientific documents, there are almost no studies focusing directly on MNCs. This result is even more surprising when we compare it with the data from Table 1, which shows a significant adherence of IR professors to IPE. Therefore, more work on MNCs was to be expected. Although there is a comparatively higher number of studies about enterprise(s) (i.e., broader than multinational enterprises) this figure is still very low. At most, 77 works on enterprise(s) were found, that is, only 1.9 per cent of the total (77/4093). Regarding ICT MNCs, no documents were found, even though some of them used the words *internet* and *technology* in their titles.

---

[17]These companies were: Apple, Google, Microsoft, IBM, DELL, INTEL, HP, Cisco, Facebook, and Oracle. However, none of the 4093 works from the FUNAG database made reference to any of these companies in their titles. The 2018 Fortune 500 list is available from: http://fortune.com/fortune500/list/filtered?sector=Technology Accessed November 13th 2018.

Table 2. Keywords present in the scientific works available at the FUNAG database, 1968–2016

Keyword	Works from PPG-RI	Works from all PPG	All works in the FUNAG database
trade	52	125	169
enterprise	19	67	77
international trade	15	39	47
enterprises	11	38	45
technology	11	24	34
internet	2	10	13
business/businesses	1	10	12
digital	3	8	11
multinational(s)	3	8	9
foreign direct investment/FDI	-	2	6
company/companies	1	5	5
multinational enterprise(s)	1	3	4
transnational enterprise(s)	1	4	4
value chains / global value chains	2	3	3
international business	-	2	2
corporation(s)	-	2	2
information and communication technology(ies)	-	1	2
ICT(s)	-	1	2
rare earth	1	2	2
information age	1	1	1
transnational corporation(s)	-	1	1
information technology	-	-	1
supply chain(s)	-	1	1
multinational corporation(s)	-	-	-
multinational company(ies)	-	-	-
transnational company(ies)	-	-	-
firm/firms	-	-	-
multinational firm(s)	-	-	-
transnational firm(s)	-	-	-
artificial intelligence / AI	-	-	-
machine learning	-	-	-
information economy	-	-	-
industry 4.0	-	-	-
fourth industrial revolution	-	-	-
production networks / global production networks	-	-	-
ICT(s) manufacturing	-	-	-
ICT supply chain(s)	-	-	-
ICT value chain(s)	-	-	-
commodity chain(s)	-	-	-
ICT commodity chain(s)	-	-	-
digital economy	-	-	-

Source: Author.

I also used the keywords from Table 2 to analyze the scientific production of the 79 IPE professors regarding MNCs and ICT MNCs. I consulted the Lattes CV of all of them, looking for the keywords in the titles of books and scientific papers published in Brazil and abroad, in IR/IPE journals and in other sectoral journals, between 2009–2018. The results of this search corroborate the negligence regarding MNCs and ICT MNCs: summing the production of all 79 professors, at maximum 5 works on those topics were published per year (in 2010, 2017 and 2018) and at minimum 2 works were published in 2016.

In order to evaluate the regularity of this negligence, I analyzed the publications on ICT MNCs in the three Brazilian journals of the highest quality (within the Brazilian ranking system) in the fields of IR/IPE, over a period of 10 years (2009–2018). I also analyzed publications on the 10 most important international IR journals, according to Seabrooke and

Table 3. Keywords for search in scientific journals.

ICT	internet, digital, information and communication technology(ies), ICT(s), rare earth, information age, information technology, artificial intelligence/AI, machine learning, big data, computer(s), robots, information economy, industry 4.0, fourth industrial revolution, internet of things, ICT(s) manufacturing, digital economy
MNC	foreign direct investment/FDI, multinational(s), multinational enterprise(s), transnational enterprise(s), value chains/global value chain(s), international business, transnational corporation(s), supply chain(s), multinational corporation(s), multinational company(ies), transnational company(ies), multinational firm(s), transnational firm(s), production network(s)/global production network(s)
ICT MNC	ICT supply chain(s), ICT value chain(s), ICT commodity chain(s), ICT MNCs, specific names of prominent ICT MNCs (Google/Alphabet, Facebook, Amazon, Apple, Microsoft, Huawei, Alibaba, AT and T, SAP, Intel).

Source: Author.

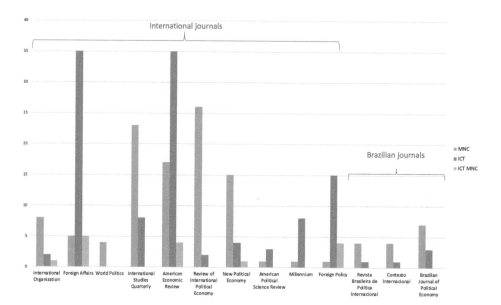

Chart 1. Papers published in International and Brazilian IR Journals, 2009–18. Source: Author.

Young (2017), in order to have a more accurate and comparative understanding of the international publications on the topic. Thus, I read the titles of all articles published in the Brazilian and international journals in that period in search of keywords extracted from Table 2, and categorized according to their main affinity regarding MNCs, ICT, or ICT MNCs. This categorization is illustrated in Table 3. I searched for the keywords both in English and in Portuguese.

The results are shown in Chart 1. As we can see, the Brazilian Journal of Political Economy was the one that published the highest number of papers on MNCs (7 papers) and ICT (3 papers), while *Revista Brasileira de Política Internacional* and *Contexto Internacional* published 4 papers on MNCs each, and only 1 paper on ICT each, in the period considered. Neither one of these 3 journals published papers on ICT MNCs. When comparing these results with publications in international journals, we noticed a higher number of papers on these foreign journals, particularly in the American Economic Review and in Foreign Affairs.

Table 4. Papers published in the Annals of ABRI, 2007–2018.

Year	Number of papers
2007	3
2009	-
2011	8
2012	3
2013	5
2014	-
2015	6
2016	7
2017	7
2018	5

Source: Author.

I also performed a keyword search in all the published Annals of the ABRI annual conferences.[18] I looked for the same keywords used in the searches on the journal's titles, both in Portuguese and in English. The results are shown in Table 4. Again, the low number of papers regarding MNCs and ICT MNCs is pretty evident. Even though we can identify papers published in every year, and the number of papers is slightly higher than in the Brazilian journals, these numbers are well below the total of papers regarding more prominent topics in Brazilian IR, such as Brazilian foreign policy and international security (TRIP 2014).

The data shown in Tables 2–4 and in Chart 1 are congruent regarding the very low number of studies on MNCs and ICT MNCs published in the realm of IR in Brazil. Based on this data we can state that Brazilian IR research has demonstrated a serious neglect of attention regarding these MNCs, thus overlooking their relevance in international politics.

Conclusion

The digital revolution brings considerable implications for the field of IR. At first, it spurs a set of new research agendas: e.g. the battle between China and the U.S. toward global technological leadership; the challenges for the construction of an international regime for global internet governance; the emergence of giant ICT MNCs such as Google and Amazon, unleashing new patterns of global trade and investments; the rebirth of discussions regarding the digital divide and the technological setback of developing countries; to name a few. These issues challenge previous dynamics of power between states and markets, inasmuch as digital technologies blur distinctions between public and private authority, at the same that old productive and financial structures are being considerably reshaped in international political economy.

In terms of productive structures, 'digitalization tends to break the operational nexus between foreign sales and foreign assets' because ICT MNCs reach foreign markets with fewer assets and fewer employees overseas comparative to traditional MNCs (UNCTAD 2017a, 172; Brun, Gereffi, and Zhan 2019). Traditional MNCs are also

[18]The Annals of ABRI can be retrieved in: https://www.abri.org.br/conteudo/view?ID_CONTEUDO=1145. The only two missing are the Annals of the 2nd Annual Meeting of ABRI/ISA, 2009 (which is not available online, thus I did not perform the search in this conference's papers) and the Annals of the 4th Seminar of ABRI, which are available from https://www.seminario2018.abri.org.br/download/download?ID_DOWNLOAD=2 Accessed February 10th 2019.

moving towards the digitalization of commercial activities, since ICTs are general purpose technologies, therefore can be applied in a variety of downstream sectors (Zylberberg 2016). Regarding financial structures, different types of FDI are becoming more important (knowledge-seeking, financial- and tax-driven FDI), insomuch as ICT MNCs' limited international production footprints diminishes their dependence on traditional types of FDI. By means of digitalization, MNCs from various other sectors tend to follow a similar path (UNCTAD 2017a). As a result, the rise of ICT MNCs is followed by a trend towards the concentration of productive investments in a few developed economies, especially the U.S. (UNCTAD 2017a).

This brings considerable implications for developing countries such as Brazil. The case of Brazil is relevant because it is home to subsidiaries of leading ICT multinationals and contract manufacturers, and for some decades now has propelled its software industry. The country ranks 6th globally as regards investments in ICTs, and 1st in Latin America. Besides, the sector is expected to reach 10.7 per cent of Brazil's GDP by 2020 (Zylberberg 2016; Agência Brasil 2018). However, current trends in GVCs and investments brought up by digitalization can bring negative impacts to the country in at least two respects. First, by dislocating FDI from the ICT sector back to developed countries. Second, by increasing the technological requirements on Brazil's software industry to an unachievable level, leading to a loss of international competitiveness and eventually to a deindustrialization in this sector. The Brazilian government has been responding to such challenges by propelling ICTs and digitalization in its domestic and foreign policy agendas. However, the effectiveness of such initiatives was not evaluated in this paper.

In this article I showed that, despite the growing importance of ICTs and ICT MNCs globally, and their implication for Brazil's politics and economy, the Brazilian IR community has substantially neglected research on these topics. Overall, this research shows that even MNCs from traditional sectors have been very little studied in Brazilian IR. This is a serious limitation of the IR knowledge produced in Brazil. As I show throughout the paper, IR can contribute to the understanding of the operations, strategies and social implications of MNCs and ICT MNCs in Brazil in ways that complement studies produced by economists and management scholars. Therefore, these topics need to be addressed more seriously by Brazilian IR scholars.

Acknowledgments

I wish to thank the two anonymous reviewers for their attentive and valuable comments. Many thanks also to Eduardo Viola, Antonio Carlos Lessa, and Niels Søndergaard for their comments on an earlier version of this manuscript.

Disclosure Statement

No potential conflict of interest was reported by the author(s).

Funding

This research received financial support from the Brazilian Coordination for the Improvement of Higher Education Personnel (CAPES), under Grant number 88882.347360/2019-01, and from the German Academic Exchange Service (DAAD).

ORCID

Marcos Vinícius Isaias Mendes ⓘ http://orcid.org/0000-0001-7512-8533

References

Agência Brasil. 2018. 'Investimentos no setor de tecnologia aumentam 4,5 per cent em 2017 no Brasil.' Accessed Jan 30, 2020. http://agenciabrasil.ebc.com.br/economia/noticia/2018-03/investimentos-no-setor-de-tecnologia-aumentam-45-em-2017-no-brasil.

Albuquerque, P. H., et al. 2019. 'Na era das máquinas, o emprego é de quem? Estimação da probabilidade de automação de ocupações no Brasil.' Texto para discussão IPEA. Accessed Oct 12, 2019. http://repositorio.ipea.gov.br/bitstream/11058/9116/1/td_2457.pdf.

Almeida, M., R. Oliveira, and B. Schneider. 2014. 'Política industrial e empresas estatais no Brasil: BNDES e Petrobrás.' Texto para discussão IPEA. Accessed Feb 12, 2019. http://www.ipea.gov.br/agencia/images/stories/PDFs/TDs/td_2013.pdf.

Amatucci, M., and R. Bernardes. 2008. 'O novo papel das subsidiárias de países emergentes na inovação em empresas multinacionais – o caso da General Motors do Brasil.' *Innovation and Management Review* 4 (3): 5–16.

Arrighi, G. 1994. *The Long Twentieth Century: Money, Power, and the Origins of Our Times.* New York: Verso.

Aykut, D., and A. Goldstein. 2007. 'Developing Country Multinationals: South-South Investment Comes of age.' In *Industrial Development for the 21st Century*, edited by United Nations. New York: UN Press.

Barwise, P., and L. Watkins. 2018. 'The Evolution of Digital Dominance: How and why we got to GAFA.' In *Digital Dominance: The Power of Google, Amazon, Facebook, and Apple*, edited by M. Moore, and D. Tambini. New York: Oxford University Press.

Becard, D., and B. Macedo. 2014. 'Chinese Multinational Corporations in Brazil: Strategies and Implications in Energy and Telecom Sectors.' *Revista Brasileira de Política Internacional* 57 (1): 143–161.

Brainard, L., and L. Martinez-Diaz. 2009. *Brazil as an Economic Superpower? Understanding Brazil's Changing Role in the Global Economy.* Washington D.C.: Brookings Institution Press.

Brasil. 2011. 'Plano de ação conjunta entre o governo da república federativa do Brasil e o governo da república Argentina para fazer avançar a cooperação bilateral na área de massificação do acesso à internet em banda larga (2011 - 2015).' Accessed Jan 30, 2020. http://www.itamaraty.gov.br/pt-BR/component/content/article?id=2449:atos-assinados-por-ocasiao-da-visita-da-presidenta-dilma-roussef-a-argentina-buenos-aires-31-de-janeiro-de-2011.

Brasil. 2014. 'Marco Civil da Internet.' Accessed Oct 9, 2019. https://www.planalto.gov.br/ccivil_03/_ato2011-2014/2014/lei/l12965.htm.

Brasil. 2015. 'Joint Action Plan between the government of the Federative Republic of Brazil and the government of the Peoplès Republic of China.' Accessed Jan 30, 2020. http://www.itamaraty.gov.br/pt-BR/component/content/article#pac-eng.

Brasil. 2018a. 'Estratégia de Governança Digital.' Accessed Jan. 30, 2020. http://www.planejamento.gov.br/EGD/arquivos/revisao-da-estrategia-de-governanca-digital-2015-2019.pdf.

Brasil. 2018b. 'Lei Geral de Proteção de Dados Pessoais.' Accessed Oct 9, 2019. https://www.planalto.gov.br/ccivil_03/_ato2015-2018/2018/lei/l13709.htm.

Brasil. 2019. 'Plano Nacional de Internet das Coisas.' Accessed Oct 9, 2019. http://www.planalto.gov.br/ccivil_03/_ato2019-2022/2019/decreto/D9854.htm.

Brun, L., G. Gereffi, and J. Zhan. 2019. 'The "Lightness" of Industry 4.0 Lead Firms: Implications for Global Value Chains.' In *Transforming Industrial Policy for the Digital Age*, edited by P. Bianchi, C. R. Durán, and S. Labory. London: Edward Elgar Publishing.

Buckley, P., et al. 2016. 'Cross-border Acquisitions by Indian Multinationals: Asset Exploitation or Asset Augmentation?' *International Business Review* 25 (4): 986–996.

Canabarro, D., and F. Wagner. 2014. 'A Governança da Internet: Definição, Desafios e Perspectivas.' Paper presented at 9th Meeting of the Brazilian Political Science Association – ABCP, Brasília, August 4-7.

Cohen, B. 2014. *Advanced Introduction to International Political Economy.* Northampton: Edward Elgar.

Cuervo-Cazurra, A. 2008. 'The Multinationalization of Developing Country MNEs: the Case of Multilatinas.' *Journal of International Management* 14 (1): 138–154.

Cuervo-Cazurra, A. 2012. 'Extending Theory by Analyzing Developing Country Multinational Companies: Solving the Goldilocks Debate.' *Global Strategy Journal* 2 (2): 153–167.

Curtis, S. 2009. *Global Cities and the Transformation of the International System.* London: ProQuest.

Deloitte. 2019. 'Insights about Digital Transformation and ICT Opportunities for Brazil: Report and Recommendations.' Accessed Jan 30, 2020. https://www2.deloitte.com/content/dam/Deloitte/br/Documents/technology-media-telecommunications/ICT-insights-report-eng.pdf.

Dunning, J. 1993. *The Globalization of Business.* London: Routledge.

Dunning, J., and S. Lundan. 2008. *Multinational Enterprises and The Global Economy.* 2nd Edition. Northampton: Edward Elgar.

Falkner, R. 2009. *Business Power and Conflict in International Environmental Politics.* Basingstoke: Palgrave Macmillan.

Fares, S. 2007. 'O Pragmatismo do Petróleo: as relações entre o Brasil e o Iraque.' *Revista Brasileira de Política Internacional* 50 (2): 129–145.

Ferreira, P. 2009. 'A Petrobrás e as reformas do setor de petróleo e gás no Brasil e na Argentina.' *Revista de Sociologia e Política* 17 (33): 85–96.

Fieldhouse, D. 1999. 'A new Imperial System? the Role of the Multinational Corporations Reconsidered.' In *International Political Economy: Perspectives on Global Power and Wealth,* edited by J. Frieden, and D. Lake. London: Routledge.

Franda, M. 2002. *China and India Online: Information Technology Politics and Diplomacy in the World's two Largest Nations.* New York: Rowman and Littlefield Publishers.

Fritsch, S. 2011. 'Technology and Global Affairs.' *International Studies Perspectives* 12 (1): 27–45.

Gamu, J., and P. Dauvergne. 2018. 'The Slow Violence of Corporate Social Responsibility: The Case of Mining in Peru.' *Third World Quarterly* 39 (5): 959–975.

Global Justice Now. 2016. '10 biggest corporations make more money than most countries in the world combined.' 12 Sep. Accessed Oct 12, 2018. https://www.globaljustice.org.uk//news/2016/sep/12/10-biggest-corporations-make-more-money-most-countries-world-combined.

Graglia, M., and C. Mellon. 2019. 'Blockchain and Property in 2018.' *Innovations: Technology, Governance, Globalization* 12 (1): 90–116.

GTAI German Trade and Investment. 2014. 'INDUSTRIE 4.0: Smart manufacturing for the future.' Accessed Oct 12, 2018. http://www.inovasyon.org/pdf/GTAI.industrie4.0_smart.manufact.for.future.July.2014.pdf.

Heeks, R. 2008. 'ICT4D 2.0: The Next Phase of Applying ICT for International Development.' *Computer* 41 (6): 26–33.

Hiratuka, C. 2005. 'Internacionalização de atividades de presquisa e desenvolvimento das empresas transnacionais: análise da inserção das filiais brasileiras.' *São Paulo em Perspectiva* 199 (1): 105–114.

Jamali, D. 2010. 'The CSR of MNC Subsidiaries in Developing Countries: Global, Local, Substantive or Diluted?' ' *Journal of Business Ethics* 93 (2): 181–200.

Jenkins, R. 1987. *Transnational Corporations and Uneven Development: The Internationalization of Capital and the Third World.* London: Methuen.

Johanson, J., and J. E. Vahlne. 2009. 'The Uppsala Internationalization Model Revisited – From Liability of Foreignness to Liability of Outsidership.' *Journal of International Business Studies* 40 (4): 1411–1431.

Kimura, F., and M. Ando. 2003. 'Fragmentation and Agglomeration Matter: Japanese Multinationals in Latin America and East Asia.' *The North American Journal of Economics and Finance* 14 (3): 287–317.

Klein, H. 2002. 'ICANN and Internet Governance: Leveraging Technical Coordination to Realize Global Public Policy.' *The Information Society* 18 (2): 193–207.

Kobrin, S. 2009. 'Sovereignty@Bay: Globalization, Multinational Enterprise, and the International Political System.' In *The Oxford Handbook of International Business 2nd Ed.*, edited by A. Rugman, and T. Brewer. New York: Oxford University Press.

Kshetri, N. 2015. 'Cybercrime and Cybersecurity Issues in the BRICS Economies.' *Journal of Global Information Technology Management* 18 (4): 245–249.

Levy, D., and A. Prakash. 2003. 'Bargains Old and New: Multinational Corporations in Global Governance.' *Business and Politics* 5 (2): 131–150.

Li, F., S. Frederick, and G. Gereffi. 2019. 'E-Commerce and Industrial Upgrading in the Chinese Apparel Value Chain.' *Journal of Contemporary Asia* 49 (1): 24–53.

Lu, Y. 2017. 'Industry 4.0: A Survey on Technologies, Applications and Open Research Issues.' *Journal of Industrial Information Integration* 6 (1): 1–10.

Malacarne, M. 2018. *Uma análise do desempenho econômico internacional do setor de tecnologia de informação e comunicação (TIC) no Brasil (2000–17)*. Monograph for B.Sc. in International Relations, Universidade Federal do Rio Grande do Sul.

Maynard, A. 2015. 'Navigating the Industry 4.0.' *Nature Nanotechnology* 10 (1): 1005–1006.

Mendes, M. V. I. 2018. 'Is it the end of North-American Hegemony? A Structuralist Perspective on Arrighi's Systemic Cycles of Accumulation and the Theory of Hegemonic Stability.' *Brazilian Journal of Political Economy* 38 (3): 434–449.

Miguel, J. C., and M. A. Casado. 2016. 'GAFAnomy (Google, Amazon, Facebook, and Apple): The Big Four and the b-Ecosystem.' In *Dynamics of Big Internet Industry Groups and Future Trends*, edited by M. Gómez-Uranga, J. Zabala-Iturriagagoitia, and J. Barrutia. Cham: Springer.

Mueller, M. 2010. *Networks and States: The Global Politics of Internet Governance*. Cambridge: The MIT Press.

Murtha, T., and S. Lenway. 1994. 'Country Capabilities and the Strategic State: How National Political Institutions Affect Multinational Corporations' Strategies.' *Strategic Management Journal* 15 (2): 113–129.

Ning, L. 2009. 'China's Leadership in the World ICT Industry: A Successful Story of Its "Attracting-In" and "Walking-Out" Strategy for the Development of High-Tech Industries?' *Pacific Affairs* 82 (1): 67–91.

Niosi, J., and F. T. Tschang. 2009. 'The Strategies of Chinese and Indian Software Multinationals: Implications for Internationalization Theory.' *Industrial and Corporate Change* 18 (2): 269–294.

Nwagwu, W. 2006. 'Integrating ICTs Into the Globalization of the Poor Developing Countries.' *Information Development* 22 (3): 167–179.

Nye, J. 1974. 'Multinational Corporations in World Politics.' *Foreign Affairs* 53 (1): 153–154.

Oliveira, A. J., and J. Onuki. 2007. 'Grupos de interesses e a política comercial brasileira: a atuação na arena legislativa.' *Papéis Legislativos* 8 (1): 1–20.

Ono, T., K. Lida, and S. Yamazaki. 2017. 'Achieving Sustainable Development Goals (SDGs) Through ICT Services.' *Fujitsu Science and Technology Journal* 53 (6): 17–22.

Pinto, A. 2019. 'Robôs ameaçam 54 per cent dos empregos formais no Brasil.' *Folha de São Paulo*, Jan 28 Pess Edition. https://www1.folha.uol.com.br/mercado/2019/01/robos-ameacam-54-dos-empregos-formais-no-brasil.shtml.

Pires, M. 2018. 'O Brasil, o Mundo e a Quarta Revolução Industrial: reflexões sobre os impactos econômicos e sociais.' *Revista de Economia Política e História Econômica* 39 (1): 5–36.

Queiroz, S., and R. Carvalho. 2005. 'Empresas multinacionais e inovação tecnológica no Brasil.' *São Paulo em Perspectiva* 19 (2): 51–59.

Ramamurti, R., and J. Hillemann. 2018. 'What is "Chinese" About Chinese Multinationals?' *Journal of International Business Studies* 49 (1): 34–48.

Ramsey, J., and A. Almeida. 2010. *A ascensão das multinacionais brasileiras*. Rio de Janeiro: Elsevier.

Rocha, A., and H. Ávila. 2015. 'Teoria institucional e modos de entrada de multinacionais de países emergentes.' *Revista de Administração de Empresas* 55 (3): 246–257.

Rodrigues, P. 2018. *Firms, institutions and foreign policy: the political economy of Brazilian multi-nationals*. Thesis for D.Sc. in International Relations, University of São Paulo.

Rodriguez, P., D. Siegel, A. Hillman, and L. Eden. 2006. 'Three Lenses on the Multinational Enterprise: Politics, Corruption, and Corporate Social Responsibility.' *Journal of International Business Studies* 37 (6): 733–746.

Roger, C., and P. Dauvergne. 2016. 'The Rise of Transnational Governance as a Field of Study.' *International Studies Review* 18 (3): 415–437.

Rosenau, J., and D. Johnson. 2002. 'Information Technologies and Turbulence in World Politics.' In *Technology, Development, Democracy: International Conflict and Cooperation in the Information age*, edited by J. Alisson. New York: State University of New York Press.

Sauvant, K., W. Maschek, and G. McAllister. 2010. 'Foreign Direct Investment by Emerging Market Multinational Enterprises, the Impact of the Financial Crisis and Recession, and Challenges Ahead.' In *Foreign Direct Investments from Emerging Markets*, edited by K. P. Sauvant, G. McAllister, and W. A. Maschek. New York: Palgrave Macmillan.

Schwab, K. 2016. *The Fourth Industrial Revolution*. New York: Penguin.

Seabrooke, L., and L. Young. 2017. 'The Networks and Niches of International Political Economy.' *Review of International Political Economy* 24 (2): 288–331.

Sheng, H., and J. Junior. 2017. 'The Top 20 Brazilian Multinationals: Divestment under Crisis.' Columbia Center on Sustainable Investment and Fundação Getúlio Vargas. Accessed Oct 12, 2018. http://ccsi.columbia.edu/files/2013/10/EMGP-Brazil-Report-March-21-2017-FINAL.pdf.

Silva-Rego, B., and A. C. R. Figueira. 2017. 'Business, Government and Foreign Policy: Brazilian Construction Firms Abroad.' *Brazilian Political Science Review* 11 (1): 1–28.

Stal, E., and M. Campanário. 2010. 'Empresas multinacionais de países emergentes: o crescimento das multilatinas.' *Economia Global e Gestão* 15 (1): 55–73.

Strange, S. 1970. 'International Economics and International Relations: A Case of Mutual Neglect.' *International Affairs* 46 (2): 304–315.

Strange, S. 1991. 'Big Business and the State.' *Millennium Journal of International Studies* 20 (2): 245–250.

Tapscott, D., and A. Tapscott. 2018. *Blockchain Revolution: How the Technology Behind Bitcoin and Other Cryptocurrencies is Changing the World*. New York: Penguin.

Tarzi, S. 1999. 'Third World Governments and Multinational Corporations: Dynamics of Host's Bargaining Power.' In *International Political Economy: Perspectives on Global Power and Wealth*, edited by J. Frieden, and D. Lake. London: Routledge.

Thite, M., et al. 2016. 'Internationalization of Emerging Indian Multinationals: Linkage, Leverage and Learning (LLL) Perspective.' *International Business Review* 25 (1): 435–443.

TRIP. 2014. 'Teaching, Research and International Policy: Faculty Survey in Brazil.' Accessed Feb 22, 2019. https://trip.wm.edu/charts/#/questions/12.

UNCTAD. 2017a. 'World Investment Report 2017: investment and the digital economy.' Accessed Jan 28, 2020. https://unctad.org/en/PublicationsLibrary/wir2017_en.pdf.

UNCTAD. 2017b. 'Technical annex: The top 100 digital MNEs. World investment report 2017, Chapter IV.' Accessed Oct 9, 2019. http://unctad.org/en/PublicationChapters/wir2017ch4_Annex_en.pdf.

Vernon, R. 1971. 'Sovereignty at bay: The Multinational Spread of U. S. Enterprises.' *Thunderbird International Business Review* 13 (4): 1–3.

Wang, D., et al. 2016. 'Exploring Cross-Cultural Skills for Expatriate Managers From Chinese Multinationals: Congruence and Contextualization.' *Asia Pacific Journal of Management* 34 (1): 123–146.

Wolf, M. 2017. 'Taming the masters of the tech universe.' *Financial Times*, Nov 14, Online Edition. https://www.ft.com/content/45092c5c-c872-11e7-aa33-c63fdc9b8c6c.

World Bank. 2016. 'The world's top 100 economies: 31 countries; 69 corporations.' Accessed: Oct 12, 2019. https://blogs.worldbank.org/publicsphere/world-s-top-100-economies-31-countries-69-corporations.

Wu, X., and G. Gereffi. 2018. 'Amazon and Alibaba: Internet Governance, Business Models, and Internationalization Strategies.' In *International Business in the Information and Digital Age*, edited by R. van Tulder, A. Verbeke, and L. Piscitello. Bingley: Emerald Publishing.

Zanatta, R., and R. Abramovay. 2019. 'Dados, vícios e concorrência: repensando o jogo das economias digitais.' *Estudos Avançados* 33 (96): 421–446.

Zylberberg, E. 2016. 'Redefining Brazil's Role in Information and Communication Technology Global Value Chains.' *MIT-Industrial Performance Center Working Paper* 16–003.

Keynes on State and Economic Development

Fábio Henrique Bittes Terra ⓘ, Fernando Ferrari Filho ⓘ and Pedro Cezar Dutra Fonseca ⓘ

ABSTRACT

This article has two purposes. On the one hand, it develops Keynes's concept of economic development. On the other hand, it presents Keynes's ideas about the role of State, chiefly the State *Agenda*. Keynes believed that the stage of economic development would only be attained if the State *Agenda* was in practice. In turn, to Keynes the economic development would be a stage in which the economic problems of society have been surpassed, and the motto of the individual behavior has been changed from the love of money to the love of living.

1. Introduction

John Maynard Keynes (1964) did not regard the State as the only solution to economic and social problems. Rather, the State should be an institution of collective action, built on a bottoms-up manner by both policy makers, who undertake economic policies to stabilize the economic cycles, and the productive economic classes, whose investments create employment and income. As such, the State should target economic development as its ultimate goal.

In this light, this article has two goals. The first is to present a concept of economic development that can be taken from Keynes's books, articles and pamphlets. However, to do so we also need to report Keynes's notion of the State, because he saw it as the institution that would lead the economic development (Keynes 1964, 1972).

These goals are the original contributions of this article. On the one hand, until to-day there is nothing said in the relevant literature about Keynes's concept of economic development.[1] On the other hand, although other references have dealt with the role of the State in Keynes's oeuvre, such as Cairncross (1978), Peacock (1993), Crabtree and Thirlwall (1993) and Skidelsky (1991), they did not mention the relationship between the State and the economic development. Mostly based on Keynes (1972) we develop an original argument that he saw the State as a space of conciliation between democratic will and technocratic ruling. This conciliation is key to economic development.

---

[1]For instance, Lavoie (2014), an important handbook of post-Keynesian economics, did not even include development as one of the keywords listed in the book's remissive index.

Besides this brief Introduction, this article has four other sections. Section Two reviews the notions of economic development within economics. We do not intend to compare all these notions with Keynes's concept of development. Our idea is to outline the evolution of the concept and discuss some references of what development means. Section Three presents Keynes's idea of the monetary theory of production, as this is the context from which economic development emerges, as well as we recall his views on the role of the State, which is the leading figure towards development. Also, this section briefly discusses the economic policies Keynes prescribed to ensure economic development. Section Four describes Keynes's notion of economic development. Section Five concludes.

2. Economic Development in Economic Theory

To understand Keynes's conception of economic development, it is useful to recall that this term has several meanings in economics. Sometimes it is employed as a synonym of growth whereas other works highlight its differences from growth. For instance, the purpose of the 'political economy' was to explain the reasons driving economic growth. Quesnay (1996), in his 1759 *Tableau Économique*, attempted to understand how wealth circulated and how it was created in the primary sector, that he regarded as being the only able to generate surplus. In his 1776 *The Wealth of Nations*, Adam Smith (1996) was the first to envisage the relationship between productivity and growth. Nevertheless, these classical authors did not delineate the difference between growth and development. Both terms were, and often still are, employed indistinctively to define the progressive nature of the economy, that is, the ongoing revolution of productive techniques over time and the consequent expansion of production and markets.

When the marginalist revolution took place by the end of the 19th century, the neoclassical marginalists believed that the economic change was related to the dynamics of an economy, in contrast with the previous notion of equilibrium that dismissed temporality. Still, they adopted as their method of analysis the static comparative, which compares two resting points of a system without exploring their long-term connection. Nonetheless, this method became the predominant view of economic change amongst British economists in the following decades. Even Keynes used it to deal with short-term growth in his 1936 *General Theory* (GT), taking capital stock and technology as given.

After 1930, but mainly following World War II, a differentiation emerged between growth and development — perhaps under the influence of Keynes's GT and the creation of macroeconomics. The New Deal and the Welfare State attracted attention in the US and Europe, respectively, and discussions about well-being ensued. It became obvious that the War expenditures had helped boosting employment, but doubts remained: did this necessarily create better conditions of life to people? From then on, the GDP growth became identified as an early stage of development.

Development, however, not only involves GDP growth but goes beyond it, demanding qualitative change in welfare. Robinson (1981) emphasized this distinction by arguing that the measurement of welfare using GDP growth was restricted to the economic orthodoxy. She noted several difficulties when counting GDP, such as the informal economy and the necessity of accounting for social indicators, like those referring to poverty, income distribution and access to health and education.

In the 1950s and the 1960s, the concept of economic development gained visibility in the US. Solow (1956) theorized about growth as well as Rostow (1960) elaborated his five stages growth model.[2] According to Boianovsky and Hoover (2014), Solow explained the long-run growth based on capital accumulation, that is population growth and technological progress, whereas Rostow's model went further and showed how an economy not only grows but also develops in the long-run. In Rostow's model the government is essential to the development,[3] a feature that Keynes also highlighted, as we shall show soon.

However, it was in Latin America, specifically so in the United Nations Economic Commission for Latin America and the Caribbean (CEPAL), that the concept of development emerged in the 1950s and was employed forcefully as a counterpoint to underdevelopment.[4] Celso Furtado (1983) helps to better understand the CEPAL's concept of development.

He argued that underdevelopment was not a step towards development, as Rostow (1960) believed, but an economic structure. Furtado's (1983) views are that (a) 'developed' countries have never been 'underdeveloped', so underdevelopment is a historical condition of countries whose economies are structurally specialized in agricultural production; (b) underdeveloped countries are peripherical to developed countries (also called the central economies) that are industrialized and have the state-of-the-art technology. So, they create and dominate the best productive structure; and (c) underdevelopment tends to repeat itself over time if nothing is done to surpass it. Thus, it is not a stage, it is a structural condition. Summing up '[i]n short, underdevelopment is not a necessary stage of the process of the formation of capitalist economies. It is, in itself, a peculiar situation. It is the result of the expansion of the capitalist economies, aiming at using the natural resources and the manpower of the areas of pre-capitalist economy' (Furtado 1983, p. 146).[5]

Going in the same direction of CEPAL, Thirlwall (2003, pp. 9–10) argued that the 'balance of payments consequences of trade is also one of the important reasons (...) for supposing a strong link between exports and economic growth'. He developed a balance-of-payments-constrained economic growth model in which the peripherical countries are likely to have their development restricted by their balance of payment. This would not be the case of developed countries.

Furtado (1983, pp. 78–80) made a clear distinction between growth and development, that was largely employed by theorists of the underdevelopment in Latin America.[6] He stated that 'the concept of growth should be reserved to express the expansion of real product within a subset of an economy'. However, growth without development 'would be a mental construction without correspondence to reality' (Furtado 1983,

---

[2]The five stages are the traditional society, the conditions for take-off, the take-off, the maturity process, and the period of mass-consumption.

[3]Like Rostow (1960), in his 1944 *The Great Transformation*, Karl Polanyi (2001) argued that in the modern economy, a combination of markets and State intervention through public policies is essential to development.

[4]To CEPAL, to overcome underdevelopment in Latin America and assure development were necessary industrialization, interventionism and the existence of a nation project.

[5]Quotes that were not in English in the original text were translated into English by the authors.

[6]Theotônio dos Santos, André Gunder Frank, Enzo Falleto and Fernando Henrique Cardoso, among others, developed the Dependence theory, that is a conceptual and intellectual structure to understand the Latin American thought in the 1950s. This theory constitutes the basis for the underdevelopment theory in Latin America. For additional details about the relevance of dependency theory, see Bielschowsky (2000) and Kvangraven (2020).

pp. 78 and 145) because growth modifies the productive structure as it changes the functions of production, expands markets, enhances productivity and intensifies the social division of labor — specially so when growth is led by the manufacturing sector. All these changes are needed for economic development. Furtado (1983) argued that development requires a long-run growth. The latter demands innovation, what also entails changes in income distribution and in welfare. He disbelieved that greater industrialization and labor productivity would reduce the supply of workers and thereby strengthen the bargaining power of the labor force (Furtado 1983, p. 133).

CEPAL saw development not only as a way to surpass underdevelopment. It was also the defense of a national industrialization plan that would drive the country's economic policies. In fact, this theoretical view was executed in Latin America when the developmentalist ideology dominated the political power between 1960 and 1980. Therefore, Fonseca (2014 p. 59) argued that,

> developmentalism is the political economy voluntarily formed or managed by Governments (national or subnational) to, by means of production and productivity growth, under the leading of the manufacturing sector, transform society aiming at reaching desirable ends, notably the surpass of the society's social and economic issues, within the institutional framework of the capitalist system.

Furtado's (1983) view of development relates to some of Keynes's propositions. When referring to the long-term, Keynes claimed that development is not growth, though the first depends upon the latter. He understood that progress, often a euphemism for development, would liberate men from economic restrictions, stating 'in the long-term *that mankind is solving its economic problem*' (Keynes 1972, pp. 325–326, original emphasis). Like Keynes, Furtado (1983) believe that markets could not either provide for full employment or overcome underdevelopment. Keynes's (1980a) thoughts suggested that development requires sustainable and continuous growth over time, requiring permanent State economic intervention, an idea shared with Furtado (1983).[7]

To sum up, the concept of development is not unambiguous. It has several meanings, such as (i) it is a process of surpassing some point of a country's economic progress; (ii) there is no automatic path to development; (iii) it is not a stage, but a structural condition; (iv) market forces alone are uncapable of developing a country, so that the State is needed; (v) market forces are not dismissible, and their productivity improvement is required to the development of an economy; and (vi) growth is not development, however there is no development without growth. Growth is the means to development, no development itself.

3. Monetary Theory of Production, the Role of the State and the Guidance of Fiscal and Monetary Policies

3.1. The Context in which the Development Happens: The Monetary Theory of Production

One key feature of the Keynesian revolution is its refuse of the quantitative theory of money, so that money is partly responsible for the inherent instability of capitalism. In

---

[7]In this sense, some authors have debated the differences between the 'prime the pump' policies, which are meant to reanimate the economy (Samuelson 1940), and the long-term public expenditures (Dillard 1980) to address the permanent insufficiency of effective demand.

his 1930 *Treatise on Money* (TM), Keynes outlined an asset choice theory to link the real and financial markets. To model this possibility, Keynes (1976 p. 243, original emphasis) described two spheres of the economy, namely industrial and financial, in that

> By *Industry* we mean the business of maintaining the normal process of current output, distribution and exchange and paying the factors of production their incomes […] By *Finance*, on the other hand, we mean the business of holding and exchanging existing titles to wealth […] including Stock Exchange and Money Market transactions, speculation and the process of conveying current savings and profits into the hands of entrepreneurs.

In the industrial circulation, income and business deposits assure monetary resources to boost consumption and investment; thereby, money is a means of exchange. In turn, money in the financial circulation relies on the savings-deposits circuit. This circuit depends on the speculative stances of agents, that can be either bull, those who hold securities and borrow cash, or bear, those that avoid securities and hold cash. So, money is either used as a hold against uncertainty or to speculate in the financial markets. It can be demanded to store wealth, but this type of money possession is an alternative to retaining other assets that makes asset prices oscillate and disturbs the industrial circulation. Money is not neutral as it is in the quantitative theory of money. Its circulation in the financial sphere can cause economic instability, and 'changes in the financial situation are capable of causing changes in the value of money in two ways. They have the effect of altering the quantity of money available for the Industrial Circulation; and they may have the effect of altering the attractiveness of Investment' (Keynes 1976, p. 254).

At the outset of the 1930s, Keynes (1979, pp. 77–78, original emphasis) explicitly established his monetary theory of production, presenting an economic taxonomy where,

> a *real-wage* or *co-operative economy* as one in which the factors of production are rewarded by dividing up in agreed proportions the actual output of their co-operative efforts. […] [when] the factors are hired by entrepreneurs for money but where there is a mechanism of some kind to ensure that the exchange value of the money incomes of the factors is always equal in the aggregate to the proportion of current output which would have been the factor's share in a co-operative economy, we will call a *neutral entrepreneur economy*, or a *neutral economy* […] [when] the entrepreneurs hire the factors for money but without such a mechanism as the above, we will call a *money-wage* or *entrepreneur economy*.

The difference between the neutral and entrepreneur economies is that Say's Law prevails in the first, so that supply creates its own demand and there is no obstacle to full employment. In the second, production only takes place when the costs of production are smaller than the expected return. In entrepreneurial economies, '[a] process of production will not be started up, unless the money proceeds expected from the sale of the output are at least equal to the money costs which could be avoided by not starting up the process' (Keynes 1979, p. 78). While the purpose of a co-operative economy is the accumulation of goods, monetary accumulation is the aim of businesspeople in Keynes's entrepreneur economy.

On the way to his final concept of a monetary economy, in the GT Keynes (1964, p. vii) argued that this sort of economy is 'essentially one in which changing views about the future are capable of influencing the quantity of employment and not merely its direction'. Expectations cause fluctuations in effective demand because they modify money demand, making 'the use of money is a necessary condition for fluctuations in effective demand' (Keynes 1979, pp. 85–86). The GT clarified Keynes's theoretical frame-work of how a monetary economy works. He elaborated three theories regarding (a) the determination of investment, (b) the setting of interest rates and (c) the theory of money. The relationship between investment, interest rates, and money explains the instability of the economy. In face of uncertainty, the only available insurance is retaining money instead of spending. Hoarding money can happen suddenly as agents' decisions are highly sensible, once they rely on subjective elements, namely expectations and confi-dence. When agents demand money and not goods though, there is no reason to main-tain the level of employment and production that delivered the good that was not consumed.

GT's monetary theory innovatively declared money an asset different from all others because of two features. On the one hand, money's elasticity of production is negligible. Money cannot be freely produced when its demand increases, thereby, a greater prefer-ence for money does not result in higher employment. On the other hand, money's elas-ticity of substitution is null. No other asset replaces money when its price varies. These features, which are taken care of by central banks, uphold agents' trust in money and make it becomes a unit of account, a means of exchange and a reserve of wealth over time. Consequently, money has absolute liquidity through time and works as a form of wealth alternative to other financial and real assets. Hence, it is not neutral to eco-nomic activity. As Keynes (1964, p. 235) explained, 'unemployment develops, that is to say, because people want the moon; — men cannot be employed when the object of desire (i.e., money) is something which cannot be produced and the demand for which cannot be readily choked off'.

3.2. The Role of the State

Although Keynes did not develop a general theory of the State, based on his pamphlets, articles and books we delineate his views on the emergence of State entities, the directions of their actions, and to envision a proper bureaucracy. In his 1926 *The End of the Laissez-Faire*, Keynes argued that *laissez-faire* would not cause individual and social interests to coincide. He also stated that the main economic, social and political problems usually stem from 'risk, uncertainty and ignorance' (Keynes 1972, p. 291). The survival of cap-italism would rely on the 'visible hand' of the State, which is responsible for regulating the socioeconomic dysfunctions that markets promote, 'I think that capitalism, wisely managed, can probably be made more efficient for attaining economic ends than any alternative system in sight [...]. Our problem is to work out a social organization which shall be as efficient as possible without offending our notions of a satisfactory way of life' (Keynes 1972, p. 294).

In *The End of the Laissez-Faire*, and mainly in the 1925 *Am I a Liberal?*, Keynes (1972) discussed how he expected the creation of State entities. Taking as examples joint-stock companies, which are owned by a great number of individuals, he expressed his hopes that social organizations oriented to public interests should emerge from the association of individuals. This logic does not exclude the creation by the State, but highlights that their structure must be fully impersonal, just as happens with joint-stock firms, in which 'the technique of modern capitalism by the agency of collective action' prevails (Keynes 1972, pp. 292–293). Considering that the community sets rules and habits seeking public welfare, reputation and stability would be more important than the payment of dividends. In light of that, these institutions would be safe from personal dominance, something Keynes (1972) insisted upon.

Keynes (1972) conveyed this idea to State entities. They should be formed by semi-autonomous bodies. Semi-autonomy has two meanings, (a) a partial autonomy of public entities in relation to any other specific entity, but that is at the same time subordinated to the democratic powers of a free society, namely parliament and government. Moreover, (b) semi-autonomy also means that the technical bureaucracy of State entities does not set their goals, just the means to reach them.

The State entities Keynes (1972) prescribed could be private-public partnerships, with joint public and private capitals.[8] Thereby, public and private interests are matched, and the public services offered to the private sector are produced and certified by individuals who will be in touch with them. Once again, the idea of autonomy emerges, meaning State entities are, at the same time, close to, and distant from government and parliament.

Another feature that appeared in *Am I a Liberal?* is Keynes's concerns about the long-term character of public policies. He believed that they should be only partly changed at every new government. The parliament has the power to oversee the set of policies that continue and those that are changed or created respecting the interests of voters passed on to State entities through the goals chosen when people voted for a government.

A key element in *Am I Liberal?* is Keynes's proposal of the *Agenda*. It is a set of actions he expected the State to fulfill aiming at building welfare and securing the stability and social justice required for long-term progress. This set of State actions also comprehends the economic policies designed to stabilize the economic cycle, distribute wealth and income, build financial stability and enable a functional credit system.[9]

The *Agenda* should be concerned with both constructing the technically social actions and excluding technically individual ones. Technically social actions are those that would not come to be if the State were uninvolved. They have horizontal outcomes across all private sectors, once they build the productive and financial infrastructures that allow for the private initiative to constitute its productive structure with isonomic opportunities. The technically individual action, which should be avoided, is the State assisting the needs of one or a few private capitals, giving them benefits through something that should improve the public welfare.

It is possible to notice that Keynes (1972) also suggested that the *Agenda* should have tools to limit individual action when it creates unfair competition, greater ignorance and, consequently, uncertainty. The State entities should include in the *Agenda* ways to furnish the greatest set of information, in order to reduce uncertainty and its effects on private spending. Within an original argument of Ferrari-Filho and Conceição (2005), Keynes's GT notion of investment socialization can be seen as the State creating the best business environment it can possibly build, so that it may lessen uncertainty and

---

[8]For instance, the port of London was one of these joint ventures. The Bank of England, the British monetary authority, was another, both cited by Keynes in *The End of Laissez-Faire*. However, in the 1932 *The Monetary Policy of the Labour Party*, Keynes turned against the public-private partnership of the Bank of England. His concerns aimed at keeping public interests on the monetary policy protected from private lobbies.

[9]The State intervention is also noticed in Keynes's 1929 *Can Lloyd George do it?*. He argued that the State economic policies could dynamize economic activity 'whether we like it or not, it is fact that the rate of capital development in the transport system, the public utilities and the housing of this country largely depends on the policy of the Treasury and the Government of the day' (Keynes 1972, p. 113).

prompt private investment. The *Agenda* is the way to make the socialization of investment.

Regarding the State bureaucracy, Keynes (1972) stated that the *Agenda* should be endowed with a technical staff bearing public spirit, knowledge and ambition. Politicians should implement, respecting democratic processes of choices, the institutional framework able to facilitate the government's accomplishment of the *Agenda*. Likewise, in his 1932 *The Monetary Policy of the Labour Party*, Keynes (1982) engaged in similar reasoning, though he refrained from using the word *Agenda* to express it. Yet, he was still arguing that the management of economic policies was a hard task and that the members of the bureaucracy should have the right skills to undertake it. With this reasoning Keynes (1972, p. 295) showed, however, a seeming contradiction in his arguments about the technical staff of the State,

> I cannot explain it without beginning to approach my fundamental position. I believe that in the future, more than ever, questions about economic framework of society will be far and away the most important of political issues. I believe that the right solution will involve intellectual and scientific elements which must be above the heads of the vast mass of more or less illiterate voters.

Hence, there is a kind of tension between democratic wishes *vis-à-vis* the aristocratic execution of the economic guidelines of society. This is crystal clear in Keynes's writings when one reviews his arguments regarding the State technical staff. The background of this tension is the need to understand the techniques of economics, that is, the limits set by the knowledge of the relationships between its key variables. That is why Keynes was keen to provide technical autonomy for those in charge of undertaking and evaluating economic policies.

The solution Keynes envisioned to this tension between the people's democratic choice of economic goals, and the aristocratic decision of how to accomplish them, was the prevalence of public spirit and democratic exercise. The semi-autonomy of State entities, as well as their counterpart, namely the partial subordination to the democratically-elected parliament and government, necessarily imply a constant dialogue and make the State be the space of the conciliation between democratic wills and technocratic ruling. Therefore, the more immediate goals of the populace are presented for execution. However, the details of such execution (How to set these goals? When? How to pay for them?) *pari passu* to what the State has been doing — the long-term public spirit — match in a State policy rather than just in government policy. The latter is, nevertheless, the official body for the new democratic wishes to be accomplished, assisted by a technical staff designated for this purpose.

What does Keynes expect the State to aim for as its ultimate target? The State would be the solution to '[t]he outstanding faults of the economic society in which we live [which] are its failure to provide for full employment and its arbitrary and inequitable distribution of wealth and incomes' (Keynes 1964, p. 372). To do so, he argued that the State *Agenda* would be the resolution to crises of effective demand and should fight against unemployment and unequal income and wealth distribution. Regarding unemployment, 'I conceive, therefore, that a somewhat comprehensive socialization of investment will prove the only means of securing an approximation to full employment; though this need not exclude all manner of compromises and of devices by which public authority will co-operate with private initiative' (Keynes 1964, p. 378).

The *Agenda* was wider than the well-known Keynes's economic policies prescriptions. Still, they are one of the most important outcomes of the State *Agenda*. Active and countercyclical economic policies, notably fiscal and monetary ones, should be undertaken to stabilize economic cycles and sustain effective demand, ensuing employment. Let us briefly explore Keynes's propositions of the countercyclical fiscal and monetary policies.

In terms of fiscal policy, in his 1933 *The Means to Prosperity*, Keynes (1972, p. 345) explored the concept of income multiplier and argued that a 'relief to the budget', that is, an expansionary fiscal policy to stimulate economic activity, was one of the solutions to an unemployment crisis. In the 1940 *How to Pay for the War?*, Keynes (1972) suggested taxing inheritance to improve wealth distribution. As a member of the Beveridge Commission, Keynes proposed a public budget divided in two parts, namely current and capital budgets. The first finances the public services offered to a country's population. The latter enrolls long-term public investments, which Keynes expected to automatically stabilize economic cycles and build the socially technical infrastructure of the *Agenda*. This is the most important of Keynes's fiscal policy proposals. Finally, in his GT Keynes (1964, p. 373) proposed the fiscal policy as an instrument for 'increasing the community's propensity to consume' and as a means to pursue an 'optimum rate of investment (…) of securing an approximation to full employment' (Keynes 1964, p. 378).

Regarding the monetary policy, in the GT Keynes (1964) stated that its target is to influence the yield curve of the financial system attempting to stimulate private investments. This emerged from Keynes's (1964) view that the interest rate is a conventional phenomenon, dependent on the expectations of both agents and the financial system concerning the actual and future stance of the monetary policy. Keynes (1964, p. 376) figured out the 'rentier aspect of capitalism', e.g., agents prefer to stay liquid, speculating about the price of securities, which depends on the yield curve. He proposed that the monetary policy should use all the available tools to aim at determining a low interest rate, that is, 'I am advocating (…) the euthanasia of the rentier' (Keynes 1964, p. 376).

In sum, Keynes did not seek the end of capitalism, quite the opposite. He desired to save it and make its progress, its development. Rejecting the *laissez-faire* doctrine, he proposed a regulated capitalism, whose market disfunctions were dealt with through State intervention. Keynes's economic policy proposals extensively suggested regular State economic intervention to regulate economic activity and, consequently, reduce unemployment and mitigate the unequal distribution of income and wealth. State economic interference was seen by Keynes as indispensable to 'stabilize the instability' inherent to capitalism. Still, what was Keynes's major goal regarding State economic intervention? Would his final goal only be the stabilization of the economic system? Keynes's intentions were even greater. He hoped to push capitalism to a superior level, at which it would prevail what he understood as economic development. This idea is explored in the next section.

4. Keynes's Notion of Economic Development

Although the Neoclassical Synthesis of Keynes and New-Keynesians say Keynes was mostly preoccupied with the short-term and little concerned with the long-term, we believe that Keynes emphasized a short-term analysis not because he was focused on time *per se*. He was concerned with the necessity of State intervention throughout time. Keynes's view was not weighing the short-term *versus* the long-term, so much as he tailored his arguments toward the mainstream theories of his time, which claimed that the State should not act in the short-term because in the long-term, equilibrium would be reset by market forces. Keynes did not believe in this. Hence, he designed the *Agenda* so that it would work overtime and promote the long-term economic goal, development. Therefore, what is development to Keynes?

In the concluding chapter of the GT, Keynes (1964) launched his *Concluding notes on the social philosophy towards which the General Theory might lead*. After bearing a high level of theoretical rigor in economics, he decided to delve substantially into social philosophy. Andrade (2000) stated that this philosophical ending of the book is due to Keynes's view that knowledge is not contemplation, but a tool to shape reality. After theorizing employment levels, which always stand below full capacity, and explaining the importance of money and interest rates in molding this common situation of the capitalism wasting its productive resources, Keynes adopted a normative stance, suggesting how society should behave in light of his theory.

However, Keynes's (1964) social philosophy did not present a notion of development beyond scarce references to the need to modify capitalism in order to safeguard private initiatives and the individual freedom. Keynes wondered about the importance of viewing production as an individual act of entrepreneurs, whose action multiplies social wealth. Entrepreneurs risk their own wealth without knowing whether they would profit or not. Thus, Keynes's social philosophy required the *Agenda* to socialize investment risks, given its dilemma: an action whose risk is imminently individual, but whose outcomes are social.

Based on his *Essays in Persuasion* (Keynes 1972) and *Essays in Biography* (Keynes 2010), it is possible to say that Keynes's notion of development involves a stage of capitalism where economic problems, such as unemployment, unequal income and wealth distribution, the waste of productive resources, the fight for the basic necessities of life, among others, are no longer widespread. These economic issues should be surpassed to reach development, a stage in which 'the economic problem is not — if we look into the future — *the problem of the human race*' (Keynes 1972, p. 326, original emphasis). Full employment and more equal income and wealth distribution are important elements on the road to development; still, they are not development itself. They help society to attain a subsequent stage of economic and social systems. The new status quo, reached after the issues of modern capitalism are overcome, is development.[10]

What would be, to Keynes, the mindset of this new status quo and stage of development? In *The End of Laissez-Faire*, Keynes (1972) argued that the motto of individual behavior in capitalism is the love of money, what causes individuals to confuse means and ends. In *Am I a Liberal?*, *A Short View on Russia* (1925) and *Economic Possibilities for Our Grandchildren* (1928), the author recurrently rejected the love of money as the main driver of capitalist progress. So, he believed that the developed society would need 'great changes in the code of morals' (Keynes 1972, p. 329). The love of money should be eliminated as the core of individual behavior.

---

[10]The post-Keynesian macrodynamic models (Harrod 1939; Kaldor 1957; Thirlwall 1979) are concerned with long-term growth, complementing Keynes's short-run analysis in the GT. However, the long-term growth in these models did not mention any definition of development.

Hence, Keynes's utopia asked for the end of the 'love of money as a possession' (Keynes 1972, p. 329). In this stage, individuals would have resolved their economic burdens and thus have the opportunity to 'cultivate into a fuller perfection, the art of life itself and do not sell themselves for the means of life, who will be able to enjoy the abundance when it comes' (Keynes 1972, p. 328). Keynes's notion of development signifies a capitalism that 'for the first time since his creation man will be faced with his real permanent problem — how to use his freedom from pressing economic cares, how to occupy the leisure, which science and compound interest will have won for him, to live wisely and agreeably and well' (Keynes 1972, p. 328).

The roots of the love of money that drives the capitalism are not to be found at any economic problem. They are a human condition, as Freud (1930) stated.[11] Humans beings are subject to a series of psychological suffering, mostly because of some feeling of lacking that is inherent to the human race. To fulfill this unidentified but always felt desire of something, men have found money. Money furnishes a mix of realization and power, given that capitalism is the system of producing to exchange and money can buy everything.

Still, as long as money just cover the lack of a fated purpose for human beings, such as religions do, its accumulation is never ending. Covering something does not solve it and when the humankind saw in money this cover, it turned means into ends. Like Freud (1930), Keynes was trying to make humans live their real life, not one covered by any symbol, such as God or money. His attempt was to show the love of living as a substitute for the love of money.[12] That is why after explaining the nature of money in the Chapter 17 of the GT, and what it can do to the economic activity when strongly desired, Keynes ended his magnus opus with a non-economic debate, but with social philosophy.

If the young and adult Keynes strongly believed in the power of reasoning to reveal the impulses of humans' emotion, such as the love of money, the 55-old Keynes was disillusioned as he said in his 1938 *My Early Beliefs* (Keynes 1972). There, Keynes assumed his skepticism regarding the human rationality being able to guide the humankind to a more reasonable and solidary social engagement. Even being contrary to Marxism and communism, Keynes (1972) extolled the pecuniary detachment of the Soviet Union and the social pact built into the socialist experience. There, progress, understood as a route to development, was a collective goal, different from the capitalist approach, whose evolution emerges from the individual love of capital accumulation.

There is another element that reinforces Keynes's claim for collective action as fundamental to achieving economic development. In *The Economic Possibilities for our Grandchildren*, a still optimistic essay about the future, Keynes (1972) argued that the uncoordinated economic behavior of individuals was, if left by its own, unable to enhance the life of the whole community. To fight this preeminent search of individuals for fulfilling their own interests, Keynes proposed the force of the collective action of people through the State *Agenda*. He believed that the emergence of its entities by

[11]O'Donnell (1989, p. 293) stated that Keynes's idea of love of money was taken from Sigmund Freud. In his words, 'on the one hand, [Keynes started a] scientific investigation in the psychological roots of money-love [in TM]; and on the other hand, a conception of money-love as a disgusting morbidity, as a disease whose eventual elimination in the ideal could be envisaged'.

[12]It is important to mention that the idea of love of living, which means friendship, goodness, and freedom, is related to Keynes's views about philosophy and ethical principles that were influenced by the 1903 G. E. Moore's *Principia Ethica*. For additional details, see O'Donnell (1989).

means of people's aggregative action could balance egoism and altruism. This is a very different interpretation of the relationship between individuals and the whole society when compared to the orthodox tradition in economics. The latter sees the whole society (including the economy) as a mere optimum and efficient result of the 'final *reduction ad absurdum*' (Keynes 1972, p. 446) of Bentham's utilitarian calculus.

Keynes's trust in the power of rationality in guiding the collective action of people is perhaps most illustrated by his proposal for an *International Clearing Union* (Keynes 1980b). It aimed at mitigating or eliminating the love of accumulating money in a global level. Despite the fact that he was pessimistic in the late 1930s, and even with his proposal being unsuccessful in Bretton Woods, Keynes did not give up saying that another world was possible. His utopia was the stage of economic development.

History showed that Keynes's legacy was ambiguous. On the one hand, he won some battles for a while, when the Welfare State was built after World War II and the western world lived what is nonetheless called 'the gold ages of capitalism'. During these years, the State *Agenda* coordinated the economic activity and built a wide social security police. This was the time when capitalism had the greatest growth and the better distributed personal income ever. On the other hand, Keynes's legacy started to lose the battle from the 1970 onwards, although the Keynesian prospects were right. Those at the financial market began the financialization era, and as never before the love of money has ruled the mood of capitalism.

Thus, Keynes's notion of development is the stage where humankind overcomes its economic concerns, which are no longer a major problem for the general populace. The means to accomplish it is the State *Agenda*. It the locus of conciliation between the democratic wills, government intentions, society's needs, and technical knowledge to execute the public policies. The State *Agenda* should put all that together. For, collective action and public spirit are needed.

In the developed phase of society, the love of money as the dynamo of individual action in capitalism, that is, the moral of accumulating money for its own sake, is surmounted. Hence, the combination of people freed from material scarcity with a State organized for public welfare lessens the risk of the rise of totalitarian political regimes. This, however, claims for the economic stability that the *Agenda* is responsible for reaching once market forces are incapable of doing so. Totalitarian regimes submit both individuals and collective wills to dictators, who are the extreme opposite of the collective action Keynes envisioned. The development would guarantee the liberty of individuals not only to do what he or she desires, but also to elect their representatives, responsible for deliberating and carrying out the goals of the collective.

5. Final Remarks

The most remarkable contrast between growth and development only emerged after World War II, when growth came to mean GDP expansion and development to refer to people's quality of life. This common distinction establishes the long-term perspective of development, assuming a more valuative connotation than growth, though tacitly bringing both concepts together, while adding social and economic indicators, better productivity and income and wealth redistribution, amongst other elements.

Even though Keynes died before the emergence of development as a research topic in economics, he had in his mind elements that put together this idea, as we suggest hereby, a Keynesian notion of economic development. It includes a rather qualitative than quantitative view of what economic progress should produce. Keynes's monetary economy of production saw capitalism as inherently unstable so State intervention by means of the *Agenda* should be continuous. There is no division between short- and long-term in this process. The *Agenda* is needed throughout the arduous path to build a developed society — that almost one century after Keynes's death has been reached by a few countries and, apart from Canada and Japan, are exclusively western-Europeans; even the USA, which is the wealthiest country in the world, did not reach Keynes's development, given the strong inequality, structural racism, deep-financialized love of money (that caused the 2008 Great Financial Crisis) that prevails in that country. He believed that the *Agenda*, together with all the economic policies of which it is comprised, leads to stable growth, improves employment levels and enhances income and wealth equality. Yet, these are intermediary goals of the State, necessary but not enough to reach the final target: development.

Another element is integral to the path to development, perhaps the hardest of all: a change in moral codes. The love of money must be replaced by the love of living. This is what Keynes desired to arise in the mindset of the people of a developed society. He saw economic development as the historical possibility of a society of abundance, not abundance *per se* but a better way of living: a society not in love with capital accumulation, but with life's amusements and pleasures, just as Freud (1930). Abundance should be a gateway to this new society, not an end unto itself. The development would be the final stage of the regulated capitalism Keynes dreamt of. Finally, sustainable economic growth, income and wealth distribution and social justice, accomplished by the co-operative association between the State, private initiatives (generalizing, market), and Institutions (public and private agencies, rules and people/society habits are necessary to force agents, with limited insights, to adopt strategies characterized by conventions), serve as the building blocks of true development.

Acknowledgements

The authors are thankful for the financial support of the Brazilian National Council of Scientific and Technological Development (CNPq) and two anonymous referees for comments and suggestions. All remaining errors are the authors' responsibility.

Disclosure Statement

No potential conflict of interest was reported by the author(s).

ORCID

Fábio Henrique Bittes Terra ⓘ http://orcid.org/0000-0002-2747-7744
Fernando Ferrari Filho ⓘ http://orcid.org/0000-0001-5600-7058
Pedro Cezar Dutra Fonseca ⓘ http://orcid.org/0000-0002-3814-9578

References

Andrade, R. P. 2000. 'A Agenda do Keynesianismo Filosófico: Origens e Perspectivas.' *Revista de Economia Política* 20 (2): 76–94.

Bielschowsky, R. 2000. 'Cinquenta Anos de Pensamento na CEPAL: Uma resenha.' In *Cinquenta Anos de Pensamento na CEPAL*, edited by R. Bielschowsky. Rio de Janeiro: Record.

Boianovsky, M., and K. D. Hoover. 2014. 'In the Kingdom of Solovia: The Rise of Growth Economics at MIT, 1956–70.' *History of Political Economy* 46 (annual supplement): 198–228.

Cairncross, A. 1978. 'Keynes and the Planned Economy.' In *Keynes and Laissez-Faire*, edited by A. P. Thirlwall. London: Macmillan.

Crabtree, D., and A. P. Thirlwall. 1993. *Keynes and the Role of the State*. London: MacMillan.

Dillard, D. 1980. *A Teoria Econômica de John Maynard Keynes*. São Paulo: Pioneira.

Ferrari-Filho, F., and O. A. C. Conceição. 2005. 'The Concept of Uncertainty in Post Keynesian Theory and in Institutional Economics.' *Journal of Economic Issues* 39 (3): 579–594.

Fonseca, P. C. D. 2014. 'Desenvolvimentismo: A Construção do Conceito.' In *Presente e Futuro do Desenvolvimento Brasileiro*, edited by B. Calixtre, A. M. Biancarelli, and M. A. C. Cintra. Brasília: IPEA.

Freud, S. 1930. *Civilization and Its Discontents*. New York: W. W. Norton.

Furtado, C. 1983. *Teoria e Política do Desenvolvimento Econômico*. São Paulo: Abril Cultural.

Harrod, R. F. 1939. 'An Essay in Dynamic Theory.' *Economic Journal* 49 (193): 14–33.

Kaldor, N. A. 1957. 'Model of Economic Growth.' *Economic Journal* 67 (268): 591–564.

Keynes, J. M. 1964. *The General Theory of Employment, Interest and Money*. New York: HBJ.

Keynes, J. M. 1972. *Essays in Persuasion. The Collected Writings of John Maynard Keynes*, vol. IX. London: Macmillan/Royal Economic Society.

Keynes, J. M. 1976. *A Treatise on Money: Volume I. The Pure Theory of Money*. New York: AMS Press.

Keynes, J. M. 1979. *The General Theory and After: A Supplement. The Collected Writings of John Maynard Keynes*, vol XXIX. London: Macmillan/Royal Economic Society.

Keynes, J. M. 1980a. *Activities 1940–1946: Shaping the Post-War World — Employment and Commodities. The Collected Writings of John Maynard Keynes*, vol XXVII. London: Macmillan/Royal Economic Society.

Keynes, J. M. 1980b. *Activities 1940–1944: Shaping the Post-War World, the Clearing Union. The Collected Writings of John Maynard Keynes*, vol XXV. London: Macmillan/Royal Economic Society.

Keynes, J. M. 1982. *Activities 1931–1939: World Crises and Policies in Britain and America. London: Royal Economic Society. The Collected Writings of John Maynard Keynes*, vol XXI. London: Macmillan/Royal Economic Society.

Keynes, J. M. 2010. *Essays in Biography, The Collected Writings of John Maynard Keynes*, vol X. London: Macmillan/Royal Economic Society.

Kvangraven, I. H. 2020. 'Beyond the Stereotype: Restating the Relevance of the Dependency Research Programme.' *Development and Change*. Advance online publication. 1–37. doi:10.1111/dech.12593.

Lavoie, M. 2014. *Post Keynesian Economics: New Foundations*. Cheltenham: Edward Elgar.

O'Donnell, R. M. 1989. *Keynes: Philosophy, Economics and Politics*. New York: St. Martin's.

Peacock, A. 1993. 'Keynes and the Role of the State.' In *Keynes and the Role of the State*, edited by D. Crabtree and A. P. Thirlwall. London: Macmillan.

Polanyi, K. 2001. *The Great Transformation: The Political and Economic Origins of Our Time*. Boston: Beacon.

Quesnay, F. 1996. *Os Economistas — Quadro Econômico*. São Paulo: Nova Cultural.

Robinson, J. 1981. *Desenvolvimento e Subdesenvolvimento*. Rio de Janeiro: Zahar.

Rostow, W. W. 1960. *The Stages of Economic Growth: A Non-Communist Manifesto*. Cambridge: Cambridge University Press.

Samuelson, P. 1940. 'The Theory of Pump-Priming Reexamined.' *The American Economic Review* 30 (3): 492–506.

Skidelsky, R. 1991. 'Keynes's Philosophy of Practice and Economic Policy.' In *Keynes as Philosopher-Economist*, edited by R. O'Donnell. London: Macmillan.

Smith, A. 1996. *Os Economistas — Um Inquérito Acerca das Causas da Riqueza das Nações*. São Paulo: Nova Cultural.

Solow, R. M. 1956. 'A Contribution to the Theory of Economic Growth.' *Quarterly Journal of Economics* 70 (1): 65–94.

Thirlwall, A. P. 1979. 'The Balance of Payments Constraint as an Explanation of International Growth Rates Differences.' *Banca Nazionale del Lavoro Quarterly Review* 32 (128): 45–53.

Thirlwall, A. P. 2003. *Trade, the Balance of Payments and Exchange Rate Policy in Developing Countries*. Cheltenham: Edward Elgar.

Capital Flows to Latin America (2003–17): A Critical Survey from Prebisch's Business Cycle Theory

Roberto Lampa

ABSTRACT

The economic literature on capital flows to developing countries has shared two important commonalities since the 1990s. Published works (whether they focus on the external situation or stress the domestic determinants of capital flows) tend to assume a beneficial effect of capital inflows, which leads to an improvement of peripheral institutions, whose deficiencies are ostensibly the main cause of economic turmoil and/or failure in attracting capital flows, in continuity with New Institutional Economics. In doing so, mainstream economists deliberately overlook the asymmetric characteristics of the international monetary system and the persisting hegemony of dollar. Raul Prebisch's pioneering work on business cycles in Latin America provide an alternative view, one capable of amending the existing mainstream literature. On the one hand, Prebisch stressed the destabilizing role of capital inflows on Latin American economies, particularly short-term speculative capital. On the other hand, Prebisch designed a set of counter cyclical monetary policies in order to contrast capital volatility, particularly during downturns. An analysis of stylized facts shows that, when correctly updated, Prebisch's theory has remarkable explanatory potential when applied to Latin America's current economic and financial situation.

1. Introduction

The financial crises that hit Latin America and South-Eastern Asia in the late 1990s/early 2000s highlighted the disruptive effects of capital flows reversals on developing countries. It also triggered a lively debate among mainstream economists, from which two contrasting positions emerged. One group of authors focused on the external conditions underpinning the supply of liquidity towards underdeveloped countries. From this perspective, risk aversion in financial markets and the international price of commodities, together with the rate of economic growth and interest rate in the US, represented the main determinants of capital flows. In other words, the so-called *push factors* over capital flows were underlined (Calvo, Leiderman, and Reinhart 1993). The proponents of this stance, however, did not suggest the implementation of capital controls; rather, they stressed that financial liberalization and capital flows had several collateral (and beneficial) effects, despite the potential risks for developing countries. The solution, therefore, depended on the transformation of developing countries' institutional framework and monetary governance in response to international investors, aiming at reducing both corruption and government failures (Kose et al. 2006).

The second group of economists stressed that domestic ('pull') factors were mainly responsible for the volatility of capital flows, arguing that international investors' decisions depend on both country-risk and the return on investment (Taylor and Sarno 1997). Therefore, domestic factors play a pivotal role in determining whether capital flows *in* or *out of* a country. In other words, developing countries should have aimed to guarantee a stable and trustworthy environment for investors through (*i*) the reduction of their deficit to moderate inflation, and (*ii*) implementation of reforms to ensure a market-friendly environment.

Both mainstream arguments emphasize government failures, which in turn reflects the role played by New Institutional Economics (NIE) within development studies since the 1990s. Following Acemoglu and Robinson (2012), economic development is inherently about the 'quality' of institutions. In particular, property rights represent the necessary condition for investment, especially in uncertain technological projects and education, i.e. the main prerequisites for long-term economic growth (Lampa and Abeles 2020).

NIE's rising popularity followed several developing countries' crises in the late 1990s (East Asia 1997; Russia 1998; Brazil 1999; Turkey 2000; Argentina 2001). In this sense, NIE represented a response to various contributions questioning the deregulation that preceded those crises. Focusing on the quality of peripheral institutions represented a shift away from blaming bad economic policies recommended by international institutions (liberalization, deregulation, privatization), towards government failures resulting from weak domestic institutions (Lampa and Abeles 2020). In this respect, NIE assumed domestic institutions as *structures* transcending individuals and representing a powerful constraint on patterns of action. In doing so, NIE failed to grasp that the relationship between institutions and development is not linear; rather, it differs across societies and is subjected to changes over time within the same society (Chang 2011).

The most recent literature on capital flows, subsequently, shows no meaningful advance in relation to the original debate between push and pull determinants: several mainstream economists have debated whether the post-2008 crisis can be characterized as a global financial cycle. Proponents of the 'push' view (Bruno and Shin 2015; Rey 2015) emphasize that capital flows move cyclically, depending on uncertainty, risk aversion in international financial markets and monetary policy in advanced countries. Meanwhile, the 'pull' view, current at the IMF (Cerutti, Claessens, and Rose 2017), denies that economic policies in advanced economies of the world could determine capital flows and implicitly blames the policies enacted in peripheral countries.

Both perspectives have mainly focused on empirical issues: they have been mainly descriptive, overlooking both the changing features of capitalist institutions (both in central and peripheral countries) over the last four decades and the asymmetrical power relations of the International Monetary System. Mainstream economists have failed to provide an institutional (and *political*) focus to the drivers of capital flows between the Northern hemisphere and the Global South over the past thirty years and, more specifically, since the 2008 crisis.

Scholars from more critical schools of economics have, nonetheless, tried to overcome the limitations of the mainstream debate. Discussing traditional categories of imperialism in light of changes in international capital flows, Marxist scholars (Patnaik and Patnaik 2016; Smith 2016) have focused on the shift of production processes to low-wage countries. From this perspective, transnational corporations headquartered in the Northern Hemisphere have led the process, cutting production costs and increasing mark-ups by substituting relatively high-paid domestic labor with much cheaper foreign labor. Subsequently, capital flows from North to South was but an optical illusion, since a larger amount of capital (increased by profits) was systemically remitted to developed countries.

While recognizing that this latter critique can capture an essential feature of capital flows towards emerging economies, we are convinced that it misses a crucial point: the pivotal role played by the financial sector of both central and peripheral economies. To this end, it becomes inescapable to complement the picture by drawing on additional theoretical sources more focused on the monetary features of production (Bellofiore 2018; Toporowski 2018).

Among critical schools, monetary hegemony theory from a radical perspective (Rochon and Vernengo 2003; Vernengo 2006a, 2006b; Fields and Vernengo 2013) and currency hierarchy (Tavares 1985; Kaltenbrunner 2015; Palludeto and Abouchedid 2016; De Paula, Fritz, and Prates 2017) shed light on this matter. In their view, the end of Bretton Woods, together with the international liberalization of financial markets, strengthened the U.S. dollar hegemony as assets denominated in this currency replaced gold. Accordingly, developing countries' monetary policy became even more dependent on the rate of interest determined by the Federal Reserve, which inescapably affected the exchange rate as well. In other words, dollar hegemony and currency hierarchy acted as external constraints on peripheral economies, reducing both the degree of freedom of domestic policymakers and the possibility of implementing countercyclical policies. In such a context, the intensified flow of capital between developed and developing countries revealed the increased political and economic dependence of the Global South.

However, except for Vernengo (Caldentey, Vernengo, and Torres 2019), this group of authors, rooted mainly in Latin American academia, repeatedly stressed the discontinuity between their approach and traditional Structuralist/Developmentalist literature (Tavares 1985; Palludeto and Abouchedid 2016). In doing so, they ignore a seminal precedent of the debate, represented by Raul Prebisch's early (i.e. pre ECLA-Cepal) analysis of business cycles in Argentina, which he extended to Latin American countries between 1944 and 1948.

As director of Argentina's Central Bank in the post 1929 years, Prebisch observed a reversal in the global liquidity cycle. In that capacity, he stressed that monetary policies in peripheral countries were constrained by the economic policies implemented by developed countries. In particular, the inflow-outflow of capital was mostly the result of both the trend of central economies (whether increasing or decreasing) and their monetary policies, especially in terms of interest rate. However, in line with Marxist analyses, Prebisch emphasized that the pivotal role played by external determinants was nothing but a reflection of the broader (institutional) subjection of peripheral countries to central countries. Accordingly, he qualified the importance of inflowing capital, highlighting that it may have acted as a destabilizing factor. From this perspective, Latin American countries—particularly Argentina—had to create their specific mechanisms to respond to the new international scenario in various ways depending on individual historical and social background.

Prebisch's analysis has crucial implications for the ongoing debate, implicitly high-lighting that the present (and critical) state of Latin American economies can be inter-preted as an exacerbated version of a recurring problem they suffer from for decades. Drawing on Prebisch's reasoning, we should stress that the main consequence of political and economic subordination of Latin America is that financial and business cycles are driven by the monetary decisions of developed countries. Consequently, post-2008 capital inflows towards the region represent a potential risk rather than an opportunity, eventually leading to financial crises triggered by 'sudden stops', as evidenced by Argen-tina's 2018 turmoil.

Through the inclusion of Prebisch's insights, the entire debate could move a step forward: since the changing directions of capital flows represent a structural element of disturbance for primary commodity-dependent and financially open economies, the only lasting solution for Latin America is a set of institutional reforms to be implemented at the sub-regional, regional and international level.

Therefore—assuming a critical stance towards the limitations and biases of the main-stream debate on capital flows—this article aims at exploring whether Prebisch's periph-eral business cycle theory can represent a consistent way of addressing the omissions in the existing critical literature. More specifically, the objective is to attain a sounder inter-pretation of the structural constraint on Latin American economies due to power asym-metries embodied in the international monetary and financial systems. By analyzing the Latin American economic scenario over the last 15 years, we also discuss (i) the benefits, or lack thereof, of the significant amount of capital flown into the continent in the recent past; and (ii) if, contrary to the idea of convergence, North–South financial relationships can be interpreted as evidence of an increased financial and monetary dependence.

For that end, Section Two undertakes a critical review of the contents of the main-stream debate regarding the determinants of capital flows towards emerging economies. In light of such a premise, Section Three reassesses the critique of mainstream literature in light of Prebisch's business cycle theory. Section Four presents some empirical evi-dence on capital flows in Latin America during the past two decades (2003–17). Finally, in Section Five, we draw some conclusions.

2. Government Failures as a Constraint on Development: The Flawed View of Mainstream Economists on Capital Flows Towards Latin America

The 1990s represented a shift in the traditional approach to economic development. In light of both the change in U.S. foreign policy and the new role played by interna-tional—or, rather, 'missionary'—institutions, a process of liberalization took place in several regions, particularly South-East Asia and Latin America. This *nouvelle vague* con-sisted of a set of prescriptions for underdeveloped governments, well exemplified by John Williamson's Decalogue (1990), also known as the *Washington Consensus*—originally designed for Latin American countries. Stated succinctly, the Decalogue combined the following measures:(1) Fiscal adjustment; (2) Elimination of subsidies; (3) Reduction of tax burden; (4) Moderate real interest rates; (5) Competitive exchange rates; (6) Trade liberalization (7) Liberalization of capital account to attract Foreign Direct Investment (FDI) (8) Privatization of state companies; (9) Deregulation of markets for goods and services (10) Legal security for private property rights (Williamson 1990; Lampa 2018).

In other words, development became a matter of *right* vs. *wrong* domestic policies, strictly related to trade and financial liberalization as well as the creation of a 'market friendly' environment in order to attract capital flows. Implementation meant that the degree of trade and financial openness of Latin American countries grew sharply.

In addition, sub-regional agreements reinforced such a tendency. In the case of MERCOSUR, for instance, trade regulations implied the convergence towards a common external tariff, as well as the liberalization of intra-member trade and a quasi-perfect mobility of labor. Consequently, an unprecedented process of financial deregulation took place in Latin America. With capital mobility becoming operative, exchange rates and balance of payments' net position became both deeply reliant upon capital inflows (Lampa 2018). Any reversal in capital flows immediately produced severe consequences, as evidenced by the impact of the Mexican *Tequila crisis* in 1994, representing the most outstanding example of financial contagion within Latin American countries.

In the following years, similar events (in East Asia, Russia, Turkey, and Argentina) highlighted the crucial role of capital flows, triggering a debate about their impact in developing countries. Economists particularly discussed whether flows were driven by external or domestic factors; that is, were investment in Latin America prompted by the the early 1990s recession in the U.S. or were they due to improvement of domestic fundamentals in these economies (Swarnaly 2018).

Fernandez-Arias (1996) and Calvo, Leiderman, and Reinhart (1993), on the one hand, argued that external conditions determined the supply of capital towards the region meaning that the recession in the U.S. had been the predominant driver of capital flows towards Latin American countries in the early 1990s. The recession had led to a sharp decrease in U.S. interest rates, which, in turn, induced a change in investment decisions, well reflected by the private capital account (foreign direct investment, stocks, bonds, bank loans etc.) of the U.S. balance of payments. In other words, the main determinants of capital flows were considered to be risk aversion in financial markets, the global trend of commodity prices, the U.S. growth rate and rate of interest. In other words, so-called *push factors* were stressed over capital flows, having unexpected implications in terms of policy.

Contrary, from what one may expect, in light of their analytical premise, these economists did not prescribe certain degree of capital account management in order to avoid *sudden stops* of capital flows. They rather stressed the collateral benefits of financial liberalization for developing countries, which included, first, the predictable increase in foreign ownership of peripheral banks would foster international insertion and 'better' (i.e. western type) regulations of the credit branch, resulting in more secure deposits and a reduced cost of capital. Second, financial openness would induce peripheral countries to adjust their public governance and, thus, increase transparency and reduce corruption. Finally, the new scenario would discipline macro policies, reducing the incentives for inflation policies and fixed exchange rate regimes. In other words, the increased intensity of capital flows would not represent a menace for developing countries because financial openness would also enhance their capability of dealing with capital volatility (Kose et al. 2006).

Lopez Mejia (1999), Taylor and Sarno (1997) and the IMF (1993), on the other hand, asserted that domestic factors were mostly responsible for the direction of capital flows.[1] In their view, international investors' decisions are influenced by both risk and return on investment, which are largely determined by the intrinsic characteristics of a particular economy. Therefore, domestic factors would play a pivotal role in determining whether capital flows *into* or *out* of a developing country. More specifically, macroeconomic fundamentals (economic growth and interest rate) and country-specific structural factors (trade and capital openness, international reserves, exchange rate regime, institutional quality, per capita income and financial development) represent crucial features in attracting foreign investors (Swarnaly 2018). It followed then that the key factor in Latin America's ability to attract capital flows was the radical turn in the political and economic sphere. The dramatic reduction in both deficits and rates of inflation, together with the neoliberal reforms of the early 1990s, create a market friendly environment which presents a stable and trustworthy scenario for investors. According to this view, *pull factors* become the main determinants of capital flows.

In other words, the whole debate reflected the 'bipartisan belief' that government failures represented a major issue in Latin America, diverging explanation notwithstanding. In a sense, capital flows became a measure of a country's overall economic performance. In fact, debt insolvency, unpredictable macroeconomic policies, the inability to maintain a public surplus and a weak rule of law represented the most important obstacles to capital inflows and provided evidence of the government's inability to implement a consistent development agenda (Williamson 1990; Reinhart 2005).

The solution to capital volatility for both groups of mainstream economists, therefore, consisted of institutional reforms aimed at modifying the detrimental features of peripheral economies. More precisely, the strict adoption of *western-made institutions* became the inevitable path to development for Latin America and other underdeveloped countries. The debate, thus, represented a clear example of the broader role played by NIE within development studies since the 1990s. Incentives for economic agents, property rights and a market-friendly environment became prerequisites for foreign investment that would unavoidably lead Latin American countries to economic prosperity. Notably the agenda of the most important international institutions was re-shaped in accordance with NIE's tenets.

Figure 1 shows the evolution of the World Bank's (W.B.) lending to developing countries from 1960 to 2019. Broadly speaking, the W.B. finances two kinds of measures. First, *Investment loans* that, according to the official definition, finance a wide range of activities aimed at creating the physical and social infrastructure necessary for poverty alleviation and sustainable development. Second, *Development policy lending* (known as 'adjustment loans' until 2004), which consists of rapidly disbursed policy-based financing typically supporting a program of policy and institutional actions, for example, actions aimed at improving the 'investment climate' and meeting 'international

---

[1] This debate led to an amendment to the IMF Articles of Agreement in September 1997, according to which the Fund had to promote the orderly liberalization of capital movements. See Fischer (1997) and, for a critical stance on capital liberalization, see also Stiglitz (2000).

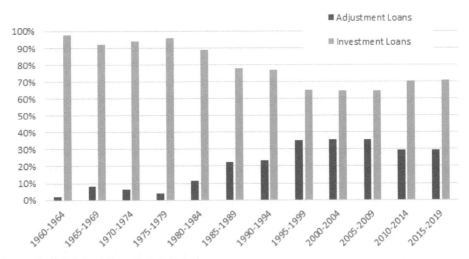

Source: Projects & Operations, The World Bank

Figure 1. World Bank's lending to developing countries.

commitments'. Whereas *Investment loans* represent traditional support for investment, *Development Policy Lending* seeks to create the conditions for capital inflows, in line with NIE's point of view. For decades, *Investment loans* corresponded to over 90 per cent of the W.B. lending budget. However, from the mid-1980s on, they started to decline, shrinking to approximately 65 per cent in 2005. Conversely, *adjustment loans* rose sharply in the same period.

The most recent controversies between the pull and push determinants of capital flows also adhere to the same pattern. Rey (2015) made considerable progress in theorizing the existence of a cyclical trend in capital flows after the 2008 global crisis, driven by uncertainty and risk aversion in financial markets and the extraordinary monetary policies of developed countries. In the author's view, in the post 2008 scenario, the traditional trilemma of a floating exchange rate as the only possible way to conjugate free mobility of capital and independent monetary policy is misleading. Rather, we should discuss a dilemma according to which independent monetary policy becomes possible if and only if the capital account is managed. In other words, it is necessary to introduce capital account management, as well as a countercyclical credit policy during upturns, because of the special circumstances determined by the 2008 crisis. A similar reconsideration also characterizes Reinhart, Reinhart, and Trebesch (2016), which shows a connection between capital flows, commodity cycles, and economic crises, thus highlighting that many emerging markets are currently vulnerable to crises, as they face an abrupt fall in both capital inflows and commodity prices.

However, several researchers from the IMF (e.g. Cerutti, Claessens, and Rose 2017) state that empirical evidence does not support Rey's conclusions, since only a quarter of capital flows can be explained by a variation in the monetary policy of developed countries. Accordingly, the existence of a financial cycle cannot be taken for granted, and capital account management is unnecessary.

The debate on capital flows determinants produced no fundamental advances. Beyond the diverging opinions on the drivers of capital flows, the prevailing idea shaping the agenda of international institutions still stresses that capital inflows must be paired with good practices and institutional empowerment implemented by developing countries. From this angle, one may conclude that mainstream economists understand capital flows merely as a *technical* problem, and they assume free capital mobility. At this level, they disagree about the drivers of capital flows. Nevertheless, at the policy level, they show a remarkable consensus on financial liberalization in emerging economies. In other words, they conceive capital flows as an allocative problem, irrespective of its cause; that is, whenever capital is misallocated, policy makers should focus on the poor institutional quality of developing countries. In this sense, government failures and corruption in the periphery occupy center stage, becoming a permanent source of disturbance for development. By deliberately ignoring the interplay between peripheral and central institutions, mainstream economists do not question, or even analyze, the agenda of international monetary institutions as possible causes for said disturbances, thus neglecting that they embody power asymmetries between countries. This oversight amounts to a deliberate removal of the political dimension from the question of capital flows.

3. Prebisch's Heretical Vision as a Blueprint for Critical Literature

All the works reviewed in the previous section completely overlook that money is first and foremost a social convention. As such, any economic theory must provide an adequate specification of its social and structural conditions of existence (Ingham 1996). In this sense, the starting point for any analysis of capital flows between developed and underdeveloped countries should be that money is socially produced. Therefore, since it does not emerge from nature, money is a social convention that is 'natural' to any society: in a nutshell, money embodies both social and power relations (Polanyi 1968).

These kinds of considerations are fundamental when discussing problems inextricably linked to the current international monetary system's asymmetric features, mainly because of the privileged status of the U.S. dollar, together with a group of other currencies in the Northern hemisphere. In fact, any development process inevitably implies an adequate supply of international currency reserves, a condition that no underdeveloped country can take for granted since no underdeveloped country issues such currency, with the very partial exception of China that finances itself (Bortz and Kaltenbrunner 2018). All the mentioned articles fail to grasp such a topical issue, implicitly assuming that either the *right* policies or some kind of capital account management would imply, by definition, an unlimited inflow of capitals, automatically driving peripheral countries to develop. Accordingly, the international monetary system becomes an exogenous datum, and the correct domestic policies, rather than the existing international monetary framework define the conditions for development.

A similar flaw also emerges in the controversy surrounding the 'end of imperialism', recently re-ignited by David Harvey's comment to Patnaik and Patnaik (in Patnaik and

Patnaik 2016). In line with his previous work, Harvey stresses that current flows of capital are constantly changing direction as a reflection of industrial outsourcing towards emerging markets, thus reversing the historical draining of wealth from East to West. According to him, the use of the theory of imperialism to interpret the structural imbalances of international monetary and financial system should be dismissed.

Despite Harvey's controversial stance, critical literature has generally evidenced a deeper awareness of the asymmetrical features of the international order. In recent years, many Marxists have rejected Harvey's thesis (Bond 2004; Sutcliffe 2006; Higginbottom 2013; Patnaik and Patnaik 2016; Smith 2016), while distancing themselves from mainstream views on the determinants of capital flows. In contrast to these latter works, Marxists have stressed the political and institutional (rather than technical) supremacy of central countries. Assuming that a global labor arbitrage is the key driver of contemporary globalization, Marxist literature has argued that the increase in FDI is a reflection of wide scale productive outsourcing, which is beneficial for developed countries, since capital drawn from the outsourced markets exceeds in-flown capital. Since South–North repatriated profits are greater than North–South FDI, the dynamics in capital flows reinforce imperialist domination over peripheral economies and the extraction of surplus value. Additionally, even South-South capital flows are not in contradiction with the theory of imperialism, since they represent what the Latin American dependency theory had defined as 'sub-imperialism'; that is, a search for valorization of the in-flown capital by the domestic elite of developing countries, normally towards fewer developed countries. From this angle, for instance, capital flow from BRICS countries (particularly Brazil and China) to Africa is an optical illusion rather than an evidence against imperialism, as the elites of BRICS countries resorted to massive capital flight (either to tax havens or to developed countries) once capital previously flown to Africa was repatriated.

Its merits notwithstanding, the re-interpretation of capital flows provided by Marxist literature is circumscribed to the *real* economy. In doing so, Marxist discourse overlooks a crucial point, i.e. that the supremacy of developed countries is also monetary and financial. In this sense, even a powerful and explanatory theory such as imperialism— when correctly interpreted as *financial* imperialism, along the pioneering lines of Rudolf Hilferding—loses its potential. From this angle, one may state that Marxists forgot the lesson of Samir Amin (1976), who described the cyclical trend of capital flows in light of the role played by peripheral countries in international recovery. During depressions, the periphery receives capital flows from developed countries looking for valorization. However, as soon as central economies recover, there occurs a reversal of capital flows, bringing serious consequences for peripheral countries. Similar considerations, nonetheless, can be found among other critical schools, particularly in those authors who focused on monetary hegemony (from a radical angle) and on currency hierarchy.

The former group (Rochon and Vernengo 2003; Vernengo 2006a, 2006b; Fields and Vernengo 2013) stresses that a country is hegemonic when its money is universally accepted at the international level as a means of exchange, a store of value and a unit of account. Being hegemonic means that the country is liberated from any constraint on its balance of payments. From this perspective, the post-Bretton Woods world is undoubtedly characterized by a stronger U.S. hegemony, since the U.S. are not indebted in any currency other than the U.S. dollar. Consequently, the Federal Reserve will always be able, by definition, to buy assets denominated in the domestic currency. In other words, there is no technical possibility of a default for the United States of America. Latin American countries, by contrast, are exposed to a constant risk represented by the scarce supply of U.S. dollars.

On the one hand, sustained economic growth immediately translates into an enormous increase in imports (also because of the pivotal role of transnational corporations within the imports branch). On the other hand, external debt has to be serviced in U.S. dollar. As a result, an insufficient stock of dollars acts as a constraint on the balance of payments, which inevitably conditions economic growth to the direction of capital flows.

Along similar lines, the currency hierarchy approach (Tavares 1985; Kaltenbrunner 2015; Palludeto and Abouchedid 2016; De Paula, Fritz, and Prates 2017) emphasizes the negative effects on peripheral countries of the U.S. dollar hegemony. In their view, the end of Bretton Woods, together with Paul Volcker's 'dollar diplomacy'—the massive issuance of U.S. debt in the late 70s /early 80s followed by an abrupt increase in the rate of interest—, acted as a disciplining factor on the central banks of the rest of the world, whose rate of interest had to adhere to the Fed's pattern. In addition, the increasing degree of financial openness also implied a greater volatility of exchange rates, depending on the direction of international capital flows. In other words, in the post-Bretton Woods era, the higher hierarchy of the U.S. dollar implied that emerging countries lost control over the most determining factors of their interest and exchange rates. As a consequence, the periphery became a 'business cycle taker' (De Paula, Fritz, and Prates 2017): the illiquid condition of peripheral countries (i.e. the inability of peripheral currencies to internationally fulfill the three traditional functions of money, determined by currency hierarchy) had to be compensated with financial profitability. Capital flows then followed a cyclical trend, depending on the interest rate differentials between the Northern hemisphere and Latin American countries. When developed countries lowered interest rates, monetary conservatism to attract capital flows were in vogue in Latin America—a policy that represented major constraints to Keynesian/ expansionary policies. Inversely, as soon as the monetary policy of developed countries changed, key currencies got stronger, triggering currency crises in peripheral countries.

Despite their illumination of the specificities of Latin America, with the exception of Vernengo (Caldentey, Vernengo, and Torres 2019), these two groups of authors neglect a seminal precedent for the debate: Raul Prebisch's early (i.e. pre ECLA-Cepal) analysis of business cycles in Argentina and, later, in Latin American countries. They actually stress the discontinuity between their approach and traditional Structuralist/Developmentalist literature (Tavares 1985; Palludeto and Abouchedid 2016). As early as 1921, Prebisch demonstrated that all the crises that had previously affected Argentina were essentially the consequence of its subordination to the developed world in the international monetary system. In Prebisch's eyes, the crises' driver had always been the unstable international inflow of capital (more precisely, gold) typical to Argentina. As a former Spanish colony subsequently turned into a *de facto* British colony, between 1862 and 1921, Argentina was unable to obtain a stable flow of capital by means of its exports. The age of empire had created a structural distortion in international trade, according to which Argentina had to rely on the unstable price of exported primary goods or on international loans to sustain sufficient gold reserves (Prebisch 1921–22; Sember

2010). Following Tugan-Baranovsky, Prebisch, then, stated that a financial cycle characterized the Argentinian economy. Stated succinctly, the transmission mechanism consisted of the following stages: when risk aversion was low (which implied a low interest rate in central countries), new loans arrived from developed countries; such loans triggered a monetary expansion and an increase in imports; the balance of payments turned negative, pushing Argentina to ask for new loans to correct external imbalances, which worsened external conditions; loans, then, suddenly stopped, initiating a reversal of capital flows; and a crisis hit the country. In other words, the ultimate causes of Argentine instability were not internal. Quite the contrary, fluctuations in capital inflows were the source of the country's instability and they largely depended on lending countries. Furthermore, Prebisch observed that the inflows of capitals had an adverse effect on domestic banks. Given the productive backwardness of Argentina, the increased capital supply fed speculative activities, which represented an opportunity for rapid enrichment, thus increasing the country's financial fragility. In other words, the disposition of European and American capitalists to lend was the ultimate cause of speculative bubbles in the periphery (Sember 2010). Therefore, the asymmetric monetary relationship between center and periphery converted capital flows into a detrimental element, permanently menacing Argentina's stability.

A decade later, Prebisch contributed to the birth of the Central Bank of Argentina (BCRA). With his theory of financial cycle in mind, he conceived BCRA as a powerful tool to reduce external vulnerability. As a member of the military government, Prebisch took part in the 1932 Geneva conference of the League of Nations, as well as the 1933 London Conference that led to the Roca-Runciman Treaty. In both cases, he realized that Argentina had no international relevance. The solution to its economic problems depended then on a set of anti-cyclical measures to be implemented during the upswing and the downturn of its cycle. Consequently, Prebisch built up a draft of a 'central bank for primary exporting countries', thus rejecting the idea of one-size-fits-all institutional setting proposed by the U.K.. In line with British interests, this consisted of an 'orthodox' Central Bank, merely implementing a fixed exchange regime; a guarantee for financial stability of the numerous British companies investing abroad, against the risk of devaluations.

The birth of BCRA corresponded to a new stage of Argentina's economy in which controls over capital flows reduced fluctuations and instability. As general manager of the BCRA, Prebisch aimed at expanding international reserves in times of prosperity in order to counterweight the outflow of capital during downturns. He also repeatedly insisted on the necessity of limiting bank credit during the upswing. In particular, Prebisch differentiates short-term speculative capital from other types of inflow. In his view, short-term capital originated from lack of speculative opportunities in developed countries. As such, when they entered peripheral economies, their disruptive effects were twofold: first, they expanded imports and second, they had to be repaid promptly, at a higher cost due to interest payments. The overall effect was a sharp reduction of international reserves, which put Argentina in an insolvent position during the subsequent downturns (Prebisch 1939; O'Connell 2001; Sember 2018). In 1937, therefore, BCRA forbade the payment of any interest to short-term capital entering the country. In 1941–42, further capital controls were introduced: remittances were subjected to a formal authorization and had to be compensated in terms of international reserves.

When compared to mainstream literature, Prebisch's work contains several insights still relevant today. First, he puts into perspective the alleged beneficial effect of capital inflows, highlighting the risks connected to an open capital account, as well as the danger short-term capital represented to a peripheral country. Second, Prebisch's description of liquidity cycle rests on different ontological assumptions as the ultimate cause of the cycle is the division of the world into *subordinated* and *dominant* countries, rather than the misallocation of capital due to (peripheral) government failures. Given such premises, Prebisch's conclusions are diametrically opposed to mainstream economists: both central and international institutions are the main actors responsible for capital volatility in the periphery; reversal in capital flows are not an exceptional and isolated fact, triggered by economic crises, but a permanent element of disturbance for peripheral economies.

Prebisch's work represents, moreover, a consistent way of also amending critical literature. A careful rereading of Prebisch shows that the current (and critical) state of Latin American economies is not an unprecedented problem or an unexpected consequence of the monetary turn of the Federal Reserve in the late 70s / early 80s. On the contrary, the post-2008 cyclical trend of capital flows is an exacerbated version of a recurrent problem that has been affecting Latin America since the gold standard era. In Prebisch's days, capital outflow was strictly related to the colonial and post-colonial features of Latin American countries, which, in a sense, are still consequential to present days.

As financial and business cycles are driven by the monetary decisions of developed countries, the post-2008 inflows of capital towards the region represent a potential risk, rather than an opportunity, eventually leading to financial crises triggered by 'sudden stops', as evidenced by Argentina's 2018 turmoil (Lampa and Zeolla 2019).

If this line of thought were upheld, the critical debate might move a step forward: since changing capital flows represent a structural element of disturbance for primary commodity-dependent and financially-open economies, only a set of institutional reforms to be implemented at the sub-regional, regional and international level could offer a long-lasting solution for Latin America.

In the short run—since primary commodity-dependent and underdeveloped economies cannot be modified *ex-nihilo* due to financial and exchange market volatility—such reforms would consist of bilateral payment systems to boost the use of national currencies in sub-regional and regional trade, together with a regional/sub-regional lender of last resort of international reserve currencies (such as the unfinished Banco del Sur project). This would reduce Latin American dependence on the dollar and international financial flows, creating room for higher capital controls.

In the medium-run, both the increased international reserves and the lower financial volatility resulting from the reforms mentioned above, would allow a more resolute transformation of Latin American economies. In this sense, the most remarkable step forward for this group of countries still consists of planned industrialization, focused on the substitution of dollar-saving imports. Along these lines, it is possible to achieve regional self-financing, which results in lower political subordination.

This idea played a pivotal role in Prebisch's mature work, since the publication of the well-known *Cepal's Manifesto* (Prebisch 1949). Despite controversies around Prebisch's solution, a careful analysis of the current situation suggests that no meaningful advancement can be achieved if these problems do not occupy the center of the debate.

4. Capital Flows to Latin America (2003–17): Drawing an Alternative Interpretation from Stylized Facts

In the previous section, we have shown how Prebisch's theory is still today able to account for some detrimental features of capital flows to Latin American countries. However, it is important to emphasize that the 'solutions' Prebisch implemented—as a central banker—should not be meant as definitive answers to these structural problems, or to expect them to magically convert capital flows into a beneficial tool for economic growth.

Quite the contrary: the anti-cyclical monetary policy, together with a strict set of capital controls, represented a sort of 'second best': the possibility of reducing capital flows. Since Latin American countries could not revert their subordinated role in the international trade and monetary system (i.e. the main determinant of capital flows' disruptive effect, according to Prebisch), capital account management had to be a judgment call to avoid major issues such as the recurrent crises of the balance of payments. However, while potentially reducing the financial fragility of Latin American countries, such measures also carried severe consequences on their economies. In particular, restrictions to credit and imports during the upswings (to increase the stock of international reserves) implied the impossibility of developing an industrial sector, which would diversify the productive structure of these primary exporting countries.[2] Besides, in order to prevent capital outflows and/or capital flights, Prebisch implemented a set of exchange control measures, which further hindered the process of industrialization by discouraging imports of capital goods. In sum, in Prebisch's pessimistic analysis, accumulation of reserves and monetary conservatism turned into the price that the periphery had to pay to minimize the systemic risk, well represented by the volatility of capital flows.

A careful review of Latin American economies during the last fifteen years suggests that Prebisch's pessimistic stance still influences the economic reality of the region. Figure 2 shows the sharp increase—approximately +50 per cent—in the international reserves/GDP ratio of eight Latin American countries (LAC8)—Argentina; Brazil; Chile; Colombia; Mexico; Peru; Uruguay and Venezuela—in the 2003–17 period. It is a remarkable piece of data, particularly if we consider that neither Argentina nor Venezuela have actively increased their reserves, for different reasons (debt restructuring and massive capital flight triggered by political instability, respectively). The increase in international reserves has been rather passive; engendered by prolonged surpluses in financial accounts due to capital flows towards Latin America.

Rather than triggering a sharp increase in investment, capital inflows were matched with the accumulation of reserves, which functioned as a typical macroprudential regulation. A similar anti-cyclical policy illustrates that monetary authorities of Latin America, just as in Prebisch's days, have treated capital inflows like a potential risk rather than an opportunity and, have accordingly adopted prudential policies inspired by monetary conservatism.

Differently from Prebisch's days, the whole region did not adopt capital account management based on individual national specificity: it was rather a product of the

---

[2] In fact, Prebisch abandoned his role at the BCRA because of a clash with the Argentinean 1943 *de facto* government, which explicitly aimed to industrialize the country.

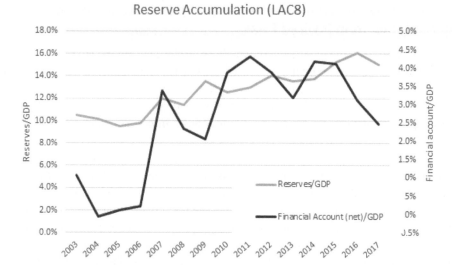

Source: IMF- BOP statistics and CEPAL

Figure 2. Reserve Accumulation in Latin America.

coordinated actions of central banks. From this perspective, Latin American central banks followed the example of Taiwan, Singapore, Malaysia, India and China, who had previously shown the beneficial effects of limiting capital volatility by means of capital account management (Epstein, Grabel, and Jomo 2005; Epstein 2009). At first sight, this might suggest that also Latin American countries were able to detach their domestic policies from the international liquidity cycle, reinforcing the autonomy of macro and micro-economic policy and shifting investment toward the long-term (Epstein, Grabel, and Jomo 2005; Epstein 2009).

Unfortunately, this has not been the case: as shown by Painceira (2008), within the existing financial framework, international reserves could not be used to finance sovereign policies or even countercyclical fiscal policies in times of severe recession, as evidenced by Brazil in 2015–16 (Lampa 2018). Since the degree of financial openness remained high, international reserves acted as a 'collateral' for foreign investors (both financial and corporations), guaranteeing that the country receiving capital flows would not suffer financial turmoil, sudden stops and/or abrupt devaluations.

From this perspective, the accumulation of reserves represented a logical outcome of the inflation targeting regimes effective since the early 2000s. After a wave of sovereign debt crises hit Latin America, mainstream policies meant a new defensive attitude was adopted to preserve financial liberalization at all costs. Inflation control and the prevention of balance-of-payments crises then became necessary conditions to keep almost free capital mobility (Frenkel 2006). In this sense, the autonomy of macroeconomic policy in Latin America mostly depended on the price of commodities, rather than capital account management, even if the latter tool effectively prevented financial crises and sudden stops.

In other words, as stated by Palludeto and Abouchedid (2016, p. 71), currency hierarchy meant that, even when a peripheral currency market has a high turnover during a liquidity boom, the abundant capital flowing into the country does not translated into a greater ability of its currency to internationally fulfill the three traditional functions of money, and thus achieving a higher political autonomy.

While capital flows to emerging countries did not affect dollar hegemony, they still acted as a 'safety valve mechanism preserving the international role of the dollar,' preventing global imbalances, resulting from the generation of global liquidity fostered by financialization (Vasudevan 2009). In other words, there has been 'no panacea' for the destabilizing role of dollar hegemony in Latin American countries (Vernengo 2006b).

Table 1 focuses on Brazil, probably the most evident example of such a tendency. Even during the years of the most severe GDP contraction (2015–16), the rate of interest remained high, acting as an obstacle on credit and domestic investors. Only in June 2017 did the Central Bank of Brazil progressively lowered the interest rate, which remained high compared to developed countries. The explanation lies in the necessity to feed capital inflows to achieve a surplus in the financial account capable of compensating the country's current account deficit. The overall importance of this capital inflow was such that total reserves in the U.S. dollar had already reached an unprecedented level of $373 billion by 2012.

Goncalves (2007) reached similar conclusions concerning Uruguay: despite the high level of reserves, a small country with a relatively big and highly dollarized—financial sector always needs reserve accumulation. Contrary to mainstream economic view, by allowing the unrestricted inflow of foreign capital, Latin American countries have often undermined their own domestic market and increased their dependence on inflowing capital to sustain economic growth.

Additionally, since 2005 capital inflows have been matched by a thorough outflow of capital, even if the net result was a surplus. This is not surprising in itself; financial transactions, by definition, enter the balance sheets twice. As purchases of foreign assets are matched by accumulation of liabilities, it is, thus, expected for gross inflows and outflows (including F.X. reserves) to grow simultaneously. However, as highlighted by Borio and Disyatat (2011), the post-2008 scenario shows an excess elasticity in the

Table 1. Brazil's financialisation in a sketch.

Year	GDP growth (%)	Annual nominal interest rate	Current account (USD mln)	Financial account (USD mln)	Total reserves (USD mln)
2003	1.1%	16.3%	4,177	−157	49,300
2004	5.8%	17.7%	11,679	−3,532	52,900
2005	3.2%	18.0%	13,985	13,144	53,800
2006	4.0%	13.2%	13,643	16,152	85,800
2007	6.1%	11.2%	1,551	88,330	180,300
2008	5.1%	13.7%	−28,192	28,302	193,800
2009	−0.1%	8.7%	−24,302	70,172	238,500
2010	7.5%	10.7%	−75,824	125,112	287,600
2011	4.0%	10.9%	−77,032	137,879	352,000
2012	1.9%	7.1%	−74,218	92,853	373,200
2013	3.0%	9.9%	−74,839	67,877	358,800
2014	0.5%	11.7%	−104,204	111,454	363,600
2015	−3.5%	14.2%	−59,450	56,730	356,500
2016	−3.3%	13.7%	−23,684	25,791	365,016
2017	1.1%	6.9%	−9,805	11,267	373,972
2018	N/A	6.4%	N/A	N/A	374,715

Source: CEPAL, Banco Central do Brasil and Lampa (2018).

international financial system—i.e. remarkably low degree to which monetary regimes constrain the credit creation process and the availability of external funding. The increasing amount of gross capital flows resulting from excessive financial elasticity may potentially foster financial fluctuations or crises in the periphery. Along these lines, Azis and Shin (2015) remark that in the post-2008 scenario, the 'easy money' policy in advanced economies has negatively affected emerging markets, creating widespread financial instability. In few words, this outcome depended on the negative interest rate policy of developed countries, which massively displaced speculative capitals towards emerging markets.

Aligned with Prebisch's views, short-term capital acted as a continuous factor of volatility in Latin American economies in the observed period. The same can be said about Asian countries (especially Japan), the arbitrage/speculative opportunities in Latin American countries were mainly represented by carry trade, which rapidly turned into a structural feature of the international monetary system (Kaltenbrunner and Painceira 2016). Carry trade consists of borrowing in a low-interest rate currency (e.g. USD) and converting the borrowed amount into another high-interest rate currency (e.g. BRL) with the purpose to: (a) place the amount on deposit in the second currency offering a higher rate of interest, or (b) invest it into assets (stocks, commodities, bonds etc.) denominated in the second currency. After this financial valorization, the (increased) amount is changed back into the low-interest-rate currency, netting the speculators an easy capital gain (Lampa 2018).

In September 2016, Argentina, Uruguay and Brazil still occupied the three highest positions in the global ranking of carry trade. The annual expected gain in USD was +5,84, +5,13 and +4,2 per cent respectively: a tremendous capital gain when compared to the corresponding values in the U.K. (−0,07 per cent) and the Eurozone (−1,88 per cent) (Barberia 2017; Lampa 2018), which prompts short-term speculation in the exchange markets of the Latin American countries, especially Argentina.

Figure 3 shows the total private flows—the total gross disbursements by the private sector of the creditor country to the recipient country (i.e. equity assets, purchase of debt plus derivatives)—as a percentage of GDP entering and exiting Latin America. It is possible to observe that both curves follow a similar trend characterizing; namely, there is a sharp increase in both outflow and inflow of capitals that correspond to the quantitative easing programs implemented by the Federal Reserve and the Bank of England (March, 2009), on one hand, and the European Central Bank (end of 2011), on the other.

Short-term capital played an important role in the years examined, having a sharp increase in the volatility of both capital and exchange rates as its main consequence: speculative capitals entered Latin America in search of easy gains, however, as soon as they increased their value, they were repatriated (Painceira 2008).

A final crucial point, going beyond the scope of Prebisch's work, must be discussed: the stocks of capital accumulated in Latin America largely turned into a flow of capital from Latin America to developed countries and tax havens. As evidenced by Table 2, from 2000 to 2015, total financial assets (F.X. reserves; purchase of debt plus other investment; purchase of equity assets) of Latin American countries expanded from 22 to 40 per cent of their GDP.

Figure 4 focuses on a point raised by Bonizzi and Toporowski (2017), showing that in Latin America, F.X. reserves and purchases debt and hard currencies (i.e. 'other

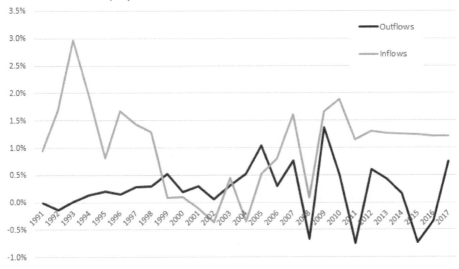

Source: IMF- BOP statistics and CEPAL

Figure 3. Total private capital flows in Latin America.

investment') of developed countries had a tremendous expansion, particularly in the post-crisis years.

This empirical evidence makes it clear that the most used macroprudential regulation for Latin American countries still consists of purchasing bonds, assets, or currency of developed countries, implicitly assuming that they represent the safest possible investment—certainly not a lack of evidence of the persisting dollar hegemony. In other

Table 2. The increasing importance of capital flows in Latin America.

Country	Total/GDP	Equity assets/GDP	Debt + OI assets/GDP	Derivatives assets/GDP	FX reserves/GDP
			2000		
Argentina	38%	2%	28%	0%	7%
Brazil	10%	0%	5%	0%	5%
Chile	49%	12%	18%	0%	19%
Colombia	23%	1%	14%	0%	9%
Mexico	15%	0%	10%	0%	5%
Peru	27%	3%	7%	0%	16%
Uruguay	59%	0%	48%	0%	11%
Venezuela	46%	2%	33%	0%	11%
LAC8	**22%**	**1%**	**14%**	**0%**	**7%**
			2015		
Argentina	38%	2%	32%	0%	4%
Brazil	26%	1%	5%	0%	20%
Chile	86%	42%	25%	2%	16%
Colombia	41%	6%	19%	0%	16%
Mexico	39%	3%	20%	0%	15%
Peru	51%	13%	7%	0%	31%
Uruguay	71%	1%	41%	0%	29%
Venezuela	93%	1%	89%	0%	3%
LAC8	**40%**	**5%**	**19%**	**0%**	**16%**

Source: Updated and extended version of dataset constructed by Lane and Milesi-Ferretti (2007).

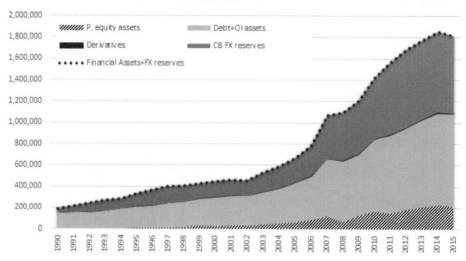

Source: Lane & Milesi Ferretti (2007)

Figure 4. Gross Capital Flows in Latin America.

words, not only did the asymmetric features of the international monetary system not disappear when compared to Prebisch's times, but they also deepened as a consequence of financialization. As if in a sort of 'international division of financial circulation', developed countries turned into providers of cheap global liquidity, flowing into the continent in search of speculative arbitrages. The stock of capital thus accumulated in Latin American central banks turned into a massive purchase of assets, bonds, and currency of developed countries. In a striking similarity to Prebisch's days, the post-2008 scenario was characterized by an increasing financial coupling (Saad-Filho 2014) between central and Latin American countries. However, this tendency was also associated to falling fixed investment, resulting in early de-industrialization and re-primarization, i.e. a real decoupling. Therefore, any kind of optimism about the alleged reversal of capital flows from central to peripheral countries seems largely unjustified. Quite the contrary, the stylized facts presented above support the conclusions of Bruno and Shin (2015): the global role of the U.S. dollar and the prevalence of debt instruments issued in U.S. dollar by borrowers from emerging markets. The implications are evident: since restricting capital flows is also a political decision, the current situation suggests that Latin American countries are not only economically but also politically subordinated to the central countries.

On the other hand, we arrive at results in line with Tooze (2018) and Bonizzi and Toporowski (2017), which highlighted developing countries' role as 'drainers' of assets and bonds from the European and North Atlantic systems. It is worth noting, however, that our data tend to be underestimated, since we do not consider unrecorded and illegal capital flows. Recent studies (G.F. Integrity 2015) have shown that, 'black' and 'grey' transactions reinforce the thesis that developing countries have acted as net creditors to the developed world from the late 1990s onwards.

From this perspective, the profound changes in financial markets have deepened the paradoxical case of capital flows between Latin America and developed countries over the last thirty years. In his inaugural address to the extraordinary CECLA session, Chilean Chancellor Gabriel Valdes (1969) exemplified this paradox in the clearest of ways:

> It is commonly believed that our continent receives actual financial aid from abroad. The data show the opposite. It is possible to state that Latin America contributes to the financing of the United States and other developed countries. Private investment in Latin America has always meant, and still means, that the amount of capital flown out of the continent is several times greater than that invested.[3]

5. Concluding Remarks

This article highlights the limitations of traditional views stemming from mainstream economics—about both the determinants and the consequences of capital flows towards Latin America.

Apart from a clear disagreement about the predominance of pull vs. push factors over capital flows, mainstream literature has uncritically accepted the idea that financial liberalization represents a consistent solution to the government failures and bottlenecks (mainly within the capital market) of peripheral economies. Accordingly, the prevailing idea shaping the agenda of international institutions continues to be that the effects of capital inflows are highly associated with good practices and institutional empowerment implemented by developing countries. In line with NIE, economic prosperity becomes inexorably linked to the existence of 'good' or 'bad' institutions, which is to say that the adoption of western institutions by Latin America is conceived as the most fruitful path to development. We have critically discussed the aforementioned literature for its technocratic flaw, which implies a lack of institutional and political analysis of the phenomenon.

Given this premise, we have reviewed the critical literature on capital flows. First, we have shown that, in opposition to mainstream economists, several Marxists have stressed that the main driver of capital flows is the political and institutional supremacy of central countries, exemplified by a wide-scale productive outsourcing driven by labor arbitrage. Second—since the supremacy of developed countries is also monetary and financial—we have recalled other critical schools, particularly those authors who focused on monetary hegemony (from a radical angle) and currency hierarchy. In their view, in the post-Bretton Woods era, the higher hierarchy of the U.S. dollar has implied that most of the relevant factors in determining interest and exchange rates have become external to emerging countries. Consequently, the periphery has become a 'business cycle taker'.

However, we have also highlighted that critical literature ignores a seminal precedent for the debate, represented by Raul Prebisch's early (i.e. pre-ECLA-Cepal) analysis of the business cycle in Latin American countries, which can be considered as an alternative to the traditional western views on capital flows and development. On the theoretical plane, Prebisch stressed the destabilizing role played by inflowing capital on Latin American economies since capital flows in the periphery were characterized by a financial cycle. When risk aversion was low, new loans arrived from developed countries, determining

---

[3]Valdes (1969, pp. 46–47). Own translation, cited in Lampa (2018).

a monetary expansion and an increase in imports. Accordingly, the balance of payments became negative, and the peripheral country asked for new loans to correct external imbalances. Finally, as soon as external conditions worsened, loans suddenly stopped and a reversal of capital flows arose, eventually developing into a crisis. In this context, at the policy level, Prebisch aimed to expand international reserves in times of prosperity in order to contrast the outflow of capital during downturns. He also stressed the necessity of limiting bank credit during upswings, particularly insisting on the importance of contrasting the inflow of speculative short-term capital. Prebisch's work is based on the underlying idea that the asymmetric monetary relationship between the center and periphery converted capital flows into a detrimental element, permanently menacing Argentina's stability. Prebisch's analysis was particularly influenced by the post-1929 scenario, a moment of systemic disruption in the Global North. His solution also represented the first mechanisms created by a Latin American country to respond to the fatal consequences of the crisis in developed countries.

We have also suggested a possible interpretation of the recent (2003–17) capital flows to/from Latin America along Prebisch's lines. First, capital inflows served international reserve accumulation, which is a typical macroprudential regulation driven by high rates of interest, acting as a constraint to expansionary policies. In the past fifteen years, monetary authorities of Latin America have, in effect, treated capital inflows as a potential risk rather than an opportunity. Second, short-term capital acted as a continuous factor of volatility in Latin American economies within the period studied. Third, the stock of capital accumulated in Latin America largely turned into a reverse flow of capital from Latin America to developed countries and tax havens, since F.X. reserves and debt and hard currency purchases (i.e. 'other investment') expanded enormously.

In conclusion, the significant amount of capital flown into Latin America during the recent past has not produced the beneficial effects assumed by mainstream economics. In fact, the unlimited capital inflow has often negatively impacted the domestic market and increased dependence on foreign investors to sustain economic growth. This result can be interpreted as evidence of an increased financial and monetary dependence, rather than an alleged convergence process towards developed countries. Prebisch's theory can, therefore, still represent a consistent contribution in amending critical literature in times of financialization, thus making sense of the debate on capital flows to developing markets.

Rather than adopting western type solutions, Latin American countries would benefit from a profound transformation of the existing international, regional and sub-regional monetary institutions to reduce the hegemonic role of dollar, which still represents a much formidable obstacle to their growth. Whether such a radical reform would be compatible with the present economic order or not exceeds the scope of this article.

Acknowledgements

The author wishes to thank Dr. Florencia Sember (CONICET-Universidad de Buenos Aires), Dr. Pablo Bortz (Universidad Nacional de San Martin, Buenos Aires), Nicolas Zeolla (Ph.D candidate, CONICET), the journal's editor Louis-Philippe Rochon, the symposium's editor Natalia Bracarense and two anonymous referees for their valuable advice. The usual disclaimer applies.

Disclosure Statement

No potential conflict of interest was reported by the author(s).

References

Acemoglu, D., and J. Robinson. 2012. *Why Nations Fail: the Origins of Power, Prosperity and Poverty*. London: Profile Books.

Amin, S. 1976. *Unequal Development: An Essay on the Social Formations of Peripheral Capitalism*. New York: Monthly Review Press.

Azis, I., and H. S. Shin. 2015. *Managing Elevated Risk, Asian Development Bank*. New York: Springer-Verlag.

Barberia, M. 2017. 'Argentina, Segunda entre los Países más Atractivos para el 'Carry Trade'.' *El Cronista*, March 23. https://www.cronista.com/finanzasmercados/Argentina-segunda-entre-los-paises-mas-atractivos-para-el-carry-trade-20170323-0011.html.

Bellofiore, R. 2018. *Le Avventure della Socializzazione. Dalla Teoria Monetaria del Valore alla Teoria Macro-Monetaria della Produzione Capitalistica*. Milan: Mimesis.

Bond, P. 2004. 'Bankrupt Africa: Imperialism, Sub-Imperialism and the Politics of Finance.' *Historical Materialism* 12 (4): 145–172.

Bonizzi, B., and J. Toporowski. 2017. 'Developing and Emerging Countries as Finance Providers: Foreign Exchange Reserves and Direct Investment to the European Union.' In *Financialization and the Economy*, edited by A. Gemzik-Salwach, and K. Opolski. London: Routledge.

Borio, C., and P. Disyatat. 2011. 'Global Imbalances and the Financial Crisis: Link or no Link?' *BIS Working Papers* no. 346.

Bortz, P. G., and A. Kaltenbrunner. 2018. 'The International Dimension of Financialization in Developing and Emerging Economies.' *Development and Change* 49 (2): 375–393.

Bruno, V., and H. S. Shin. 2015. 'Global Dollar Credit and Carry Trades: a Firm-Level Analysis.' *BIS Working Papers* no. 510.

Caldentey, E. P., M. Vernengo, and M. Torres. 2019. *Raúl Prebisch y su Faceta de Banquero Central y Doctor Monetario (Textos Publicados e Inéditos de la Década de 1940)*. Santiago, Chile: Cepal.

Calvo, G. A., L. Leiderman, and C. M. Reinhart. 1993. 'Capital Inflows and Real Exchange Rate Appreciation in Latin America: the Role of External Factors.' *Staff Papers – International Monetary Fund* 40 (1): 108–151.

Cerutti, E., S. Claessens, and A. K. Rose. 2017. 'How Important is the Global Financial Cycle? Evidence from Capital Flows.' *IMF Working Papers* 17/193.

Chang, H. J. 2011. 'Institutions and Economic Development: Theory, Policy and History.' *Journal of Institutional Economics* 7 (4): 473–498.

De Paula, L. F., B. Fritz, and D. M. Prates. 2017. 'Keynes at the Periphery: Currency Hierarchy and Challenges for Economic Policy in Emerging Economies.' *Journal of Post Keynesian Economics* 40 (2): 183–202.

Epstein, G. 2009. 'Should Financial Flows Be Regulated? Yes.' *DESA Working Paper* No. 77.

Epstein, G., I. Grabel, and K. M. Jomo. 2005. 'Capital Management Techniques in Developing Countries: an Assessment of Experiences from the 1990s and Lessons for the Future.' In *Capital Flight and Capital Controls in Developing Countries*, edited by G. Epstein. Northampton: Edward Elgar Press.

Fernandez-Arias, E. 1996. 'The New Wave of Private Capital Inflows: Push or Pull?' *Journal of Development Economics* 48 (2): 389–418.

Fields, D., and M. Vernengo. 2013. 'Hegemonic Currencies During the Crisis: The Dollar Versus the Euro in a Cartalist Perspective.' *Review of International Political Economy* 20 (4): 740–759.

Fischer, S. 1997. 'Capital Account Liberalization and the Role of the IMF.' Paper presented at the IMF Asian Seminar, Honk Kong, September 19. https://www.imf.org/en/News/Articles/2015/09/28/04/53/sp091997.

Frenkel, R. 2006. 'An Alternative to Inflation Targeting in Latin America: Macroeconomic Policies Focused on Employment.' *Journal of Post Keynesian Economics* 28 (4): 573–591.

G.F. Integrity. 2015. *Financial Flows and Tax Havens: Combining to Limit the Lives of Billions of People*. Washington, DC: Global Financial Integrity.

Goncalves, F. M. 2007. 'The Optimal Level of Foreign Reserves in Financially Dollarized Economies: The Case of Uruguay.' *IMF Working Paper* 07/265.

Higginbottom, A. 2013. 'The Political Economy of Foreign Investment in Latin America: Dependency Revisited.' *Latin American Perspectives* 40 (3): 184–206.

IMF. 1993. 'Recent Experiences with Surges in Capital Inflows.' *Occasional Paper* No. 108.

Ingham, G. 1996. 'Money is a Social Relation.' *Review of Social Economy* 54 (4): 507–529.

Kaltenbrunner, A. 2015. 'A Post Keynesian Framework of Exchange Rate Determination: A Minskyan Approach.' *Journal of Post Keynesian Economics* 38 (3): 426–448.

Kaltenbrunner, A., and J. P. Painceira. 2016. 'International and Domestic Financialisation in Middle Income Countries: the Brazilian Experience.' *Fessud Working Paper Series*, 146.

Kose, M. A., E. Prasad, K. Rogoff, and S. J. Wei. 2006. 'Financial Globalization: a Reappraisal.' *IMF Working Paper* 06/189.

Lampa, R. 2018. 'Economic Crises and Political Downturns in the Southern Cone: are MERCOSUR's Neoliberal Roots a Constraint on Development?' In *Global Economic Governance and the Challenge of Human Development*, edited by S. Raudino, and A. Poletti. London: Routledge.

Lampa, R. and M. Abeles 2020. 'From Ontological Orientation to Axiomatic Habitus? An Historical Reappraisal of Contemporary Political Economy from a Marxian Angle.' *Cambridge Journal of Economics* 44 (5): 1013–1030.

Lampa, R., and N. H. Zeolla. 2019. 'Dalla Crisi del Cambio al Salvataggio del FMI: Cronaca del Naufragio Argentino.' *Moneta e Credito* 72 (287): 275–293.

Lane, P. R., and G. M. Milesi-Ferretti. 2007. 'The External Wealth of Nations Mark II: Revised and Extended Estimates of Foreign Assets and Liabilities, 1970-2004.' *Journal of International Economics* 73: 223–250.

Lopez Mejia, A. 1999. 'Large Capital Flows: A Survey of the Causes, Consequences, and Policy Responses.' *IMF Working Papers* 99/17.

O'Connell, A. S. 2001. 'El Regreso de la Vulnerabilidad y las Ideas Tempranas de Prebisch sobre el "Ciclo Argentino".' *Revista de la Cepal* 2001 (75): 53–67.

Painceira, J. P. 2008. 'Developing Countries in the Era of Financialisation: From Deficit Accumulation to Reserve Accumulation.' In *Financialisation in Crisis*, edited by C. Lapavitsas. Leiden: Brill.

Palludeto, A. W. A., and S. C. Abouchedid. 2016. 'The Currency Hierarchy in Center-Periphery Relationships.' *Analytical Gains of Geopolitical Economy (Research in Political Economy)* 30 (B): 53–90.

Patnaik, U., and P. Patnaik. 2016. *A Theory of Imperialism*. New York: Columbia University Press.

Polanyi, K. 1968 [1957]. 'The Semantics of Money Use.' In *Primitive, Archaic and Modern Economies: Essays of Karl Polanyi*, edited by G. Dalton. Boston: Beacon Press.

Prebisch, R. 1921–22. 'Anotaciones sobre Nuestro Medio Circulante. A Propósito del Último Libro del Doctor Norberto Piñero.' In *Raúl Prebisch Obras 1919-1948, Vol. 1*, edited by M. Fernández López. Buenos Aires: Fundación Raúl Prebisch.

Prebisch, R. 1939. *Memoria Anual BCRA. Quinto Ejercicio*. Buenos Aires: BCRA.

Prebisch, R. 1949. *El Desarrollo Económico de la América Latina y Algunos de sus Principales Problemas*. Santiago de Chile: CEPAL.

Reinhart, C. M. 2005. 'Some Perspective on Capital Flows to Emerging Market Economies.' NBER Reporter Online. Summer 2005. https://www.nber.org/reporter/summer05/reinhart.html.

Reinhart, C. M., V. Reinhart, and C. Trebesch. 2016. 'Global Cycles: Capital Flows, Commodities, and Sovereign Defaults, 1815-2015.' *American Economic Review* 106 (5): 574–580.

Rey, H. 2015. 'Dilemma not Trilemma: The Global Financial Cycle and Monetary Policy Independence.' *NBER Working Paper* No. 21162.

Rochon, L. P., and M. Vernengo. 2003. 'State Money and the Real World: or Chartalism and its Discontents.' *Journal of Post Keynesian Economics* 26 (1): 57–67.

Saad-Filho, A. 2014. 'The 'Rise of the South': Global Convergence at Last?' *New Political Economy* 19 (4): 578–600.

Sember, F. R. 2010. 'The Origins and Evolution of the Monetary Thought of Raúl Prebisch.' Ph.D dissertation, University of Paris 1 Pantheon Sorbonne.

Sember, F. R. 2018. 'El Banco Mixto. 1930–1945: Entre la Ortodoxia y la Búsqueda de un Nuevo Sendero de Crecimiento.' In *Historia Necesaria del Banco Central de la República Argentina*, edited by M. Rougier, and F. R. Sember. Buenos Aires: Ciccus-Lenguaje Claro.

Smith, J. C. 2016. *Imperialism in the Twenty-First Century*. New York: Monthly Review Press.

Stiglitz, J. 2000. 'Capital Market Liberalization, Economic Growth, and Instability.' *World Development* 28 (6): 1075–1086.

Sutcliffe, B. 2006. 'Imperialism Old and New: A Comment on David Harvey's *The New Imperialism* and Ellen Meiksins Wood's *Empire of Capital*.' *Historical Materialism* 14 (4): 59–78.

Swarnaly, A. H. 2018. 'Revisiting the Determinants of Capital Flows to Emerging Markets—A Survey of the Evolving Literature.' *IMF Working Papers* 18/214.

Tavares, M. D. C. 1985. 'A Retomada da Hegemonia Norte Americana.' *Revista de Economia Politica* 5 (2): 5–15.

Taylor, M. P., and L. Sarno. 1997. 'Capital Flows to Developing Countries: Long- and Short-Term Determinants.' *The World Bank Economic Review* 11 (3): 451–470.

Tooze, A. 2018. *Crashed: How a Decade of Financial Crises Changed the World*. New York: Viking Press.

Toporowski, J. 2018. 'Marx, Finance and Political Economy.' *Review of Political Economy* 30 (3): 416–427.

Valdes, S. G. 1969. 'Discurso del Canciller Gabriel Valdés S. en la Inauguración de la Sesión Extraordinaria de CECLA.' *Memorias del Ministerio de Relaciones Exteriores. Año 1969*, Santiago de Chile.

Vasudevan, R. 2009. 'Dollar Hegemony, Financialization and the Credit Crisis.' *Review of Radical Political Economics* 41 (3): 291–304.

Vernengo, M. 2006a. 'Technology, Finance, and Dependency: Latin American Radical Political Economy in Retrospect.' *Review of Radical Political Economics* 38 (4): 551–568.

Vernengo, M., ed. 2006b. *Monetary Integration and Dollarization: No Panacea*. Northampton: Edward Elgar.

Williamson, J. 1990. 'What Washington Means by Policy Reform.' In *Latin American Adjustment: How Much Has Happened?*, edited by J. Williamson. Washington: Institute for International Economics.

Institutions and Development From a Historical Perspective: the Case of the Brazilian Development Bank

Alex Wilhans Antonio Palludeto and Roberto Alexandre Zanchetta Borghi

ABSTRACT

This paper analyzes the role played by the Brazilian Development Bank (BNDES) in different periods of Brazil's development process since its founding in 1952. The bank's history is nonlinear, varying with socio-economic and political changes over time. Four major periods in its history are: (i) from its creation to the debt crisis in the 1980s, a period known as 'developmentalism'; (ii) the neoliberal movement of the 1990s; (iii) the reintroduction of the BNDES as a relevant tool for development in the 2000s; and (iv) a new neoliberal movement that arose beginning in mid-2016. Each of these periods is characterized by certain development conventions that shape how institutions, such as the BNDES, operate, and at the same time are shaped by them. In contrast to mainstream economics, which focuses on a one-size-fits-all institution for development, this paper evaluates the interactions between development and institutions as historical processes, with an emphasis on the prevailing development conventions. The trajectory and different roles assumed by the BNDES over time exemplify this permanent relationship, rejecting the idea that particular types of institutions are related to development.

1. Introduction

Mainstream economics sees institutions as one of the main reasons why growth trajectories have differed between countries. In particular, this literature regards market-oriented institutions as the basis of economic development (Acemoglu and Robinson 2010). Critical approaches, however, emphasize the historical process of different institutions and a mutual causality between institutions and development (Chang 2011).

This paper analyzes the trajectory of a key institution of long-term financing in Brazil, namely the National Development Bank (BNDES). Following an 'Old Institutionalist' approach, it takes into account the changes in the bank's orientation. It also highlights the interaction between the role assumed by the BNDES and the prevailing development conventions over time.

The bank's history is seen as nonlinear, varying according to the socio-economic and political context. Four major periods can be highlighted following each phase of Brazil's development process: (i) from the creation of the BNDES in 1952 to the debt crisis in the 1980s, a period known as 'developmentalism'; (ii) the neoliberal movement of the 1990s; (iii) the reintroduction of the BNDES as a relevant tool for development in the 2000s; and (iv) a new neoliberal movement since mid-2016. Each of these periods is marked by a certain political and socio-economic convention regarding development that shapes (and is shaped by) institutions, such as the BNDES.

Based on literature review and data analysis, this work sheds light on the role of the bank in the historical context of Brazilian development. The remainder of the paper is divided into three sections. The first section reviews the literature on economic development and institutions. In contrast to the mainstream economics that considers a one-size-fits-all institution for development, a critical approach is adopted by highlighting the interactions between development and institutions as historical processes, inspired by the 'Old Institutional Economics' approach. The second section analyzes the role played by the BNDES in the aforementioned periods, in order to show how it shapes and at the same time is conditioned by different historical contexts. The third section details BNDES policies since the 2000s, particularly its role as a countercyclical force in the face of the 2008 global financial crisis and the introduction of new directives in recent years. Concluding remarks follow.

2. Institutions and Economic Development: a Critical Approach

Mainstream economics evolved from analyzing physical capital accumulation to focusing on technology and human capital as possible explanations for economic development. In this context, the inherently institutional character of socio-economic relations was absent (Hodgson 2009).

This scenario has changed since the mid-1970s. Works on institutions and institutional change linked to neoclassical, Austrian and game-theoretic approaches, have become increasingly popular (Rutherford 1999). Covering a wide range of topics, this literature is known as the 'New Institutional Economics'.[1]

Since then, the introduction of institutions, together with cultural and geographical issues, into the development debate has been widespread in mainstream economics (North 1981, 1990, 1994; Rodrik, Subramanian, and Trebbi 2002; Acemoglu and Robinson 2010). As Acemoglu and Robinson (2010) point out, this broad set of works attempts to separate proximate causes of development (e.g., technology, human and physical capital) from fundamental causes of development (e.g., institutions).

The definition of what institutions are or what economists regard as institutions is a crucial matter. Van Arkadie (1990) stresses that economists interpret institutions in two different ways — namely 'the rules of the game' and organizations. In the first sense, institutions provide the context in which markets operate and, as such, define the terms under which different actors make decisions. In the second sense, institutions are systems of non-market relations, as organizations refer to nonmarket coordination arrangements that make production and transaction activities possible.

---

[1] The term 'New Institutional Economics' was coined by Williamson (1975) with the deliberate attempt of disassociating the newer approach from the 'Old Institutional Economics', based on the works of Thorstein Veblen, Wesley Mitchell, John R. Commons, and Clarence Ayres (Rutherford 1999; Hodgson 2009). For more on the 'New Institutional Economics', see Williamson (2000) and Jütting (2003).

One of the most widespread and well-known definitions of institutions has been put forward by Douglass North in many of his works. Acemoglu and Robinson (2010), for example, use North's first definition:

> Institutions are the rules of the game in a society or, more formally, are the humanly devised constraints that shape human interaction. In consequence they structure incentives in human exchange, whether political, social, or economic. Institutional change shapes the way societies evolve through time and hence is the key to understanding historical change. (North 1990, p. 3)

In this definition, Acemoglu and Robinson (2010) highlight three key points: (i) the human nature of institutions, contrasting with other possible fundamental causes of growth out of human control, such as geographical conditions; (ii) the fact that institutions can set constraints on human behavior, as 'rules of the game'; and (iii) the idea that institutions lie behind a series of incentives through which human interaction take place.

An extended definition of institutions is given in another passage from North:

> Institutions are the humanly devised constraints that structure political, economic and social interaction. They consist of both informal constraints (sanctions, taboos, customs, traditions, and codes of conduct), and formal rules (constitutions, laws, property rights). Throughout history, institutions have been devised by human beings to create order and reduce uncertainty in exchange. [...] Institutions provide the incentive structure of an economy; as that structure evolves, it shapes the direction of economic change toward growth, stagnation, or decline. (North 1991, p. 97)

North (1990, 1994, 2005) also highlights the difference between institutions and organizations. In several works, he identifies institutions as 'the rules of the game' and organizations as 'the players'. According to North (1990, p. 5), 'both what organizations come into existence and how they evolve are fundamentally influenced by the institutional framework. In turn they influence how the institutional framework evolves'.

Several critiques of the 'New Institutional Economics' have come from heterodox economists. As Rutherford (1999, p. 4) points out, authors inspired by the 'Old Institutional Economics' argue that the new approach is too formal, abstract, 'individualist, reductionist, orientated toward rational choice and economizing models, and generally anti-interventionist'.[2]

Regarding the role of institutions in economic development in mainstream economics, two main proposals are discussed in greater depth, as follows. First, a good deal of this literature has tried to identify institutions as the ultimate, or fundamental, cause of development. This implies a one-way causality from institutions to development (Shirley 2008; Acemoglu and Robinson 2010). Multilateral organizations began to spread the idea that development requires the prevalence of certain institutions, arguing that nations fail to catch-up with advanced economies since they lack these institutions (Evans 2003; Chang 2006, 2011). As Blankenburg and Palma (2012, p. 142) put it, 'neoclassical theory has shifted its argument from "getting prices right" to "getting institutions right"'.

---

[2] It is important to note that, like any general characterization of a diverse literature, these labels apply more to some authors and works than others. Williamson and North, although representatives of the neoclassical approach to institutions, explicitly recognize its limitations (Rutherford 1999). North's contributions, in particular, can be likened to the 'Old Institutional Economics' in his later works as he began to emphasize the importance of path dependence, bounded rationality and shared mental models in the understanding of institutions and institutional change (Hodgson 2009).

Normative guidelines for poorer economies would lie in adopting the 'right' institutions and governance-related reforms. This 'institutional monocropping', as Evans (2003) calls it, usually refers to the Western neoliberal institutions that underlie free-market reforms, such as contract laws, property rights and law enforcement (Shirley 2008; Chang 2011; Blankenburg and Palma 2012). In this regard, development is reliant on the implementation of such 'rules of the game'. As Shirley (2008, p. 3) emphasizes, 'the vast majority of humans today live in countries that failed to create or sustain strong institutions to foster exchange and protect property'. Therefore, institutions are understood from a supply-side economics approach (Vernengo and Caldentey 2017).

From a critical perspective, Chang (2011) highlights a two-way causality between institutions and development. Historical evidence shows that many of today's developed economies only adopted market-friendly institutions after achieving a certain level of development. This shows that developed countries today did not necessarily adopt market-friendly institutions initially.

In this regard, there is a clear chicken-and-egg problem, as a two-way causality between institutions and development leads to a high level of indeterminacy (Paldam and Gundlach 2007). Institutions can help to promote development, but development can also be a condition for institutions to arise and become stronger (or weaker) in a way that development can be reinforced (or hindered). Many institutions arise (or adapt) after certain levels of development are achieved, thus reflecting political, economic and social arrangements. Additionally, institutions are important for economic development if they are able to expand demand in a Keynesian fashion, as highlighted by Vernengo and Caldentey (2017).

Second, the political nature of institutions is recognized, even in more recent mainstream works (North 1994, 2005; Acemoglu, Johnson, and Robinson 2005; Acemoglu and Robinson 2010). For instance, Acemoglu, Johnson, and Robinson (2005) and Acemoglu and Robinson (2010) argue that development depends on certain economic institutions that are highly influenced by political institutions. In turn, these institutions face conflicts of interest among various groups and individuals over the choice of economic institution to be adopted, with the political power being the deciding factor. So, particular interests can capture political institutions and consequently economic institutions. Rent-seeking behavior can lead institutions to work inefficiently, with a possible adverse effect on economic growth. In this regard, a close link to the previous discussion is established, in which a governance-related agenda should be implemented in less developed economies as reforms to prevent such behavior from occurring.

Institutions, if considered as an organization or a set of formal and informal rules or norms that constrain or enable individuals' actions, present a structure that is dynamic rather than static (North 2005). The political nature of institutions acts as a force to frame institutions and institutional changes, but this does not necessarily mean that institutions are permanently subject to the control of rent-seeking groups. However, conflicts of interest and political power can lie behind decisions and orientation taken over time.

In order to properly deal with these issues, a conception of institutions inspired by the 'Old Institutional Economics' seems more theoretically consistent and empirically relevant to the purpose at hand. Hodgson (2006, p. 6), for example, broadly defines institutions as 'systems of established and prevalent social rules that structure social interactions' or alternatively as a 'socially embedded system of rules' (Hodgson 2006, p. 8). Therefore, institutions not only constrain, but also enable behavior (Hodgson 2006, 2009). In this framework, organizations, such as the BNDES, are a kind of institution with the following particular features: '(a) criteria to establish their boundaries and to distinguish their members from nonmembers, (b) principles of sovereignty concerning who is in charge, and (c) chains of command delineating responsibilities within the organization' (Hodgson 2006, p. 8).

Similarly, institutions can be regarded 'as socially shared systems of rules of behavior or of thought that have some recurrence' (Dequech 2013, p. 85). Social reality can be seen as a set of interrelated institutions. For this reason, it is important to consider the dominant development conventions that, at each point in time, shape other institutions, while simultaneously being shaped by them and by the socio-economic outcomes of these interactions.

> Development conventions can be broadly defined as socially shared systems of rules of thought or behavior regarding development, with the properties of conformity with conformity and arbitrariness. Development conventions involve issues that are relevant in both developing and developed countries. Among these issues are: growth, inequality, poverty, inflation, technological change, sustainability, the role of the state in the economy, the exchange rate regime, fiscal policy, monetary policy, international trade policy, industrial policy, social policy, environmental policy, etc.[3] (Dequech 2017, p. 290)

Therefore, class interests, struggles and alliances, political and economic power, resources and capacities of coordination and legitimation of social actors are crucial to understanding the surge and diffusion of a particular development convention as well as how it becomes embedded into other institutions, particularly organizations. In the following section, we argue that different guidelines followed by the BNDES over time can be understood under prevailing development conventions.

3. A Historical Overview of the Role of the BNDES in the Brazilian Economy

Founded in 1952, the BNDES[4] was created according to a development convention based on heavy state intervention in the economy. This development convention could be observed in several Latin American countries between 1950 and 1980[5], and was known as 'developmentalism'.

According to Fonseca (2014, p. 59; authors' translation), 'developmentalism' can be understood as:

> the economic policy formulated and/or deliberately implemented by governments (national or subnational) to transform society, notably to overcome economic and social problems,

---

[3] 'Conventions are socially shared systems of rules of thought or behavior (i.e., institutions) with two defining properties: conformity with conformity – or the conformity of one with the (actual or expected) conformity of others – and arbitrariness. Conformity with conformity means that the fact that other agents have adopted a convention, or are expected to adopt it, plays a role in leading someone else to also adopt it, at least when behaving or thinking consciously. Arbitrariness means that a non-inferior alternative to the prevailing rule or system of rules exists or is conceivable. These two properties imply that not every kind of socially shared system of rules or mental construct qualifies as a convention' (Dequech 2017, p. 290).

[4] Originally created as the BNDE, the 'S' referring to social was added to the bank's name 30 years later, in 1982, in the wake of Brazil's redemocratization process and increasing pressures to improve social conditions after a military dictatorship (1964–1985).

[5] It is also important to note that this historical context and its dominant development convention are closely related to the emergence of several development theories, such as Latin American Structuralism, as a way of dealing with the poverty and inequality of post-war peripheral economies (Bracarense 2012).

through the growth of production and productivity in the industrial sector, within the institutional frameworks of the capitalist system.

Historically, this model of economic development comprises a broad set of instruments managed by the state, such as credit subsidies, tax incentives, favorable exchange rates and interest rates, as a way to stimulate capital accumulation. These incentives aimed to boost import-substitution industrialization.

In order to deal with the lack of long-term private finance, many underdeveloped countries have established development banks, like the BNDES.[6] The Brazilian Development Bank was founded during Vargas' second term (1951–1954), following suggestions from the Brazil-United States Joint Commission (1951–1953). The Commission sought to identify the main bottlenecks within the Brazilian economy and set forth projects to overcome them, particularly in the energy and transportation infrastructure sectors (Ferreira and Rosa 2017). These projects envisaged financial support from the United States through the Export-Import Bank and the International Bank for Reconstruction and Development, which would account for half of the required funds. The other half would be raised within Brazil, in the national currency. In order to finance and manage the resources of these projects, the BNDES was founded. Over time, the BNDES has become the main source of long-term finance in Brazil, and one of the largest and most profitable development banks in the world (Musacchio and Lazzarini 2014; Gallagher and Kring 2017).

However, its history is nonlinear, reflecting changes in development conventions that materialized in changes in economic policy and even in the political-economic orientation of the bank's selected presidents (Torres Filho and Costa 2012). These changes can be seen in the bank's financing priorities and sources of funding over time (Doctor 2015). Four major phases can be highlighted: (i) from the bank's foundation to the debt crisis in the 1980s, a period marked by 'developmentalism'; (ii) the neoliberal movement during the 1980s and 1990s; (iii) the reintroduction of the BNDES as a relevant tool for development in the 2000s; and (iv) a new neoliberal movement, discernible since mid-2016. The bank's disbursements illustrate this movement (Figure 1).

The first phase can be subdivided into two periods: a democratic period from 1952 to the mid-1960s and a military regime period from the mid-1960s to the early 1980s. The first period was characterized by relatively low BNDES disbursements, as a result of a lack of funding from the bank at that time (Cavalcante 2018). In the following period, disbursements rose at an accelerated rate, accompanied by an increase in its sources of funding.

The bank's main sources of funding were relatively unstable and based on income tax transfers and government deposits from the so-called 'monetary reserves' up until 1974 (Prochnik 1995). In addition to these sources, part of the funding between 1952 and 1966 came from sector-specific funds, such as the Federal Fund for Electrification and the National Paving Fund. In the same period, the BNDES also began to manage the resources of the Railways Renewal and Improvement Fund, the Merchant Navy Fund and the National Port Fund (Ferreira and Rosa 2017).

During the 1950s, loans were mainly directed toward the public sector itself in the wake of the projects implemented by Kubitschek's Government (1956–1960), known as the 'Goals Plan' (Figure 1, Part 1A). In the face of the main bottlenecks in transportation

---

[6]See World Bank (2018) for a survey of national development banks.

Figure 1. BNDES total disbursements and as a percentage of GDP, 1952–2018.

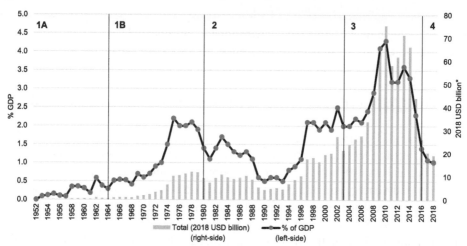

Source: From 1952 to 1969, own elaboration based on BNDES (1992); from 1970 to 2016, Além (1997) and BNDES (2017, pp. 50–51); from 2017 to 2018, BNDES (2019). * BRL at constant terms of 2018, converted into USD using the average exchange rate of 2018 (BRL/USD = 0.2737).

and energy, loans approved during the 1950s focused on the infrastructure sector (Figure 2). Railways and electric power were prioritized (BNDES 1992).

The elaboration of the 'Goals Plan' also counted on technical support provided by the bank's staff, thus revealing another important dimension of the BNDES activity: to provide technical support and policy advice to private and public sectors for the elaboration of

Figure 2. Loan approvals by sector as a percentage of total, BNDES, 1952–2018.

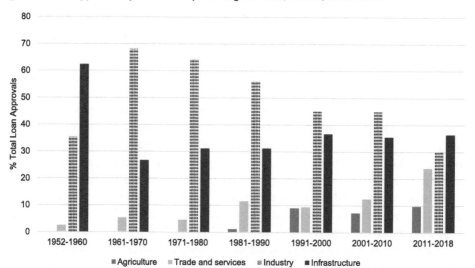

Note: As Barboza, Furtado, and Gabrielli (2019) highlight, this classification should be interpreted with caution. For example, various activities that were carried out within the industrial firm in the 1960s began to be outsourced and often classified in the services sector instead of the industrial sector. Source: Own elaboration based on BNDES data — https://www.bndes.gov.br/wps/portal/site/home/transparencia/centraldedownloads.

investment projects, including those aimed at attracting external funding (Doctor 2015; Cavalcante 2018).

Due to the deepening of the industrialization process throughout the 1960s, the industry began to account for a significant part of the bank's loans. The steel and metallurgy sectors received an expressive share of the bank's loans in this period. The BNDES even became informally known as the 'Steel Bank' (Schneider 2015). From the mid-1960s, during the military government (1964–1985), BNDES loans were largely directed to the private sector. According to Cavalcante (2018), BNDES disbursements to the public sector, which corresponded to approximately 90 per cent of the total between 1952 and 1964, declined thereafter, stabilizing at around 20 per cent in the 1970s. Loans approved during this period were concentrated in the industrial sector (Figure 2) and BNDES disbursements grew at a higher rate (Figure 1, Part 1B).

An important initiative to boost the import-substitution industrialization was the creation of the Financing Fund for the Acquisition of Industrial Machinery and Equipment (FINAME).[7] Founded in 1964, FINAME became an autarchy in 1966 and has been one of the bank's main subsidiaries since then. The aim was to stimulate national machinery and equipment sectors by requiring a minimum level of local content to obtain a BNDES loan (BNDES 2002).

In the 1970s, the BNDES sources of funding underwent major changes, allowing the bank to expand its financial activities, particularly to support the new round of planned investments under the so-called II National Development Plan (1975–1979) (II PND). In 1974, the BNDES began managing resources from workers' compulsory savings systems: the Social Integration Program and the Patrimony of the Public Servant (PIS and Pasep, respectively, both created in the early 1970s).[8] As a result, the bank not only had a more stable source of funds, but also a larger pool of resources for its operations. In addition, the bank's operations have become more flexible as funds linked to specific investment projects have their share reduced in the bank's total funding (Prochnik and Pereira 2008). Also in 1974, three new subsidiaries were created for capital market operations, mainly equity participation: Mecânica Brasileira SA (Embramec), Insumos Básicos SA Financiamentos e Participações (Fibase) and Investimentos Brasileiros SA (Ibrasa). In 1982, these three subsidiaries were merged into BNDES Participações SA (BNDESPar), one of the bank's main branches.

Between the end of the 1970s and beginning of the 1980s, the Brazilian economy entered a new phase in which the BNDES activities changed. At the international level, the fall of the Bretton Woods system and increased international competition contributed to the rise of political and economic forces pushing for market deregulation and liberalization (Helleiner 1994; Belluzzo 1995; Glyn 2006). Due to Volcker's interest rate shock in 1979, the oil shock in the same year and the Latin American debt crisis that followed in the early 1980s, the Brazilian economy experienced a decade of low economic growth, high inflation and external constraints. In the context of intense international transformations and under pressure from the International Monetary Fund and international creditors, new development conventions based on a neoliberal reconfiguration of the role of the

---

[7] A number of other funds were created under the BNDES during this period, although their relative importance was lower than that of the FINAME (BNDES 2002).

[8] The 1988 Federal Constitution, already in a democratic regime, established that PIS-Pasep funds became integrated into the Workers' Assistance Fund (FAT), 40% of which was managed by the BNDES.

state in the economy were formed. The Washington Consensus and its policy guidelines for economic liberalization seemed to be the building blocks of the development model adopted by several developing countries (Williamson 1990; Lapavitsas 2005; Wylde 2017).

This broad neoliberal orientation also characterized the governmental policies in Brazil. In the 1980s, the level of BNDES disbursements stagnated (Figure 1, Part 2) and the bank began supporting a process of privatization of state-owned enterprises (BNDES 2002). The successful privatization operations at that time led the BNDES to manage the National Privatization Fund in the 1990s. Due to growing privatization-related operations that marked Brazil's economic liberalization and deregulation in the 1990s, BNDES disbursements increased again from 1993 onward. In fact, the BNDES became the main financial coordinator of the Brazilian privatization process, particularly during the presidency of Fernando Henrique Cardoso (1995–2002) (Doctor 2015; Lazzarini et al. 2015; Cavalcante 2018).

In 1995, a constitutional amendment that blurred the legal distinction between national and foreign companies favored privatization-related operations by granting foreign companies access to government credit agencies, including the BNDES (Costa, Melo, and Araujo 2016). Another institutional change in the same period that was important to the BNDES activities was the introduction of the Long-Term Interest Rate (TJLP) as the benchmark interest rate for BNDES loans.[9] From the mid-1990s, BNDES disbursements — with no clear sector-specific development strategy — increased not only due to privatizations but also to promote exports in general (Torres Filho and Costa 2012; Ferreira and Rosa 2017).

From 2003, with the rise of the Workers' Party to government (2003–2016), the BNDES entered a third phase. While it is true that traces of 'developmentalism' never disappeared completely during the neoliberal period, it is also possible to identify the 2000s as a turning point in the prevailing development conventions, especially during Lula's second term (2007–2010). A kind of renewed 'developmentalism' came to dominate the government's strategies (Cavalcante 2018). As Hochstetler and Montero (2013) argue, the period was marked by a combination of the strengthening of certain market-oriented macroeconomic policies[10], inherited from the previous period, and an attempt to form global players focused on increasing industrial competitiveness and innovation policies. Small and medium-sized enterprises (SMEs) were also an important part of the bank's operations (BNDES 2017). This process led to a strong increase in BNDES disbursements (Figure 1, Part 3), as well as greater diversity in the sectors it supported (Figure 2). The bank's increasing size also reflected the role it played in the government's countercyclical policies in the face of the global financial crisis, as discussed further in the following section.

4. The BNDES in the 2000s Under Changing Development Conventions

National development banks can play important roles in the economy. These roles include: filling the gap of domestic financial systems by offering loans with longer maturities; promoting industrial policies and directing loans to firms that can boost

---

[9]Initially, the TJLP calculation was based on the average interest rate of external and internal public debt securities. However, due to its high volatility, from 1999 the TJLP has been calculated based on two components: (i) the target inflation rate for the following 12 months; and (ii) an institutionally fixed risk premium. In the absence of private long-term financing, the TJLP was systematically set below the market interest rate, albeit at a relatively high level during the 1990s.

[10]In this regard, it is worth mentioning the Brazilian macroeconomic 'tripod' based on (i) inflation targeting, (ii) managed floating exchange rate regime, and (iii) primary surplus targets.

productivity, technological progress and exports (in this latter case, generating foreign currency revenues); producing positive externalities by financing infrastructure and 'green' technologies; smoothing out the business cycle by acting quickly in recession periods; and promoting social inclusion through credit to agents that would otherwise not have access (Guadagno 2016; Scherrer 2017).

Ferraz and Coutinho (2019, p. 87, authors' emphasis) summarize these multiple roles according to three main features of development banks over the business cycle:

> [...] as investment is a pro-cycle phenomenon, in upswings and complementary to the private industry, *development banks are pro-cyclical*; in times of finance retrenchment from other sources (see last financial crisis), *development banks act countercyclically* and, *development banks play a pre-cycle role*, when supporting investments (especially where investment uncertainty is strong) that may bear fruits in an upcoming cycle.

It is possible to observe these different roles performed by the BNDES during the 2000s. The bank has assumed unprecedented importance, especially since the outbreak of the global financial crisis (Figure 1, Part 3). Its assets nearly tripled between 2007 and 2014 (Figure 3), indicating the high growth rate of its financing operations since 2008.

The bank has been key to public policy considering both the diversity of financed activities and the government's restored capacity to channel funds to priority areas. The orientation of the BNDES during this period can be considered from two complementary analytical perspectives: a *structural* and a *conjunctural* perspective.

A broader scope of action can be defined under the *structural* dimension, given the diversification of the bank's loans, the bank's focus on investments in infrastructure, and the support for the consolidation of big businesses and SMEs, with a particular focus on innovation (Mazzucato and Penna 2015). Part of this orientation, however, was redefined — or even intensified — under the *conjuncture* of the widespread effects of the global crisis on the Brazilian economy, when BNDES financial operations worked countercyclically, as detailed below.

From the *structural* perspective, the BNDES had been following a strategic position in Brazilian investment financing before the crisis. Due to the expansion of available

Figure 3. Total assets, BNDES, 2002–2018.

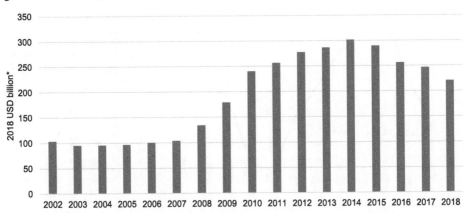

Source: Own elaboration based on BNDES data — https://www.bndes.gov.br/wps/portal/site/home/transparencia/centraldedownloads. * BRL at constant rate of 2018, converted into USD using the 2018 average exchange rate (BRL/USD = 0.2737).

instruments for private financing, the BNDES share in total credit stock fell in the 2003–2007 period from 24 per cent to 16.4 per cent. Despite this decline, which resulted from a large increase in credit from private institutions (Figure 4), the BNDES continued as the main supplier of long-term financing in Brazil (Oliveira 2015). As Hanley et al. (2016, p. 844) emphasize:

> Before 2008, greater involvement of private capital markets in long-term finance allowed BNDES to reduce its participation in total credit operations in the economy. However, by 2007, funding and support for the Growth Acceleration Programme (PAC) and Programme for Productive Development (PDP) came to be part of BNDES operational policies. In this way, the bank became the central actor in the country's policies of development and investment support.

The bank's disbursements increased significantly over the period, thus contributing to the credit expansion observed during the Brazilian economic boom. As a proportion of GDP, total credit reached almost 40 per cent by 2008 and would rise even more after the global financial crisis, especially through credit from state-owned institutions, the BNDES included (Figure 4). The pre-crisis movement followed a strong decline in the basic interest rate and better loan conditions, including BNDES subsidized credit policy, expansion of formal employment and rising income in Brazil.

BNDES disbursements have presented a clear positive correlation with Brazilian gross fixed capital formation over time, as shown in Figure 5. However, there is a heated debate about the bank's possible crowding-in or crowding-out effects on domestic investment and output. According to Albuquerque et al. (2018), empirical studies show mixed results of the impact of BNDES disbursements on gross fixed capital formation depending on the specification of the econometric model used. On the one hand, Salvador (2017) stresses that BNDES activities between 2002 and 2015 only caused a change in the sources of funding in private companies. Firms replaced their obligations to the private

Figure 4. Outstanding credit as a percentage of GDP by institution, Brazil, 2000–2017.

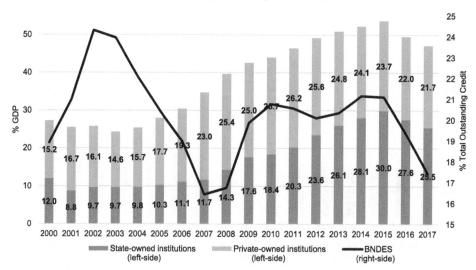

Source: Own elaboration based on Brazilian Central Bank data — https://www.bcb.gov.br/.

Figure 5. BNDES disbursements and Gross Fixed Capital Formation as a percentage of GDP, 1952–2018.

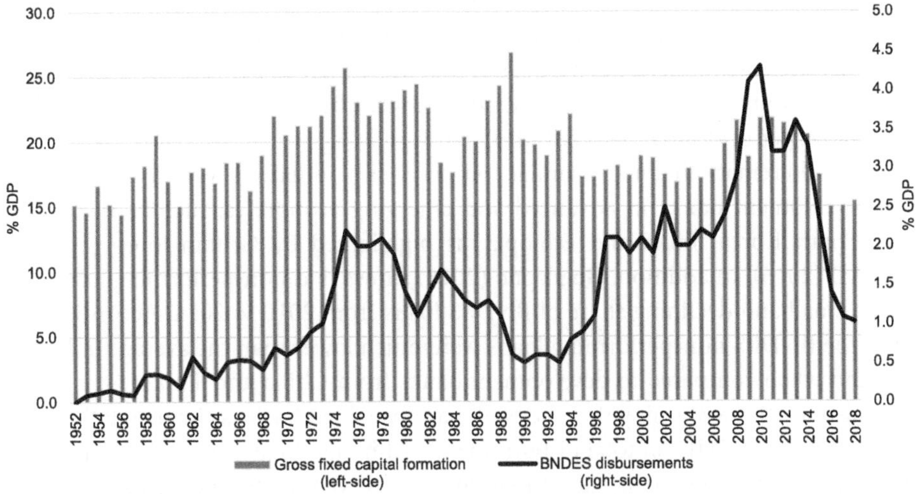

Source: BNDES disbursements — from 1952 to 1969, own elaboration based on BNDES data (1992); from 1970 to 2016, Além (1997) and BNDES (2017, pp. 50–51); from 2017 to 2018, BNDES (2019); Gross fixed capital formation — own elaboration based on Ipeadata — https://www.ipeadata.gov.br/.

financial market with subsidized BNDES loans, which did not necessarily result in an increase in investments.

On the other hand, Rezende (2015) emphasizes the role of the BNDES as a public bank that contributes to attenuating the endogenous instability of private financial markets and to providing long-term financing, given the high short-termism of the private financial system in Brazil. This role became evident in the face of the 2008 global economic crisis. Countercyclical performance of public banks is also highlighted in Scherrer (2017).[11] Far from blocking private credit during the growth period in Brazil before the financial crisis, the BNDES helped to support long-term financing. It also clearly expanded its operations during the economic downturn. At that time, while Brazilian private commercial banks curbed the rate of expansion of their loans, shortening terms and increasing guarantees, the countercyclical role of the BNDES helped to prevent the economy from entering into a deeper downturn and liquidity crisis.

From the *conjunctural* perspective, the BNDES has played a key role in dealing with the international crisis and its transmission to the Brazilian economy. In 2009, the Brazilian government launched the Investment Maintenance Program (PSI) in order to revert the fall in the investment rate. The program sought to stimulate gross fixed capital formation through a temporary reduction of BNDES interest rates on credit lines to capital goods sectors (Machado, Grimaldi, and Albuquerque 2018; Ferraz and Coutinho 2019). The PSI was in force until 2015, after nine renewals.

According to Barboza et al. (2017), the PSI — while in effect — was the main reason for the rapid growth in BNDES operations. In the wake of international economic turmoil, the

---

[11]Several works show the positive impact of BNDES disbursements on investment. See, for instance, Barboza and Vasconcelos (2019), Cavalcanti and Vaz (2017), Grimaldi et al. (2018), Machado, Grimaldi, and Albuquerque (2018), Machado and Roitman (2015), and Oliveira (2014).

PSI played a crucial role in preventing the decline in investment rates, especially in its early years[12] (Machado and Roitman 2015; Barboza et al. 2017; Machado, Grimaldi, and Albuquerque 2018). Under the program, BNDES disbursements accounted for 18 per cent of sources of financing for investments in 2009 and more than 13 per cent from 2010 to 2014 in Brazil. By contrast, they stood at around 8 per cent between 2004 and 2006, and were lower than 6 per cent after 2016 (CEMEC 2018).

One should remark that many similar countercyclical initiatives were also performed by other development banks in advanced and emerging economies, such as in Germany, China, South Korea, India and Ethiopia, as highlighted by Griffith-Jones (2016) and UNCTAD (2016). In addition, Guadagno (2016) shows that non-performing loans represented a small and declining share of BNDES loans from 2010 to 2014. According to the author, the BNDES non-performing loans were much lower than the average of Brazilian banks and when compared to development banks from China and Turkey.

It is also worth mentioning that the bank has diversified business financing through an increasing share of SMEs in total disbursements. Although in absolute terms large corporations still correspond to a substantial share of BNDES disbursements, SMEs have assumed a position of great relevance in the bank's operations, especially since the global financial crisis. For example, between 2009 and 2014, the share of BNDES disbursements to SMEs increased to nearly 30 per cent while between 2003 and 2008 it oscillated at around 25 per cent. The BNDES financial support for SMEs is particularly important given the evidence that the direct impact of the BNDES on SMEs' capital accumulation and productivity is usually greater than on large corporations, which have lower financial constraints (Oliveira 2014; Cavalcanti and Vaz 2017).

Nonetheless, a policy to consolidate large players at the international level has also remained at the core of BNDES directives, with the bank supporting the internationalization of large Brazilian conglomerates. In fact, the international crisis opened up the opportunity for the acquisition of cheaper assets abroad. Table 1 illustrates the main credit borrowers from the bank over the 2000s, including not only Brazilian public and private internationalized groups, but also subsidiaries of large foreign companies of different sectors. Ten companies accounted for 49.3 per cent of the total credit taken by the bank's 50 largest clients from 2004 to 2018, which together accounted for approximately 20 per cent of the bank's loans in the period.

The key role assumed by the BNDES was largely a consequence of political decisions taken under the prevailing development conventions and changing economic conditions at the time, including the decision to expand its sources of funding. In this regard, it is worth highlighting the position assumed by the National Treasury as the main funding provider of the BNDES, a position that would later be criticized by Brazilian mainstream economists[13] (Figure 6). The implicit fiscal cost involved in this operation, given the difference in interest rates between the Treasury and the BNDES, is frequently debated. However, some authors, such as Pereira, Simões, and Carvalhal (2011), highlight that, if the fiscal revenues resulting from the bank's operations are considered, the net balance would positively contribute to public accounts.

---

[12]Barboza et al. (2017) and Machado, Grimaldi, and Albuquerque (2018) argue that over the years the deterioration of public accounts and the adoption of a more restrictive monetary policy have raised the cost of the PSI and reduced its impact on the economy.

[13]See, for instance, Bolle (2015).

Table 1. Ten largest borrowers of BNDES, 2004–2018 (USD billion*).

Company	Sector	Amount	%**
Petrobras***	Oil	17.1	12.9
Embraer	Aviation	13.5	10.2
Norte Energia	Energy	6.9	5.3
Vale****	Mining	6.2	4.7
Odebrecht	Construction	5.0	3.8
State of São Paulo	Government	4.0	3.0
TAG	Gas transportation	3.6	2.8
TIM	Telecommunications	3.3	2.5
Telefonica	Telecommunications	2.8	2.1
FCA Fiat Chrysler	Automotive	2.7	2.1

* Current BRL converted into USD using the average exchange rate of 2018 (BRL/USD = 0.2737).
** In relation to the total amount of USD 132.1 billion borrowed by the 50 largest borrowers of the BNDES.
*** 60.3% of the total amount refers to loans and 39.7% to variable income.
**** 90.2% of the total amount refers to loans and 9.8% to variable income.
Source: Own elaboration based on BNDES data — https://www.bndes.gov.br/wps/portal/site/home/transparencia/consulta-operacoes-bndes/maiores-clientes.

Figure 6. Liabilities by source, BNDES, 2002–2018.

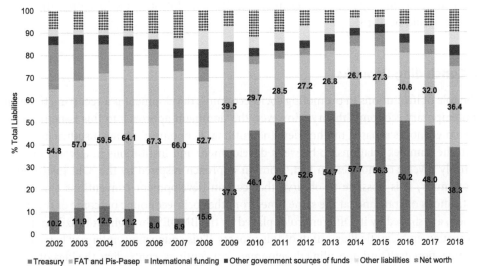

Source: Own elaboration based on BNDES data — https://www.bndes.gov.br/wps/portal/site/home/relacoes-com-investidores/informacoes-financeiras.

Therefore, the position assumed by the Treasury as a source of funding should be understood within the context of the global financial crisis and the government's responses, particularly to smooth out the business cycle, assure quick demand recovery and restore companies' liquidity. At that time, Treasury transfers were seen the easiest way in the short run to expand the bank's lending capacity considering a drastic and sudden reduction in credit from private financial institutions.

Another matter of debate regarding the bank's operations is related to the limitation that government-driven credit supposedly imposes on monetary policy, thereby reducing its effectiveness and preventing the basic interest rate in Brazil from falling (Bonomo and Martins 2016). In contrast, Vieira and Modenesi (2019) compare monetary policy power, defined as the sensitivity of inflation to changes in the basic interest rate, in periods of loose and tight credit and do not find evidence that monetary policy is less powerful when public banks expand their credit.

Since 2016, the BNDES has assumed a new orientation aligned with the renewed neo-liberal development convention shared by recent Brazilian governments. The bank shrunk in size (Figure 1, Part 4) under the perception that its previous guidelines were flawed. Large amounts of resources have already been paid back to the Treasury. From 2016 to 2019, the amount totaled USD 116.6 billion.[14] In this scenario, investment and growth fell. Additionally, in 2018, the TJLP was replaced by the Long-Term Rate (TLP), which aimed to reduce the implicit subsidy on BNDES financial operations and bring the benchmark interest rate closer to market levels. The TLP is pegged to the inflation target rate and the interest rate of a government five-year bond.

Therefore, a wave of market-oriented policies is underway and the role of the BNDES is already changing accordingly. The renewed dominant neoliberal development convention includes new rounds of privatization of public-owned enterprises, in which the BNDES can play a key role (Campos 2019). Finally, discussions on reducing the bank's sources of funding, including FAT funds (Vasconcelos 2019), show that part of its historical operations in financing long-term investments in Brazil and its key role in supporting development could be at risk.

5. Concluding Remarks

The role of institutions in promoting socio-economic development is a recurring theme in contemporary economic theory. However, the dominant approach to this issue in mainstream economics, based on the 'New Institutional Economics', seems insufficient to deal with the complex relationship between development and institutions in a world of qualitatively diverse economies. In fact, from an approach inspired by the 'Old Institutional Economics', it is possible to observe that certain development conventions shape how institutions operate and, at the same time, from the socio-economic outcome of this interaction, are shaped by it. Different roles played by the BNDES throughout Brazilian history present an emblematic illustration of this process. This endogenous interplay between the organization itself and prevailing development conventions, contradicts the idea of predetermined types of institutions for development and reinforces a two-way mutually dependent and self-reinforcing causality between institutions and development.

From the analysis of the role played by the BNDES over time, the importance of its main activities regarding long-term financing in Brazil, its sources of funding and the economic sectors supported, four major phases were identified: (i) from its creation in 1952 to the debt crisis in the 1980s, a period known as 'developmentalism'; (ii) the neoliberal movement of the 1990s; (iii) the reintroduction of the BNDES as a relevant tool for development in the 2000s, especially in the face of the global crisis; and (iv) a new neoliberal movement in place since mid-2016.

Each of these periods corresponds to dominant development conventions and, to some extent, can be also associated with the contribution of the BNDES to Brazilian growth; more positively during the first and third 'developmental' periods, since crowding-in

---

[14]Current BRL converted into USD at the average exchange rate of 2018 (BRL/USD = 0.2737). Available at: https://www.bndes.gov.br/wps/portal/site/home/transparencia/recursos-do-tesouro-nacional.

effects were generated, and more negatively during the second and fourth neoliberal periods, when the role of the BNDES was refocused toward privatization. During the first phase, permeated by a 'developmental' convention, the bank began to finance important infrastructure projects and basic industries, contributing to the consolidation of the Brazilian productive structure. The second phase, which began with the 1980s debt crisis and gained momentum during the 1990s economic liberalization, was marked by a relative decline in the bank's credit operations and its central role in the privatization process during that time. Although the bank still supported long-term financing operations, its role has changed under the prevailing context of a neoliberal development convention.

In the 2000s, the BNDES entered a new phase, when its operations expanded significantly. A kind of renewed 'developmental' convention came to dominate the government's strategies. A combination of certain market-oriented macroeconomic policies and active social and industrial policies prevailed. In this context, the BNDES reinforced its role in financing infrastructure but also redirected efforts to support Brazilian global players focused on increasing industrial competitiveness and innovation policies. Small and medium-sized enterprises were also an important part of the bank's operations. This intensified after the widespread consequences of the international crisis on the Brazilian economy. BNDES financial operations worked countercyclically in the aftermath of the global crisis. In fact, the crisis allowed for accelerated internationalization of Brazilian business groups in sectors in which they already had competitive advantages.

In the wake of recent market-oriented policies, the role of the BNDES changed after 2016 due to a deliberate reduction in its financial activities and sources of funding. The renewed dominant neoliberal development convention is likely to lead to new rounds of privatization of public-owned enterprises and the BNDES may once again be one of the main pillars of this process.

Acknowledgments

We are grateful to Steven Pressman and two anonymous referees for their comments and suggestions. The usual caveats apply.

Disclosure Statement

No potential conflict of interest was reported by the author(s).

References

Acemoglu, D., S. Johnson, and J. A. Robinson. 2005. 'Institutions as a Fundamental Cause of Long-Run Growth.' In *Handbook of Economic Growth*, vol. 1A, edited by P. Aghion, and S. N. Durlauf. Amsterdam: North Holland/Elsevier.

Acemoglu, D., and J. Robinson. 2010. 'The Role of Institutions in Growth and Development.' *Review of Economics and Institutions* 1 (2): 1–33.

Albuquerque, B. E., D. S. Grimaldi, F. Giambiagi, and R. M. Barboza. 2018. 'Os Bancos de Desenvolvimento e o Papel do BNDES.' *Textos para Discussão do BNDES* 133.

Além, A. C. 1997. 'BNDES: Papel, Desempenho e Desafios para o Futuro.' *Textos para Discussão do BNDES* 62.

Barboza, R. M., G. R. Borça Junior, G. T. L. Horta, J. M. B. Cunha, and F. G. Maciel. 2017. 'A Indústria, o PSI, o BNDES e Algumas Propostas.' *Textos para Discussão do BNDES* 114.

Barboza, R. M., M. Furtado, and H. Gabrielli. 2019. 'A Atuação Histórica do BNDES: O que os Dados Têm a Nos Dizer?' *Revista de Economia Política* 39 (3): 544–560.

Barboza, R. M., and G. F. R. Vasconcelos. 2019. 'Measuring the Aggregate Effects of the Brazilian Development Bank on Investment.' *North American Journal of Economics and Finance* 47: 223–236.

Belluzzo, L. G. M. 1995. 'O Declínio de Bretton Woods e a Emergência dos Mercados Globalizados.' *Economia e Sociedade* 4 (1): 11–20.

Blankenburg, S., and J. G. Palma. 2012. 'Economic Development.' In *The Elgar Companion to Post-Keynesian Economics*, edited by J. E. King. 2nd ed. Cheltenham: Edward Elgar.

BNDES (Banco Nacional de Desenvolvimento Econômico e Social). 1992. *BNDES, 40 anos: Um Agente de Mudanças*. Rio de Janeiro: BNDES.

BNDES (Banco Nacional de Desenvolvimento Econômico e Social). 2002. *BNDES, 50 anos: Um Agente de Mudanças*. Rio de Janeiro: BNDES.

BNDES (Banco Nacional de Desenvolvimento Econômico e Social). 2017. *Livro Verde: Nossa História tal como Ela é (65 anos)*. Rio de Janeiro: BNDES.

BNDES (Banco Nacional de Desenvolvimento Econômico e Social). 2019. *Notas para a Imprensa: Março de 2019*. Rio de Janeiro: BNDES.

Bolle, M. 2015. 'Do Public Development Banks Hurt Growth? Evidence from Brazil.' *Peterson Institute for International Economics Policy Brief*, 15–16.

Bonomo, M., and B. Martins. 2016. 'The Impact of Government-Driven Loans in the Monetary Transmission Mechanism: What Can We Learn from Firm-Level Data?' *BCB Working Paper* 419.

Bracarense, N. M. 2012. 'Development Theory and the Cold War: The Influence of Politics on Latin American Structuralism.' *Review of Political Economy* 24 (3): 375–398.

Campos, R. 2019. 'CEO of BNDES Says Privatizations Likely to Speed Up in 2020.' *Reuters*, September 17. https://www.reuters.com/article/us-bndes-privatization/ceo-of-bndes-says-privatizations-likely-to-speed-up-in-2020-idUSKBN1W227 T.

Cavalcante, L. R. 2018. 'The Brazilian Development Bank.' In *The Oxford Handbook of the Brazilian Economy*, edited by E. Amann, C. R. Azzoni, and W. Baer. New York: Oxford University Press.

Cavalcanti, T., and P. H. Vaz. 2017. 'Access to Long-Term Credit and Productivity of Small and Medium Firms: A Causal Evidence.' *Economic Letters* 150: 21–25.

CEMEC (Centro de Estudos de Mercado de Capitais). 2018. 'Relatório Trimestral de Financiamento dos Investimentos no Brasil.' *Nota CEMEC* 06/2018.

Chang, H.-J. 2006. 'La Relación entre las Instituciones y el Desarrollo Económico. Problemas Teóricos Claves.' *Revista de Economía Institucional* 8 (14): 125–136.

Chang, H.-J. 2011. 'Institutions and Economic Development: Theory, Policy and History.' *Journal of Institutional Economics* 7 (4): 473–498.

Costa, G. M. M., H. P. Melo, and V. L. Araujo. 2016. 'BNDES: Entre o Desenvolvimentismo e o Neoliberalismo (1982-2004).' *Memórias do Desenvolvimento* 5 (5): 1–564.

Dequech, D. 2013. 'Economic Institutions: Explanations for Conformity and Room for Deviation.' *Journal of Institutional Economics* 9 (1): 81–108.

Dequech, D. 2017. 'The Concept of Development Conventions: Some Suggestions for a Research Agenda.' *Journal of Economic Issues* 51 (2): 285–296.

Doctor, M. 2015. 'Assessing the Changing Roles of the Brazilian Development Bank.' *Bulletin of Latin American Research* 34 (2): 197–213.

Evans, P. 2003. 'Além da Monocultura Institucional: Instituições, Capacidades e o Desenvolvimento Deliberativo.' *Sociologias* 5 (9): 20–63.

Ferraz, J. C., and L. Coutinho. 2019. 'Investment Policies, Development Finance and Economic Transformation: Lessons from BNDES.' *Structural Change and Economic Dynamics* 48: 86–102.

Ferreira, A. N., and E. S. T. Rosa. 2017. 'The Role of the Brazilian Development Bank (BNDES) in Brazilian Development Policy.' In *Public Banks in the Age of Financialization: A Comparative Perspective*, edited by C. Scherrer. Cheltenham: Edward Elgar.

Fonseca, P. C. D. 2014. 'Desenvolvimentismo: A Construção do Conceito.' In *Presente e Futuro do Desenvolvimento Brasileiro*, edited by A. B. Calixtre, A. M. Biancarelli, and M. A. M. Cintra. Brasília: IPEA (Instituto de Pesquisa Econômica Aplicada).

Gallagher, K. P., and W. N. Kring. 2017. 'Remapping Global Economic Governance: Rising Powers and Global Development Finance.' *GEGI Policy Brief* 4-10/2017.

Glyn, A. 2006. *Capitalism Unleashed: Finance, Globalization, and Welfare*. New York: Oxford University Press.

Griffith-Jones, S. 2016. 'Development Banks and their Key Roles: Supporting Investment, Structural Transformation and Sustainable Development.' *Brot für die Welt Discussion Paper Analysis* 59.

Grimaldi, D. S., A. R. Pinto, B. E. Albuquerque, F. Buchbinder, J. P. O. Pereira, L. O. Nascimento, M. Tortorelli, and R. A. Martini. 2018. 'Uma Solução Automatizada para Avaliações Quantitativas de Impacto: Primeiros Resultados do MARVIm.' *Textos para Discussão do BNDES* 128.

Guadagno, F. 2016. 'The Role of Industrial Development Banking in Spurring Structural Change.' *UNIDO ISID Working Paper* 08/2016.

Hanley, A. G., J. M. Pires, M. J. P. Souza, R. L. Marcondes, R. N. Faria, and S. N. Sakurai. 2016. 'Critiquing the Bank: 60 Years of BNDES in the Academy.' *Journal of Latin American Studies* 48 (4): 823–850.

Helleiner, E. 1994. *States and the Reemergence of Global Finance: From Bretton Woods to the 1990s*. London: Cornell University Press.

Hochstetler, K., and A. P. Montero. 2013. 'The Renewed Developmental State: The National Development Bank and the Brazil Model.' *Journal of Development Studies* 49 (11): 1484–1499.

Hodgson, G. M. 2006. 'What are Institutions?' *Journal of Economic Issues* 40 (1): 1–25.

Hodgson, G. M. 2009. 'Institutional Economics into the Twenty-First Century.' *Studi e Note di Economia* 14 (1): 3–26.

Jütting, J. 2003. 'Institutions and Development: A Critical Review.' *OECD Development Centre Working Paper* 210.

Lapavitsas, C. 2005. 'Mainstream Economics in the Neoliberal Era.' In *Neoliberalism: A Critical Reader*, edited by A. Saad-Filho, and D. Johnston. London: Pluto Press.

Lazzarini, S. G., A. Musacchio, R. Bandeira-de-Mello, and R. Marcon. 2015. 'What do State-Owned Development Banks do? Evidence from BNDES, 2002–09.' *World Development* 66: 237–253.

Machado, L., D. S. Grimaldi, and B. E. Albuquerque. 2018. 'Additionality of Countercyclical Credit: A Cost-Effectiveness Analysis of the Investment Maintenance Program (PSI).' *Textos para Discussão do BNDES* 129.

Machado, L., and F. B. Roitman. 2015. 'Os Efeitos do BNDES PSI sobre o Investimento Corrente e Futuro das Firmas Industriais.' *Revista do BNDES* 44: 89–122.

Mazzucato, M., and C. C. R. Penna. 2015. 'The Rise of Mission-Oriented State Investment Banks: The Cases of Germany's KfW and Brazil's BNDES.' *ISI Growth Working Paper* 1/2015.

Musacchio, A., and S. G. Lazzarini. 2014. *Reinventing State Capitalism: Leviathan in Business, Brazil and Beyond*. London: Harvard University Press.

North, D. C. 1981. *Structure and Change in Economic History*. New York: Norton.

North, D. C. 1990. *Institutions, Institutional Change and Economic Performance*. Cambridge: Cambridge University Press.

North, D. C. 1991. 'Institutions.' *Journal of Economic Perspectives* 5 (1): 97–112.

North, D. C. 1994. 'Economic Performance through Time.' *American Economic Review* 84 (3): 359–368.

North, D. C. 2005. 'Institutions and Performance of Economies over Time.' In *Handbook of New Institutional Economics*, edited by C. Ménard, and M. M. Shirley. Amsterdam: Springer.

Oliveira, F. N. 2014. 'Investment of Firms in Brazil: Do Financial Restrictions, Unexpected Monetary Shocks and BNDES Play Important Roles?.' *Textos para Discussão do BCB* 366.

Oliveira, G. C. 2015. 'A Estrutura Patrimonial do Sistema Bancário no Brasil no Período Recente (I-2007/I-2014).' *Texto para Discussão do IPEA* 2162.

Paldam, M., and E. Gundlach. 2007. 'Two Views on Institutions and Development: The Grand Transition vs. the Primacy of Institutions.' *Kiel Institute for the World Economy (IfW) Working Paper* 1315.

Pereira, T. R., A. Simões, and A. Carvalhal. 2011. 'Mensurando o Resultado Fiscal das Operações de Empréstimo do Tesouro ao BNDES: Custo ou Ganho Líquido Esperado para a União?.' *Texto para Discussão do IPEA* 1665.

Prochnik, M. 1995. 'Fonte de Recursos do BNDES.' *Revista do BNDES* 2 (4): 143–180.

Prochnik, M., and V. M. S. C. Pereira. 2008. 'Fontes de Recursos do BNDES 1995-2007.' *Revista do BNDES* 14 (29): 3–33.

Rezende, F. 2015. 'Why Does Brazil's Banking Sector Need Public Banks? What Should BNDES Do?' *Levy Economics Institute Working Paper* 825.

Rodrik, D., A. Subramanian, and F. Trebbi. 2002. 'Institutions Rule: The Primacy of Institutions over Geography and Integration in Economic Development.' *NBER Working Paper* 9305.

Rutherford, M. 1999. *Institutions in Economics: The Old and the New Institutionalism.* Cambridge: Cambridge University Press.

Salvador, P. I. C. A. 2017. 'O Efeito Crowding-Out via BNDES no Mercado Brasileiro, no Século XXI.' *Revista Espacios* 38 (61): 8–27.

Scherrer, C., ed. 2017. *Public Banks in the Age of Financialization: A Comparative Perspective.* Cheltenham: Edward Elgar.

Schneider, B. R. 2015. 'The Developmental State in Brazil: Comparative and Historical Perspectives.' *Revista de Economia Política* 35 (1): 114–132.

Shirley, M. M. 2008. *Institutions and Development: Advances in New Institutional Analysis.* Cheltenham: Edward Elgar.

Torres Filho, E. T., and F. N. Costa. 2012. 'BNDES e o Financiamento do Desenvolvimento.' *Economia e Sociedade* 21 (4): 975–1009.

UNCTAD (United Nations Conference on Trade and Development). 2016. 'The Role of Development Banks in Promoting Growth and Sustainable Development in the South.' *UNCTAD Report* December 2016.

Van Arkadie, B. 1990. 'The Role of Institutions in Development.' *Proceedings of the World Bank Annual Conference on Development Economics* 1989.

Vasconcelos, G. 2019. 'Ex-Presidentes do BNDES Criticam Extinção dos Repasses do FAT ao Banco.' *Valor Econômico*, June 19. https://www.valor.com.br/brasil/6312845/ex-presidentes-do-bndes-criticam-extincao-dos-repasses-do-fat-ao-banco.

Vernengo, M., and E. P. Caldentey. 2017. 'Introduction.' In *Why Latin American Nations Fail: Development Strategies in the Twenty-First Century*, edited by E. P. Caldentey, and M. Vernengo. Oakland: University of California Press.

Vieira, N. P. P., and A. M. Modenesi. 2019. 'Bancos Públicos e Política Monetária: Um Estudo Utilizando Projeções Locais Dependentes de Estado.' Paper presented at XII Encontro Internacional da Associação Keynesiana Brasileira, Campinas, August, 30.

Williamson, O. E. 1975. *Markets and Hierarchies: Analysis and Antitrust Implications.* New York: Free Press.

Williamson, J. 1990. *Latin American Adjustment: How Much has Happened?* Washington: Institute for International Economics.

Williamson, O. E. 2000. 'The New Institutional Economics: Taking Stock, Looking Ahead.' *Journal of Economic Literature* 38 (3): 595–613.

World Bank. 2018. *2017 Survey of National Development Banks.* Washington: World Bank.

Wylde, C. 2017. *Emerging Markets and the State: Developmentalism in the 21st Century.* London: Palgrave Macmillan.

Institutional Change in Nepal: Liberalization, Maoist Movement, Rise of Political Consciousness and Constitutional Change

Kalpana Khanal and Natalia Bracarense

ABSTRACT
Contradicting the rest of the world's promptness to discredit communism as an alternative and Francis Fukuyama's (1992) teleological account of 'the end of history,' Nepal witnessed a Maoist revolution between 1996 and 2006. Such a 'deviation' from what Fukuyama and others have viewed as the path of development raises questions about the linear progression of history and its implicit dualism of market vs. government. As several Original Institutional Economists have discussed, analytical dichotomies lead to a simplistic understanding of transformation that disregards the multilayered nature of society and, thus, concludes that history unfolds linearly to arrive at a predetermined and homogeneous end. This paper analyzes the social transformation of Nepal that preceded the Maoist revolution, through the lens of Feminist Institutionalism, utilizing a multidisciplinary approach to understand the complexity of the impacts of liberalism-protectionism political changes on Nepali institutions.

1. Introduction

Nepal has undergone radical political and institutional transformation since the 1980s. As Prashant Jha (2014, p. xxv) notes: 'From war to peace, from monarchy to republicanism, from being a Hindu Kingdom to secularism, from being unitary to a potentially federal state, and from a narrow hill-centric notion of nationalism to an inclusive sense of citizenship — Nepal's transformation was, and is, among the most ambitious political experiments in recent years in South Asia.' While there are many causes of these deep transformative processes, the main trigger was the *Jana Andolan* I (People's Movement) of 1990 — led by a coalition of political parties, including both the Nepali Congress and various communist parties, especially the center-left Communist Party of Nepal, Unified Marxist Leninist — which ushered Nepal to a new era of democracy. *Jana Andolan I* put an end to the *Panchayat* system (a thirty-year autocratic reign under the Shah monarchy), restoring multi-party democracy to, subsequently, implement a new constitution and democratic elections at national and local levels.

The establishment of a multi-party parliamentary system, the ten-year Maoist insurgency from 1996 to 2006 and the stymieing of a 2005 'royal coup' by *Jana Andolan II* in the spring of 2006 constitute the most remarkable changes in Nepali political institutions between 1990 and 2013. Nonetheless, other important political events took place during this period, including two rebellions in the Madhes/Terai (Nepal's southern plains) in 2007 and 2008, two elections to the Constitution Assembly in 2008 and 2013, and the abolition of the monarchy in 2008 (Hutt 1994; Malagodi 2013; Hachhethu 2015). Such political transformations gained force in 1996 when Maoists — who previously were only a small communist faction among a number of extremist communist parties — received support from the poorest portions of the population whose social awareness was reawakened by the meek economic and social outcomes of a widely adopted neoliberal strategy.

In fact, in the 1990s, Nepal started to adopt a Structural Adjustment Program (SAP) focused on privatization and financial liberalization. Neoliberalism coupled with democratic changes rendered the population optimistic about playing an active role in the political process through economic opportunities and social justice. However, even after its transition to democracy, the Nepali state remained an extractive patrimonial state that institutionally neglected people living in rural areas and failed to address their grievances (Joshi 2010). One of the shortcomings of the SAP policies based on recommendations from the International Monetary Fund (IMF) and the World Bank was the dismantling of the old national development plans without launching a new and sustainable development strategy.

In the past decade or so, the general consensus that neoliberal policies failed to sustain economic development in Nepal, and in the Global South in general, led the IMF and the World Bank to reformulate their policy recommendations to focus on the role of institutional improvement in achieving development (Chang 2007; Chang 2011). The revival of interest in institutions for the promotion of development is linked to New Institutional Economics (NIEs), which prescribes protecting private property rights and enforcing contracts, coupled with policies that remove government restrictions on free markets in order to promote private investment and economic growth. To sustain its claims, NIE relies on diametrically opposed dichotomies: private-public, good-bad institutions, developed-underdeveloped, extreme cultural voluntarism-fatalism to prescribe homogenizing policies towards the development of market institutions (Acemoglu, Johnson, and Robinson 2001; Acemoglu, Johnson, and Robinson 2003). The relationship between institutions and economic development, however, has proven to be far more complex than this framework can encompass.

The aforementioned approach simplistically treats economic institutions and development strategies as mere structures, ignoring their characteristic as processes that evolve over time (Waller 1988). Another related issue is its dualist view of the 'pendulum of history' swinging back and forth from protectionism to liberalism — a perspective that neglects other possible directions through which history may unfold (Waller and Wrenn 2019). Although not necessarily wedded to this particular dualism, some Original Institutionalist Economists (OEIs) have not been fully attentive to the theoretical impact of protectionism-liberalism dyad. In an attempt to fill this lacuna, proponents of Feminist Institutionalism propose a reformulation of Karl Polanyi's framework based on three main points: (i) the rescue of the concept of domination and its disassociation from commodification (Selwyn and Miyamura 2014); (ii) a stronger emphasis on the theoretical consequences of the separation between family and economy (Waller and Jennings 1991); (iii) and an explicit recognition that marketization may have emancipatory effects (Fraser 2014). Each one of these ideas are explored in detail in the next section.

The remainder of the paper uses Nepal as a case study to support Feminist Institutionalism's claim that dualist frameworks cannot grasp historical processes (Waller and Jennings 1991) and support Nancy Fraser's (2013, 2014) push for a critical theory of contemporary crises that encompasses not only the economy and financialization (i.e., the domination of money), but also the environment and society, dealing also with the domination of both land and productive labor as well as the subordination of 'unproductive' labor either due to gender or ethnicity.

2. Nepal: A Unique Post-Colonial, Feudal, Caste based Society in the Context of Institutional Economics

The institutional transformations that took place in Nepal since the 1980s could be judged as 'deviations' if gazed at in isolation and through linear-progression-historical lens, whose implicit dualism of market vs. government favors the development of market institutions. However, when placed within a broader context, both historically and theoretically, Nepal serves as an example of the general phenomenon noted by Fraser (2013): the current economic, political, ecological and sociological worldwide crisis. Several OIEs have argued that analytical dichotomies lead to simplistic understandings of transformation that disregard the multilayered nature of society and, thus, conclude that history unfolds linearly to arrive at a desired/homogenous end. For that, among other reasons, OIE maintains that the shortcomings of development economics have not been resolved by the mainstream status conceited to NIE in the past twenty years (Tamanaha 2015, p. 89).

In the global context, NIE represents global economic transformation/development as a natural and benign outcome of markets. OIEs, on the contrary, have been at the forefront of documenting how economic development is moored to particular places by political and cultural means and how it is mediated by the actions of individuals and institutions at different scales (Schneider and Nega 2016; Bracarense and Gil-Vasquez 2018). The emphasis on agency offers several key analytical advantages to the study of local-global articulations (Rankin 2004). In the cultural domain, on the ground, local experiences and interpretations play a crucial role in sustaining, challenging, or adapting large-scale political economic processes. It follows that institutions are embedded (Polanyi [1944] 2001, p. 57; Polanyi 1957, p. 250) within particular political and cultural contexts. Understanding these specificities is, thus, crucial for improving human and social wellbeing — especially in countries like Nepal where market institutions are not fully broached.

Nepal's agriculture, for instance, is responsible for more than 30 percent of the GDP and employs about 65 percent of the population (World Bank 2019). Of these agricultural entities about 55.3 percent are characterized as subsistence farming (MOAC 2014, p. 26). Using different methodologies, Acharya (2003) estimated that Nepal's GDP (as reflected in official statistics) in 1991 was only 48 percent of the total GDP when non-market production was accounted for. The author also found that 93 percent of this unpaid work was done by women. These statistics indicate the importance of non-market relations in Nepal's provisioning process and underscore the influence of land tenure and access, and their evolution, on inequalities and injustices that fueled the Maoist revolution.

It is precisely to grasp with the oppression mechanisms not imposed by markets that Feminist Institutionalists propose a reformulation of Polanyi's concepts of embeddedness, double movement, and great transformation. The first modification consists of a few ontological changes and, consequently, adds another layer of complexity to the analysis: the recognition of the prevalence of exploitation/domination in different economic systems (Fraser 2014; Selwyn and Miyamura 2014).

As pointed out by Feminist Institutionalism, Polanyi (1944 [2001], pp. 76, 136–138, 201–209, 236) states that commodification of the fictitious commodities set in motion far-reaching crises; as a result, his theory of crises relies on his concept of commodity, which the author defines as a good (or service) produced for sale. Polanyi's (Polanyi 1944 [2001], p. 75) argument that land, labor and money are fictitious commodities, consequently, presupposes a market economy as their fictitious character originates from the unnaturalness and impossibility of their complete commodification. The problem with such conception is that Polanyi's definition of commodity is market-specific, so that his theory of crisis becomes constrained to the market system. Fraser (2014, p. 547) argues that these market lenses are blind to the fact that access to land, labor and money have never existed in their pure form; they have rather always been engaged in production through some sort of domination.

Additionally, according to Benjamin Selwyn and Satoshi Miyamura (2014, p. 655), Karl Polanyi (1944 [2001], p. 159) refuses to conceptualize commodification as a form of exploitation that persists in the market system. This prevents him from seeing that in the absence of commodification (as is often the case in other economic systems) exploitation/dominance is still present, facilitating the appropriation of the surplus by some people at the expense of others. The admission of commodification as a form of exploitation and recognition of its market-specificity enables the analysis to carefully study intra- and inter-systemic unfolding and transformation.

By reformulating Polanyi's (1947, p. 31) substantive approach, Feminist Institutionalists find themselves better furnished to combat ahistoricism and simplistic dualism of formalist economics and push forward a critical theory able to grasp with the complexities of the 21st century (Waller and Jennings 1991; Fraser 2014; Bracarense and Gil-Vasquez 2018). In directing their efforts at freeing the analysis from a concept that is market-specific (i.e., commodification), Feminist Institutionalists become equipped to consider a possible systemic capitalist crisis.

Their concerns, moreover, rightly apply to the case of Nepal, where the land access was based on, and the Maoist revolution was prompted by, factors — such as feudal, patriarchal, and caste relations — that extrapolate the commodification-embeddedness problematic. This leads us to the second modification suggested by Feminists Institutionalism to Polanyi's framework. According to William Waller and Ann Jennings (1991, p. 485), while Karl Polanyi's perspective is 'both promising and hospitable to feminist reformulation' and establishes a pertinent critique of the private-public dichotomy between society and the economy created by formalist economics, it does not push incisively enough on the separation between family and economy.[1] Waller and Jennings (1991) argue that the dichotomy private-public implies a double-dualism: while the economy is private vis-à-vis the government, it is public in relation to the privacy of the family, which implies that conflict is a multilayered process.

To further such framework, Fraser (2014) labels the double-dualism 'private-public' on one hand and 'domination-emancipation' on the other, from which she creates the concept of a *triple movement*. According to her, Polanyi's (1944 [2001], p. 73) double movement focuses mostly on the former dualism, seeing the movement of the economic pendulum as two-dimensional: that is, when the extension of the market system — through the commodification of land, labor and money — threatens the social ethos, a double movement takes place, creating protective devices to guarantee production and reproduction of society. When Polanyi discusses the ongoing provisioning process, however, he does not carefully consider the impact of the second aspect of the private-public dualism; that is the relationship between familial institutions, or the provisioning happening within the clan — namely, institutions that establish instances of domination unrelated to commodification, determining, for instance, types of labor that are productive or unproductive. A framework that is able to encompass this other dimension of private-public is critical in a country like Nepal, where patriarchal and caste systems determined whose labor may be commodified or not. For instance, Nepali men and women spent virtually the same hours in economic activities, but while men worked about 4–4.5 hours per week in unpaid activities, women's contribution to unpaid labor mounted to 23–30 weekly hours (Acharya 2003).

Such a two-fold reformulation of the private-public dualism shows commodification as merely one form of domination, exposing more systematically the injustices within communities — such as slavery, serfdom and patriarchy — that depend on social constructions of labor, land and money precisely as non-commodities (Fraser 2014, p. 544). Consequently, transformation is multidimensional rather than a two-dimensional pendulum between liberalism and protectionism that only deals with the tension between commodification or non-commodification.

In effect, Maoist leaders, such as Baburam Bhattarai (cited in Jha 2014, p. 22), identify patterns of dominance of land, labor and money as the main sources of tension in Nepal and the main reason for Maoist resistance. The dissidents' concerns went beyond class inequality, including extreme socio-cultural inequality that existed among numerous linguistic, ethnic, religious, caste and regional groups within Nepal.[2] It is not surprising, thus, that the support bases necessary for revolutionary insurgency came from not only the rural population, but also from other marginalized sections of the population.

These are reactions to a perpendicular system of domination. Fraser call it a *triple movement*, which brings up the third reformulation of Polanyi's theory proposed by Feminist Institutionalism. The added layer of complexity means that emancipation, depending on whether it allies with liberalism or protectionism, could respectively

---

[1] Karl Polanyi's (1947) adequacy to feminist reformulations is clear as the author entertains some questions that are currently pertinent to feminist theory. He spends, nonetheless, most of his effort rejecting the formalist separation between economy and polity rather than its denial of the familial role in the provisioning process (Waller and Jennings 1991, pp. 491–493).

[2] Nepal has four religious groups joined by 3 percent of the population or more (Hindu, Buddhist, Muslim and Kiranti), more than 100 linguistic groups and numerous caste and sub-caste groups, as well as 59 nationalities. The groups can be broadly categorized as Caste Hill Hindu Elite (31 percent), Dalits or untouchables of the Hindu caste system (15 percent), Janajati or the group who lived in the Mountains and mainly spoke Tibeto-Burman language (37 percent), and Madhesis or natives of Terai, the plains of Southern Nepal (17 percent) (Lawoti 2010, p. 25).

exacerbate individualist impulses or could reshape social relations towards an alternative to the market system (Bracarense and Gil-Vasquez 2018, p. 617; Fraser 2014). While Polanyi (1933, 1945, pp. 88–90; 1957, p. 251) has articulated possible combinations of interactive action between institutions and individuals that could lead to non-teleological outcomes (i.e., socialism, social democracy or fascism), the possible outcomes remain straightjacketed by the market-specificity of the concept of commodification (Selwyn and Miyamura 2014, p. 658).

To overcome this shortcoming, Fraser suggests a rectification of Polanyi through the adoption of Hegel's idea that society cannot be *contracted* all the way down. With this modification, Fraser (2014, p. 548) elaborates a 'structural interpretation of fictitious commodification,' which recognizes commodification as exploitation and extends the concept of domination to systems other than the market system. The grounds for Fraser's (2017) persistence in building upon Polanyi, after some considerations, is twofold: his peculiar ability, in comparison to other economists, to deal with a generalized crisis that goes beyond economic factors, bringing to attention its interactions with sociological, cultural, and ecological aspects; and, consequently, the compatibility of his framework to feminist concerns. Through a combination of 'Two Karls,' Fraser (2014, p. 551) argues that 'struggles around labor's commodification were actually three-sided: they included not just free marketeers and proponents of protection, but also partisans of "emancipation", whose primary aim was neither to promote marketization nor to protect society from it, but rather to free themselves from domination.'.

The triple movement stresses something Polanyi had seen, but had not elaborated upon. Polanyi saw that while the 'double movement' keeps the system functioning, it is not inherently beneficial to everybody, and may be oppressive (Khanal and Todorova 2019). Struggles to protect nature and society from the market are, more often than not, aimed at entrenching existent privilege and excluding 'outsiders.' Conversely, as both Karl Marx and Friedrich Engels ([1846] 1959, p. 370) and Karl Polanyi (1947, p. 107) have noted, marketization is capable at times of generating emancipatory effects. It may dissolve modes of domination external to the market and create the basis for new, more inclusive, and egalitarian solidarities.

Nepalis' fight for emancipation exemplifies Fraser's (2014, p. 551) dictum as it includes all sectors of the population who actively participated in the production and reproduction of society, but yet had their access to the provisioning process restricted through feudal subjection, social exclusion and imperial domination, as well as from sexism and patriarchy. Firstly, while injustice and inequality were aggravated by the commodification of land, labor, and money during both the liberalism of the British proto-colonial period and neoliberalism under the surveillance of the IMF and World Bank, the 1950s–1960s developmentalist policies did not mitigate these issues. Secondly, the socio-cultural inequalities existed in Nepal long before the liberal, developmentalist and neo-liberal periods. Thirdly, the commodification process of the 1990s engendered the empowerment of ethnic minorities and transformation of gender roles and relations; elements of wider shifts in the sociocultural patterns of Nepali society (Manchanda 2001; Yadav 2016).

Fraser's triple movement — through the incorporation of additional layers of complexity to Polanyi's double movement — renders the reach of embeddedness unbounded. In doing so, the pendulum of historical transformation moves multi-dimensionally, resulting in a non-teleological understanding of history and fostering a critical theory of contemporary crises. Consequently, as shown hereafter, we can visualize the process of transformation in Nepal not only as another form of protection from market institutions, but also as a triple movement that can transform the lives of many Nepali.

3. Nepal and Great Britain: A Single Dualism from Liberalism to Modernization?

Fraser's (2014, p. 544) assertion that land, labor and money have always been engaged in production through some form of domination is illustrated in 19th-century Nepal, when the country became deeply entangled with the colonial politics of South Asia. Nepal's experiences with colonial history deviate from a standard trajectory — as the country was never formally colonized — and trace back to the Anglo-Nepali War of 1814–1816.

When colonizing India, the British unsuccessfully tried to expand their territory to Nepal in 1768 by sending an expedition called 'Kinloch' (Regmi 1971). They aimed at opening up new markets for European products at a time when the East India Company was experiencing a severe currency drain due to the high administration costs in India. After his army defeated the British troops, King Prithivi Narayan Shah took measures to prevent the drain of Nepali currency: he banned imports of European and Indian goods and promoted local production (Liechty 1997).[3]

Despite Nepal's victory in the Anglo-Nepali war, the establishment of British colony in India along with the transaction of East India Company consolidated Great Britain as the strongest power on the subcontinent. Nepali sovereignty now rested on the Nepali government's willingness and capacity to support the British Raj. Starting in 1846, the Ranas' — ruling dynasty of hereditary prime ministers from 1846 to 1951 — ascension to power served the vested interest of British in two ways. First, the Nepali prime ministers offered the Gurkha regiment to suppress the mutiny of colonial Indian soldiers (Shakya 2016; Rankin 2004). Second, they developed an insatiable appetite for European goods — creating a market for imports that turned the balance of trade securely in favor of the British (Liechty 1997). Michael Herzfeld coined this paradoxical situation of political independence and economic subordination as crypto-colonies (Shakya 2016).

By 1900, almost all British trans-Himalayan trade was conducted through Sikkim, circumventing Nepal entirely (Regmi 1971, p. 24; Uprety 1980, pp. 166–167). As a result, the revenue collected by the Ranas from the Tibetan trade decreased sharply. The Ranas then turned increasingly to policies of internal economic colonization to sustain their practices of conspicuous consumption (Rankin 2004, p. 97). Their actions illustrate their views of the entire state of Nepal as 'a private feudal fiefdom to be mined for the profit of the ruling elite' (Liechty 1997, p. 59).

First of all, the Ranas created state monopolies of timber to be supplied to the expanding British railway network in India. Through extensive exploitation and domination of land resources, Nepali statesmen profited from the development of India while neglecting the development of Nepal. Secondly, they intensified domestic resources mobilization by

---

[3]In his nationalist treatise, *Dibya Upadesh* (1774), Shah linked his protectionist monetary policies to state building ambitions: Our money will not go abroad. Send our herbs to India and bring back money. When you acquire money, keep it. If the citizens are wealthy, the country is strong. The King's storehouse is his people (cited in Liechty 1997, p. 3).

taxing the peasant class — that is, through the command of money — to advance a personal expense account for the Rana elite.[4] Thirdly, in this strictly hierarchical system, one individual, the Rana prime minister, assumed all power and authority (Whelpton 2005, p. 50). The first civil code, the *Muluki Ain*, adopted in 1854 by Jung Bahadur Rana, formalized the caste system by providing a legal framework that led to the marginalization of a large portion of the population (Hachhethu 2003, p. 223; Einsiedel, David, and Pradhan 2012, p. 5). The domination of labor was organized and supported by caste hierarchy, which submitted the diverse peoples inhabiting Nepal into a nation state under the authority of Ranas (Bennett, Dahal, and Govindasamy 2008, p. 2). Power was centralized and only those nearest and dearest to the rulers — like the *Bhardars*, i.e., the ministers, aides, and officials to the king/prime minister — possessed it (Einsiedel, David, and Pradhan 2012).[5]

Illustrating Fraser's concerns, it is clear that the interaction between British colonizers and Ranas local power is permeated by the emergence of the market system; however, the Ranas' ability to mobilize resources came from their political power, which depended on social constructions of resources as non-commodities. In addition to determining the division of labor based on their castes, the *Muluki Ain* discriminated against people from different castes in the judicial system and in the distribution of state resources, which translated 'diversity into inequality' (Hachhethu 2003, p. 223). The introduction of and fascination with market relations amongst Nepali elites fastened the consolidation of their power and dominance of land, money, and labor, but it did not create it. In other words, Nepal's unique political-economic history and institutionalization of ceremonial values has significantly influenced economic institutions in the country.

With regards to land, state-society relations have been largely extractive and state ownership the traditional form of land tenure. State landlordism is labeled *Raiker*; a system in which private individuals have the right to occupy and use land, but do not own these lands and thus have no right to sell them (Regmi 1977, 16). Approximately fifty percent of total land in Nepal was reported to be under *Raiker* (or state's land and state was synonymous with the monarch) until the 1950s (HLLRC 1996, p. 11). From the 1950s onward, *Raiker* land denoted individuals' private property so that they would pay taxes to the government and gain full rights in terms of selling, using, inheriting, transferring, dividing and leasing (Adhikari 2008).

Under *Raiker*, there were four types of land occupancy through transference: *Birta*, the plots granted to individuals; *Guthi* donated to temples or monastery; *Jagir* assigned to government employees; and *Sera* appropriated to meet the requirements of the Royal palace (Regmi 1999, p. 16, 106). *Birta*, *Guthi* and *Jagir* were the most commonly granted and were usually distributed to priests, religious teachers, soldiers, nobles and members of the royal family. In this system, the domination and unequal access to land was determined by clan and kinship rather than market relations. Over time, the ownership of state land was transferred to these individuals and they became feudal landlords, in a way that private land ownership was incipiently implemented as early as the

---

[4]See Mahesh Chandra Regmi (1978) for details on the Rana taxation system.

[5]Despite the fact that Nepal was a combination of different states, where people had different cultures, languages, costume and religious backgrounds, the Shah dynasty was successful in institutionalizing a sense of nationalism, embodied by a single religion (Hinduism), a single language (Nepali), and a single costume (*Daura Suruwal* for men and *Gunyo Cholo* for women) (Regmi 1978).

1880s even though private property ownership was formalized in 1950 (Regmi 1977, pp. 176–177).

Raiker was not the only system of landownership in the country. Another clan-based land tenure was the *Kipat;* a communal land system. Based on the idea of collective rights to land, a *Kipat* beneficiaries derived rights to lands by virtue of his location and membership of specific ethnic group (i.e., *Kiratis, Danuwars, Sunuwars, Majhis, Tamanga, Sherpas, Kumhals* and *Lepchas*). In Regmi's (1999, p. 27) words '[i]ndividuals who cultivated lands in their capacity as a member of *Kipat*-owning ethnic groups owed allegiance primarily to the community, not to the state.'

Finally, the *Jimidari*, a third landownership system, introduced absentee landlordism in the Terai region.[6] This system emerged during 1862/63 when the revenue administrative system was reorganized with the objective of extending the revenue base of the government in the villages (Khanal 1995, p. 9). The political implication of the revenue collection system was that it tied the interests of local 'big men' closely to those of the central government. Their privilege went beyond tax collection; they had the authority to provide property ownership certificates. As such, they used their administrative power for their personal benefit and gradually established personal ownership on wide areas of land through such practices, becoming big landlords who provided the support base for the Ranas. While it is clear that command of land, or the lack thereof, did not rely on commodification, it rooted inequity in Nepal.

The same can be said about contracts pertinent to money, which, through the taxation system, became another aggravating source of economic disparity. As the beneficiaries of land grants and other privileged classes paid no taxes, the fiscal burden of the state rested on the large number of non-privileged classes, mainly peasants, workers, craftsmen and small traders. From the 18th to the mid-20th centuries, both Shah rulers and Rana oligarchs were successful in raising revenue and increasing agricultural surpluses for the ruling classes through such mechanisms (Seddon 1987, pp. 4–13; Ghimire 1992, p. 33).

In sum, up until the 1950s, conflicts related to land and land contracts were basically limited to disputes between central government and rural ruling elite and feudal landlords. Meanwhile, the majority of the population was excluded from this process either because of their caste, ethnicity, or gender. Since exploitation of land, labor, and money in this situation was not mainly effected by commodification, Nepal illustrates the importance of extending Polanyi's double movement beyond the analysis of how shifts to more market- or protection-oriented policies, respectively, aggravated or relieved communities' exposure to the disintegrating forces of markets (Fraser 2014, p. 547). Fraser's reformulation sheds light over the simultaneous entrenching domination within and among members of these communities.

The Rana dynasty came to an end when King Tribhuvan Bir Bikram Shah, with support from political groups such as Nepali congress and Communist Party of Nepal, assumed power in 1951 and prepared the terms for the first democratic system in Nepal. The King, however, did not follow through with the commitment to hold a democratic Constitutional Assembly and centralized power on himself and a few handpicked

---

[6]*Jimidari* is a system of appointing a functionary known as a *Jimidar* to collect taxes and promote land reclamation and settlement, whose personal liability is the full collection of the land and other taxes in the *Mouja* under his jurisdiction, even if lands remained uncultivated for any reason. A similar system in the hills was called the *Talukdari* system.

ministers instead. Under disguise of a modernization push, the 1951 interim constitution included a provision that guaranteed private property rights to the holders of *Birta* and *Jagir* land and furthered their bearers' status to permanent landowners (Regmi 1977). Besides *Shahas, Ranas* and *Thakuris*, the key beneficiaries of these ownership concessions were *Brahmin, Kshetries* and *Newars,* who became the foundation of Nepali social, political, and economic life (Khanal 1995, p. 7). In other words, while commodification reassured the dominance of some groups at the expense of ethnic minorities, women, and *Dalits,* who were deprived of the right to land ownership, the origin for the domination already existed before commodification took place.

In 1955, Mahendra Shah became king of Nepal, a position he maintained beyond the predetermined term by overthrowing the succeeding government with the support of the Royal Nepal Army in 1960 (Thapa and Sharma 2009, p. 207). Subsequently Mahendra Shah banned all political parties and instituted the partyless *Panchayat* system; a 30-year-long authoritarian regime that prohibited all other parties' political activities. This system further institutionalized the privileges of the Kathmandu-based elites, leading to the systematic marginalization of *Dalits, Janajati, Madhesis,* and religious minorities (Thapa 2012, p. 40; Yadav 2016). Similar to the period of crypto-colonialism, disparities in land ownership remained the focal point of vertical conflicts of interest in Nepal.

The modernization push to incorporate market institutions in Nepal through the commodification of land further aggravated inequality and land tenure insecurity among the rural poor. As a result, a large rural proletariat and *Sukumbasis* had their rights and livelihoods threatened by landlessness (Karki 2002, p. 206).[7] The careful observation of social relations around land in Nepal shows that regardless of the economic regime, the beneficiaries and excluded have not changed and the determination of to which of these groups an individual belongs depends on a multidimensional prism of feudal, caste, market and patriarchal systems.

The history, culture identity, and politics of the *Terai* — the southern areas along the border with India—, for instance, have often been seen in opposition to the dominant politics emanating from the hills and capital of Kathmandu. Resistance by communities living in this region is constructed around identity consciousness, particularly for the *Madhesis* and *Tharus,* who have raised the issue of internal colonization by high-caste hill Hindus (*Pahadis*), suggesting more complex dominance narratives at work (Crews 2018, pp. 1–2).[8]

The formalization of private property in Nepal has, nonetheless, sparked a triple-movement response. Since the 1950s, many social movements for emancipation involving indigenous groups and ethnic minorities have emerged. Peasant/landless unrest over these developments compelled the government to enact several reforms aimed at redistributing land in Nepal. One of the first acts passed was the 1951 Tenancy Rights Acquisition Act, intended to provide land title to tenants who paid tax or rent on the land they

---

[7]Sukumbasis (landless) can be theorized as a group of people who maintain barely *a de facto* possession over the land they occupy. It is a name given to an individual or a group of people who occupy public land such as state forest and or land actively unclaimed by other owners (Ghimire 1992, p. 11).

[8]Crews (2018) uses the lens of settler colonialism to explain these social movements and political uprising in Nepal since the 1950s. Settler colonialism functions through the replacement of indigenous populations with an invasive settler society that, over time, develops a distinctive identity and sovereignty (Veracini 2015).

cultivated. This Act, however, had the opposite effect to its intent, since the landlords very often reported the taxes they collected in their own names, enabling the landlords to claim a permanent legal title to the land they had managed (Regmi 1977). Other governmental initiatives to redistribute land included the Royal Land Reform Commission in 1952, the Land Act of 1957, the *Birta* Abolition Act of 1959, and the Land Reorganization Act of 1962 (Regmi 1977). None of these Acts, however, had a significant impact on more equitable redistribution of land, but quite the contrary; the abolition of *Kipat*, for instance, by the land reforms in the 1960s, took away the indigenous land protections (Caplan 2000; Forbes 1999).

While the dominating relations causing inequality in Nepal were stable before the 1960s, modernization policies of the 1950s and 1960s incited potential conflicts as they changed societal conditions and introduced uncertainty and fluidity (Lawoti 2010). The failure of such policies to promote stability and nation building did not go unnoticed by the Nepal Communist Party (Maoist). On the day it launched the People's War, the Party stated: 'The current rulers of Nepal, speaking tirelessly about development and nation-building for 50 years [in fact] have led Nepal to become one of the world's poorest nations, second only to Ethiopia' (*Nepal Rastriya Budwijivi Sangathan* 2054 V.S., 45; cited in Fujikura 2003, p. 25). The Maoists declared that it is now time to overthrow the 'comprador and bureaucratic capitalist classes,' who have ruled Nepal and led it into its current economic, political, and cultural crises. By pointing out failure of the existing regime to develop Nepal, the Maoists' declaration of war attempts to de-legitimatize it and present the revolutionaries as the legitimate rulers or the true representatives of the people and the real agents of development (Fujikura 2003, p. 25).

In conclusion, for two centuries, the pressure over land ownership and the aggravation of social inequities were reinforced by different types of political regimes. An understanding of the domination/emancipation of the oppressed members of society demands a multidimensional framework such as Fraser's triple movement. The latter uncovers that, in the case of Nepal, the liberal-protectionist economic dualism had no emancipatory impact on those whose subordination (i.e., women, religious minorities and members of lower castes) is sustained through the economy-clan/family duality (i.e., through productive and reproductive domination of land, labor and money as non-commodities). Intensified social pressures, fomented by institutional changes such as commodification of land and a pseudo-democracy, however, created the conditions for an emancipatory response that began in the 1950s and gained full force after the 1990s neoliberal reforms.

4. From TINA Neoliberal Policies to Maoist Movement and the Rise of Political Consciousness in Nepal

After practicing import-substitution industrialization through a protectionist trade regime for almost three decades, in mid-1980s Nepal gradually opened up its economy to liberal institutions (Athukorala and Kishor 2005). Launched in the 1987/88 fiscal year, Nepal's stabilization program was facilitated by a loan from the World Bank and the IMF, in a context in which institutions had just moved to the center stage in the debate on economic development (Stein 2008, pp. 38–42). The new focus, largely coordinated through the apparatus of Structural Adjustment Program, was based on the view

that poor-quality institutions were the root of economic problems in developing countries. Although there is no agreed upon definition of 'better' institutions, the Global Standard Institutions (GSIs) are typically based on Anglo-American countries and aim at
maximizing market freedom and protect private property rights (Chang 2011, p. 473).
International organizations followed suit and started to attach governance conditions,
which implied extensive commodification of all three fictitious commodities, to their
loans and financial aid.

Implementing GSIs required a political constituency supporting currency devaluations, trade liberalizations, and austerity measures; however, the locus of decision-
making lied with IMF and World Bank, their creditors, and dominant member
states (Kapur and Webber 2000).[9] In Nepal, the implementation of Structural Adjustment Program was expected to generate sustained output growth of 4.5 percent, reduce
inflation to 5 percent annually, and strengthen the balance of payments. Despite external shocks, such as the trade and transit gridlock with India in March 1989, Nepal's
balance of payments position did improve. The country experienced higher employment rates in both urban and rural areas and a slight improvement of revenue mobilization, but the fiscal deficit and inflation rate remained uncurbed (Acharya,
Khatiwada and Aryal 2003).

In 1991, for the first time, Nepal elected its government leaders, whose priority became
economic liberalization and incentives for Foreign Direct Investment (FDI). Between
1988 and 2001, 721 FDI projects were approved. These investments were expected to
create more than 80,000 jobs but only about 37 percent of the approved projects were
operational (Athukorala and Kishor 2005). With decreased regulation both for the
domestic and foreign capital, a large portion of FDI was directed towards privatizing
Nepal's social and infrastructure sectors.

Care was commodified as several public-run enterprises such as hospitals, schools and
other educational institutions were privatized (Acharya, Thapa, and Sharma 1998). The
marketization of care substantiates the dominance of the economy over both polity and
family (Waller and Jennings 1991). Not surprisingly, polity and family are often the focus
of feminist economists, as the expansion of the market reconfigures and destabilizes
(with the potential of replacing old dominations for commodification) existing concep-
tions of 'unproductive' labor (Folbre 2001).

The marketization of land resources was also further deepened through privatization
of national infrastructure including ground and air transport, electricity generation, tele-
communication, and imports and distribution of fertilizers. Privatization meant that
prices of publicly supplied services rose substantially as the elimination of subsidies
allowed a greater role for markets in price determination.

Due to its ability to simultaneously encompass economic, social, and ecological pre-
cariousness, Polanyi's framework seems adequate to deal with such an expansion of
the marketization of land and labor. Specially given that Polanyi also deals with the commodification of money; the main piece of the 1990s round of encounters between Nepali
ceremonial institutions and the market system.

---

[9]Heavy involvement of outside agents has exerted pressure on Nepali politics throughout history. While India and China
    play a more direct role (Mishra 2004; Baral 1994), the involvement of EU and US, along with various non-governmental
    agencies has to be explored while tracing the development journey of Nepal (Hachhethu 2009).

Nepal's financial sector reform began under particular circumstances. Prior to the reforms, there were only two commercial banks, both operated through the government sector; one was fully and the other partially owned by government (Khatiwada 2000). Both banks were tightly regulated; there was no competition, non-performing loans were mounting, and the quality of bank service was relatively poor. Nominal interest rates were controlled and real deposit rates were often negative. There were no non-bank financial institutions other than the two specialized financial institutions — Agricultural Development Bank of Nepal and Nepal Industrial Development Corporation — a few insurance companies, and one Employees Provident Fund Corporation. In brief, the state had a monopoly over the operations of the financial sector.

Financial reform initiated by the central bank of Nepal, Rastra Bank (NRB), in 1984 could be seen as the beginning of commodification of money. The reform allowed private sector entry in the banking industry, which was followed by the liberalization of interest rates, relaxation of barriers of entry for domestic and foreign banks, restructuration of public sector commercial banks, and withdrawal of central bank control over their portfolio management. Foreign capital was accepted in the banking business for the first time in 1984, with the establishment of the Nepal Arab Bank; a joint venture between foreign and local capital. The Nepal-Indo-Suez Bank and the Nepal Grindlay's Bank were established in 1986 and 1987 respectively, and an additional nine joint venture private commercial banks were founded in Nepal by the end of 2000.

Banking sector reforms in Nepal were initiated with the hope that the joint venture banks would improve the efficiency of existing banks by modernizing services for the expansion of the export and manufacture sectors (Peek and Rosengren 2000). Opening the financial sector to foreign banks was also expected to extend financial services to the rural areas. However, replicating a pattern observed in many other countries (Prebisch 1984), hosting foreign companies failed to extend the banking facilities to new areas or reduce the lending rates. Instead, the new commercial banks colluded to lower the time-length of loans and fixed deposit rates without changing the interest rates. The banks, moreover, maintained excess liquidity, while not making efforts to expand their operations by providing cheaper credit.

Financial liberalization in Nepal was unable to promote a more fluid commercial banking system. First, older and the larger commercial banks, with their wide rural networks, had to compete with new banks having no rural operations. This allowed the new banks to make large profits, as their operating costs were much lower. Second, the lucrative business of older banks, such as low-cost donor transactions and export financing, had been cornered by the new private sector bank, thus hurting the older banks' viability. The two older banks had the highest proportion of the non-performing loans in the country during the 1990s, prompting the government to sell their management to foreign private entities (Acharya, Khatiwada and Aryal 2003, p. 40).

In contrast to the disarray in the formal sector, Nepal's informal financial institutions survived and thrived. Moneylenders provided loans and much of the cross-border trade with India were financed through the traditional *hundi* system (Seddon, Gurung and Adhikari 2002).[10] Protectionism and liberalism alike did not improve the conditions of those

---

[10]Hundis were legal financial instruments that evolved on the Indian subcontinent, used as remittance instruments for the purpose of transfer of funds from one place to another.

with restricted access to loans. *Hundi* interest charges were high but they had much lower transaction and information costs built into their loan contracts when compared to the Agricultural Development Bank or commercial banks (Adams and Brunner 2003).[11] The survival of the *hundi* system did, however, not counterweight the negative impact of liberalization on credits access of the poor (Shrestha and Khorshed 2007).

Ironically, more protective initiatives, such as the low-interest-rate loans from Agricultural Development Bank, failed to make credit more easily available to peasant households (smallholders, sharecroppers and landless peasants), because these loans required a collateral (land titles in most cases).[12] In other words, the highest share of institutional credit went to landed elites, which increased their power in the political and economic hierarchy while the peasants had no other choice but to informally borrow at a high premium from the same elites (Joshi 2010).

It is not surprising, then, that, on one hand, neoliberal policies worsened inequality in Nepal. Economic growth from marketization was not evenly dispersed; rather it had a negative impact on the rural poor peasants and marginalized ethnic groups (Shrestha and Khorshed 2007). On the other hand, institutions veered towards protectionism, like the Agricultural Development Bank, also did nothing to improve the conditions of these parcels of the population.

Additionally, in line with privatization priorities, the seeds and fertilizer subsidies given to farmers were eliminated (Deraniyagala 2005, p. 59), encouraging those involved in agriculture to relocate to export-oriented sectors. The distributive effects of subsidy benefited the rural elite at the expense of the rural poor, but also changed the rural-urban distributive patterns. In fact, the subsidy cuts were mostly borne by rural households whose income depended largely unskilled labor (Cockburn 2002). The spatial operation of FDI also indicates that the benefits of the liberal market economy remained concentrated in urban areas, particularly in the capital city Kathmandu: 57 percent of the 270 operating FDI projects were concentrated in the capital (Athukorala and Kishor 2005). The structural reforms imposed by the World Bank and IMF on Nepal created economic constraints for the government and forced it to cut off welfare programs, which impacted people living in urban and rural areas very unevenly; the burden of structural reforms being disproportionately held by peasants. Between the mid-1980s and the mid-1990s, average levels of urban real income became twice as high as rural real income, which represented a deepening of the level of inequality (Deraniyagala 2005, p. 58). Even after the democratic change, the rural portion of the population was left behind — caught between ties with landed elites and institutionalized exclusion by the state.

The part of the population that had borne the costs of colonization, modernization, and liberalization was the same groups of people. Fraser's triple movement shows that despite the two-dimensional swing of the pendulum sometimes towards protectionism, other times toward liberalism, domination relationships endured for centuries in Nepal.

---

[11]The process of financial liberalization gained momentum in 1987/88 when Nepal entered into the first and second phase of SAP. The second phase started in the fiscal year 1992/93, which envisaged a greater role and reliance on the private sector (Paudel 2005). Several other initiatives were forged in order to meet the need for consumer financing requirements. By the end of mid-July, 2012, altogether 265 banks and non-bank financial institutions licensed by NRB were in operation (NRB 2012).

[12]According to Madhav Joshi (2010), the landed elites of the rural villages and urban districts have had equal access to the institutional credit.

Although *Jana Andolan I* promulgated a democratic constitution and initiated the 1990 democratic reforms, at the administrative level, exclusion of historically marginalized ethnic, caste and religious groups continued. In some cases, there was even a decline in representation in the government of some groups that had been well represented during the *Panchayat* era (Lawoti 2005). Modernization and neoliberal policies failed to reduce poverty or inequality in Nepal (Murshed and Gates 2003). Nevertheless, the reforms opened a 'space for public expression of dissent and the organization of disaffected communities, both of which had been actively suppressed during the *Panchayat* era' (Shneiderman et al. 2016, p. 2051).

Democratic transformation also created space for public critique of the state and escalated the critique of a caste-based social order, giving rise to ethnic politics in Nepal (Hangen 2010). Rage against a legacy of oppression based on caste and ethnicity as well as inequalities and lack of opportunity led previously excluded individuals to support for the Maoist insurgency: a triple movement in Nepal (Bray, Leiv, and Murshed 2003; Do and Iyer 2007). Witnessing the commodification and dismantling of some of ceremonial Nepali institutions of the 1990s, indigenous nationalities constructed a new sense of identity and legal grounds to appeal for their rights and fight for emancipation (Pandey 2005). The pro-poor approach of the Maoists had been a magnet for deprived groups, ethnicity, in turn, became an important element of the movement (Pandey 2005).

Before 1996, something similar to the 'People's War' could not have occurred because there was no unified voice in the rural areas; however, the Maoist organization tapped into existing latent conflicts, creating a collective grievance amongst the diverse Nepali population and translating this into a collective force. The result was the operation of parallel structures of government in Maoist-operated areas led by the Communist Party of Nepal-Maoist (CPN-M), who relied on violence against the state (People's War) to uphold these structures (Basnett 2009). When CPN-M launched their 'People's War' the party had fewer than 100 full-time members. With their focus on building a full-capacity military, within ten years the party had raised an army of 20,000 (Ogura 2008, p. 13).

The Nepali government was ill equipped to respond to the challenge to its legitimacy. Extreme centralization of political, administrative and governance powers in post-1990 Nepal also played a major role in turning a regional crisis into a national security crisis and then into state implosion within ten years (Pahari 2010, pp. 210–211). In fact, constitutional monarchy in Nepal meant that Nepali political parties made no use of government or the parliament to institute long-term social, economic, and political goals, thereby bolstering Maoists' claims that nothing in Nepal would change without a total revolution (Pahari 2010, p. 210). When King Gyanendra unconstitutionally resorted to direct rule, he eroded the political elite's stake and interest in continuing to defend the 1990 constitutional monarchy. Instead, with India's help, the elites formed a political alliance with the Maoists to embrace the latter's key political goals (republic, new constitution via elections to a constituent assembly, and a new federal state structure).

During the period of the Maoist movement, Nepal was one of the few countries where absolute poverty fell significantly. Between 1996 and 2004, the GDP growth averaged 4.2 percent, against a population growth rate of 2.2 percent, resulting in a per capita income growth of 2 percent. Meanwhile, the proportion of the population below the poverty line was reduced to 31 percent in 2004 from 42 percent in 1996 (Khatiwada 2012).[13] Poverty reduction, unfortunately, did not mean a decrease in inequality. Decomposing poverty reduction into economic growth and income distribution components for the period of 1996–2004 shows that growth alone contributed to a 24.1 percent decline in poverty, whereas inequality in distribution of income exacerbated poverty by 13.2 percent resulting in a net decline in poverty by 11 percent (Khatiwada 2012; Central Bureau of Statistics (CBS) 2010/2011).

During this period, traditional economic performance measurements showed a dim picture: lower growth rates due to social unrest when compared to the previous decade — around 4 percent annual GDP growth in the 1990s and 2000s, in comparison to 5 percent in the 1980s — and bigger economic burden on the poorest portion of the population. Notably, when poverty analysis is disaggregated into different ethnic groups, it is clear that the reduction of poverty was not felt by the lower strata of the population during the decade-long rebellion. As shown in Table 1, members of the upper caste experienced a decrease of 46 percent in poverty headcount, while Hill *Janajati* and *Muslims*, both minority groups, felt a much slighter reduction in poverty, 10 percent and 6 percent respectively between 1995–96 and 2003–04.

In the aftermath of the revolution, however, the important political changes took. The Nepali Maoists became the first political party in the post-cold war world to successfully use a 'People's War' to end a political regime and also bring about a change in the entire state structure (Pahari 2010, p. 211). In addition to undermining strict rules of inter-caste commensality, the People's War broke spatial boundaries separating different castes. The war was arguably the first time when the lower caste entered the houses of the higher caste *en masse* (Zharkevich 2019). It was not until the end of Maoist revolution that *Dalits* as a group had any representation in national politics. Fifty *Dalits* representatives were elected to the Constituent Assembly in 2008 (Vasily 2009).[14] Maoist demand for a

Table 1. Change in poverty measurement by caste and ethnicity.

	Poverty headcount rate			Distribution of the poor			Distribution of the population		
	1995–96	2003–04	Change in %	1995–96	2003–04	Change in %	1995–96	2003–04	Change in %
Upper Caste (Hill-Terai)	34.1	18.4	−46	26.7	15.7	−41	32.7	26.3	−20
Yadavs (Middle C. Terai)	28.7	21.3	−26	2.9	1.9	−33	4.2	2.8	−−34
Dalits (Hill-Terai)	57.8	45.5	−21	10.6	10.9	3	7.7	7.4	−4
Newar	19.3	14	−28	2.5	3.4	35	5.5	7.5	38
Hill Janajati	48.7	44	−10	19.7	27.8	41	16.9	19.5	16
Tharu (Terai janajati)	53.4	35.4	−34	10.4	9.2	−12	8.2	8.1	−1
Muslims	43.7	41.3	−6	5.7	8.7	53	5.4	6.5	19
Other	46.1	31.3	−32	21.4	22.3	4	19.4	21.9	13
Total	41.8	30.8	−26	100	100	–	100	100	–

Source: Central Bureau of Statistics(CBS). 2005.Poverty Trends in Nepal 1995–96 and 2003–04. CBS: Kathmandu, Nepal.

[13]The poverty line for Nepal has been derived on the basis of the 1995–96 Nepal Living Standard Survey (NLSS-I) using the cost-of-basic-needs (CBN) method. Changes in the cost of living have been taken into account using region-specific price indices developed on the basis of NLSS-I 1995–96 and NLSS-II 2003–04.

[14]Before the Maoist revolution, Dalits were conspicuously absent from national politics: only one Dalit served as a minister of state between 1960 and 1990 and another was elected to Parliament in the 1990s.

secular state was satisfied in 2008, which meant religion no longer served as a source of law or state ideology (Zharkevich 2019). Past efforts to ensure women's representation in politics had never exceeded 6 percent until 2008 (Nepali and Shrestha 2007), and politics was out of reach for the overwhelming majority of Nepali women. The People's War and other regional and ethnic conflicts that emerged after the Constituent Aseembly created an enabling environment for women to join politics. Yadav (2016) estimates that at least one-third of the participants were women in the second People's Movement in 2006; and women were at the front line for other movements in the country.

The dismantling of existing oppressive institutions in Nepal started in 1996. It was prompted as the marketization of land, labor, and money pressured society to extreme inequality and stripped its elitist state in a way that it created the conditions for an eman-cipatory impulse. Despite some negative consequences and the hardship people faced during the decade-long Maoist Movement in Nepal, it created an enabling space for empowerment of ethnic minorities and women while forcing a restructuring of national political institutions that represented century-long group dominance (Aguirre and Pie-tropaoli 2008; Manchanda 2001).[15] Between 1996 and 2006, Nepal provides a clear example of Fraser's triple movement.

The unfolding of such emancipatory push is still in process. The First Constitutional Assembly was dissolved in 2012 without a new constitution because of various political differences. New elections held in 2013 instituted a Second Constituent Assembly, which promulgated a contentious constitution in September 2015, sparking a new wave of polit-ical uncertainty and polarization (Shneiderman et al. 2016). In 2017, nevertheless, Nepali citizens voted in an historic election — for representation in the country's national and provincial parliaments — giving birth to one of the world's youngest democracies. The Left Alliance, an unexpected coalition between the Maoist and Marxist-Leninist parties, acquired a sweeping majority, winning nearly 70 percent of the total parliamen-tary seats and replacing the ruling, center-left, Nepali Congress. These events exemplify the non-teleological unfolding of history prompted by Nepal's emancipatory forces, the detailed analysis of which is worth examination in future research.

5. Concluding Remarks

Within a global context of economic development, policymakers have pieced together fragmentary projects to imagine development as an abstract object while letting go of the political impetus for tempering corporatism with social justice. Nepal is not excep-tional in this regard (Panday 2011). The pressure to develop led Nepal to indebtedness to foreign capital. In an effort to demonstrate their ability to repay their debts to foreign creditors, Nepali political leaders, whether liberal or protectionist, often played a repressive role on the rest of the population (Baviskar 2004, p. 36).

Some specific state policies, such as land privatization, aggravated the marginalization of some groups in Nepal on the basis of ethnicity, gender, and kinship. This displacement

[15]Gender equality is far from a reality in Nepal, a highly patriarchal country, where women report high levels of sexual violence, as well as other abuses, across castes. The country, nevertheless, is making progress to improve women's con-ditions. In the 2017 elections, women earned 40 percent representation in local governments. Also, after a new civil code in 2018, women are entitled to keep their share of their parents' property after getting married and their hus-band's share if the divorce is his fault.

eroded their identity — because oftentimes identities of family farmers are intertwined with the land — increased poverty, and destabilized communities. Nepal, like other countries (Schneider and Nega 2016; Bracarense and Gil-Vasquez 2018), thus, provides a counterexample to the NIE perspective of development, which emphasizes private property and liberalization as the means for improvement of life standards.

Another shortcoming of NIE is its view that wrong policies taken by populist states are *the* source of underdevelopment. In reality, wrongly conceived and executed policies taken by 'universalized' westernized models, whether liberal or protectionist, appear as the main cause of transformational problems. In the case of countries like Nepal, protection and liberalization alike have entailed national political and economic elites to dominate productive and unproductive labor and appropriating resources such as land, forests, minerals, water and money to their benefit (Seppälä 2014).

The way in which the population organized and reacted to these impositions was particular to Nepal's history of elitist land tenure, nationalized financial system, and caste-based social organization. The formation of the secular federal republic of Nepal, with wide ethnic and gender representation, was the result of emancipatory movements led by a part of the population that had been deprived of their rights for centuries by both liberal and protectionist policies. Rather than the imposition of private propriety and the private/public dichotomy of market/government, it was social interactions within the domination/emancipation dimension driven by collective consciousness formation at grassroots level that secured institutional transformation in Nepal.

This corresponds with Fraser's (2013, 130) triple movement, which shows that the political dismantling by market forces may trigger emancipatory reactions that may align themselves with either marketization or embeddedness, encouraging possible social erosion or ethical protection, respectively. This supports, as a result, her effort to expand Polanyi's theory to address forms of domination other than commodification and offer a multidimensional approach to institutional transformation that grasps with the complexity of the twenty-first-century in a non-teleological way.

Finally, Nepal illustrates the importance of Polanyi's understanding of a commodification-fueled crisis that is simultaneously ecological, economic, political, and social. This paper, thereby, reinforces Fraser's call for a new economic theory of contemporary crises that deals with instabilities spurred by the commodification of money, but that also captures the instabilities created by the commodification of labor and land as well.

Acknowledgements

The authors wish to thank the anonymous reviewers for their helpful comments.

Disclosure Statement

No potential conflict of interest was reported by the author(s).

References

Acemoglu, D., S. Johnson, and J. A. Robinson. 2001. 'The Colonial Origins of Comparative Development: An Empirical Investigation.' *American Economic Review* 91 (5): 1369–1401.

Acemoglu, D., S. Johnson, and J. A. Robinson. 2003. 'An African Success Story: Botswana.' In *In Search of Prosperity: Analytic Narratives on Economic Growth*, edited by D. Rodrik. Princeton, NJ: Princeton University Press.

Acharya, M. 2003. 'Time Budget Studies and Its Policy Relevance—The Case of Nepal.' Proceedings of the national seminar on applications of time use statistics, organized by central statistical organization, New Delhi, 8–9 October, 2002.

Acharya, M., Y. R. Khatiwada, and S. Aryal. 2003. *Structural Adjustment Policies and Poverty Eradication*. Kathmandu: Institute for Integrated Development Studies.

Acharya, K., N. B. Thapa, and S. Sharma. 1998. *Economic Liberalization in Nepal Sequence and Process*. Kathmandu, Nepal: Oxfam.

Adams, J., and H.-P. Brunner. 2003. 'Technology and Institutions in the Process of Economic Reform: Achieving Growth with Poverty Reduction in South Asia.' *Journal of Economic Issues* 37 (2): 363–369.

Adhikari, J. 2008. *Land Reforms in Nepal: Problem and Prospects*. Kathmandu, Nepal: Actionaid.

Aguirre, D., and I. Pietropaoli. 2008. 'Gender Equality, Development and Transnational Justice: The Case of Nepal.' *International Journal of Transnational Justice* 2 (3): 356–377.

Athukorala, P.-C., and S. Kishor. 2005. 'Foreign Investment in Nepal.' In *Economic Growth, Economic Performance and Welfare in South Asia*, edited by R. Jha. Houndmills, UK: Palgrave.

Baral, L. R. 1994. 'The Return of Party Politics in Nepal. Journal of Democracy.' *Journal of Democracy* 5 (1): 121–133.

Basnett, Y. 2009. 'From Politicization of Grievances to Political Violence: An Analysis of the Maoist Movement in Nepal.' Working Paper Series, No 7–78, Development Studies Institute, London School of Economics and Political Science.

Baviskar, A. 2004. *In the Belly of the River: Tribal Conflicts Over Development in the Narmada Valley*. New Delhi: Oxford University Press.

Bennett, L., D. R. Dahal, and P. Govindasamy. 2008. *Caste, Ethnic and Regional Identity in Nepal: Further Analysis of the 2006 Nepal Demographic and Health Survey*. Calverton, MD: Macro International.

Bracarense, N., and K. Gil-Vasquez. 2018. 'Bolivia's Institutional Transformation: Contact Zones, Social Movements, and the Emergence of an Ethnic Class Consciousness.' *Journal of Economic Issues* 52 (3): 615–636.

Bray, J., L. Leiv, and M. Murshed. 2003. 'Nepal: Economic Drivers of the Maoist Insurgency.' In *The Political Economy of Armed Conflict: Beyond Greed and Grievance*, edited by Karen Ballentine and Jake Sherman. Boulder, CO: Lynne Rienner.

Caplan, L. 2000. *Land and Social Change in East Nepal*. 2nd ed. Lalitpur: Himal Books.

Central Bureau of Statistics (CBS). 2010/2011. *Final Result of Population and Housing Census 2011*. Thapathali, Kathmandu: Government of Nepal National Planning Commission Secretariat.

Chang, H.-J. 2007. 'Institutional Change and Economic Development: An Introduction.' In *Institutional Change and Economic Development*, edited by Ha-Joon Chang. New York: United Nations University Press.

Chang, H.-J. 2011. 'Institutions and Economic Development: Theory, Policy and History.' *Journal of Institutional Economics* 7 (4): 473–498.

Cockburn, J. 2002. 'Trade Liberalization and Poverty in Nepal: A Computable General Equilibrium Micro Simulation Analysis.' *CSAE Working Paper Series*, 2002–11.

Crews, C. 2018. 'What about Postcolonial Politics in Nepal?' Paper presented at western political science association meeting, March 29–31, San Francisco.

Deraniyagala, S. 2005. 'The Political Economy of Civil Conflict in Nepal.' *Oxford Development Studies* 33 (1): 47–62.

Do, Q.-T., and L. Iyer. 2007. *Poverty, Social Divisions, and Conflict in Nepal*. Policy Research Working Paper; No. 4228. Washington, DC: World Bank.

Einsiedel, S. V., M. M. David, and S. Pradhan, eds. 2012. 'Introduction.' In *Nepal in Transition: From People's War to Fragile Peace*, edited by S. von Einsiedel, D. M. Malone, and S. Pradhan. New York: Cambridge University Press.

Folbre, N. 2001. *The Invisible Heart. Economics and Family Values*. New York: New Press.

Forbes, A. A. 1999. 'Mapping Power: Disputing Claims to Kipat Lands in Northeastern Nepal.' *American Ethnologist* 26 (1): 114–138.

Fraser, N. 2013. 'A Triple Movement? Parsing the Politics of Crisis After Polanyi.' *New Left Review* 81 (5): 119–132.

Fraser, N. 2014. 'Can Society be Commodities all the Way Down? Post-Polanyian Reflections on Capitalist Crisis.' *Economy and Society* 43 (4): 541–558.

Fraser, N. 2017. 'Why Two Karls are Better than One: Integrating Polanyi and Marx in a Critical Theory of the Current Crisis.' *Working Paper der DFG-Kollegforscher_innengruppe Postwachstumsgesellschaften.*

Fujikura, T. 2003. 'The Role of Collective Imagination in the Maoist Conflict in Nepal.' *HIMALAYA, the Journal of the Association for Nepal and Himalayan Studies* 23 (1): 21–30.

Fukuyama, F. 1992. *The End of History and the Last Man.* New York: The Free Press, A Division of Macmilan Inc.

Ghimire, K. B. 1992. *Forest or Farm? The Politics of Poverty and Land Hunger in Nepal.* Delhi: Oxford University Press.

Hachhethu, K. 2003. 'Democracy and Nationalism: Interface Between State and Ethnicity in Nepal.' *CNAS* 30 (2): 217–252.

Hachhethu, K. 2009. *The European Union's Role in Democracy Building in Nepal.* Stockholm: International Institute for Democracy and Electoral Assistance.

Hachhethu, K. 2015. *Trajectory of Democracy in Nepal.* New Delhi: Adroit.

Hangen, S. I. 2010. *The Rise of Ethnic Politics in Nepal: Democracy in the Margins.* Abingdon, UK: Routledge.

HLLRC. 1996. High Level Land Reform Commission (2051BS). A report submitted to the HMG/ Nepal by High level Land Reform Commission.

Hutt, M., ed. 1994. *Nepal in the Nineties: Version of the Past, Visions of the Future.* Delhi: Oxford University Press.

Jha, P. 2014. *Battles of the New Republic: A Contemporary History of Nepal.* New Delhi: Aleph Book Company.

Joshi, M. 2010. 'Between Clientelistic Dependency and Liberl Market Economy: Rural Support for the Maoist Insurgency in Nepal.' In *The Maoist Insurgency in Nepal: Revolution in the Twenty-First Century,* edited by M. Lawoti and A. K. Pahari. London: Routledge.

Kapur, D., and R. Webber. 'Governance-related Conditionalities of the IFIs.' G-24 Discussion Paper Series, 6. Geneva: UNCTAD, 2000.

Karki, A. K. 2002. 'Movements From Below: Land Rights Movement in Nepal.' *Inter-Asia Cultural Studies* 3 (2): 201–217.

Khanal, D. N. 1995. *Land Teen? System and Agrarian Structure of Nepal.* Rome: Food and Agriculture Organization.

Khanal, K., and Z. Todorova. 2019. 'Remittances and Households in the Age of Neoliberal Uncertainty.' *Journal of Economic Issues* 53 (2): 515–522.

Khatiwada, Y. R. 2000. 'An Overview of Financial Liberalization and agenda for Further Reforms.' In the Proceedings of the National Workshop, Do We Need Economic Reforms Phse II? Organized by Institute for Integrated Development Studies. June5, 1999, Kathmandu, Nepal.

Khatiwada, Y. R. 2012. 'Nepal.' In *Trade Liberalisation and Poverty in South Asia,* edited by J. S. Bandara, P. C. Athukorala, and S. Kelegama. London: Routledge.

Lawoti, M. 2005. *Towards a Democratic Nepal: Inclusive Political Institutions for a Multicultural Society.* New Delhi: Sage.

Lawoti, M. 2010. 'Evolution and Growth of the Maoist Insurgency in Nepal.' In *The Maoist Insurgency in Nepal: Revolution in the Twenty-First Century,* edited by M. Lawoti and A. K. Pahari. London: Routledge.

Liechty, M. 1997. 'Selective Exclusion: Foreigners, Foreign Goods and Foreignness in Modern Nepali History.' *Studies in Nepali History and Society* 2 (1): 5–68.

Malagodi, M. 2013. *Constitutional Nationalism and Legal Exclusion: Equality, Identity Politics, and Democracy in Nepal.* New Delhi: Oxford University Press.

Manchanda, R. 2001. 'Ambivalent Gains in South Asian Conflicts.' In *The Aftermath: Women in Post-Conflict Transformation*, edited by M. Turshen, S. Meintjes, and A. Pillay. London: Zed Books.

Marx, K., and F. Engels. 1959 [1846]. *The German Ideology*. Volume 5. Marx and Engels 1845–1847 (Karl Marx and Friedrich Engels Collected Works). Berlin: Dietz.

Mishra, R. 2004.'India's Role in Nepal's Maoist Insurgency.' *Asian Survey* 44 (5): 627–646.

MOAC. 2014. *Agriculture Development Strategy*. Nepali Ministry of Agricultural Development. http://extwprlegs1.fao.org/docs/pdf/nep159180.pdf.

Murshed, S. M., and S. Gates. 2003. *Spatial-Horizontal Inequality and the Maoist Insurgency in Nepal*. Washington, DC: World Bank. February.

Nepal Rastra Bank. 2012. Banking and Financial Statistics, No.58, July.

Nepali, R. K., and P. Shrestha. 2007. *Unfolding the Reality: Silenced Voices of Women in Politics*. Kathmandu: South Asia Partnership.

Ogura, K. 2008. *Seeking State Power: The Communist Party of Nepal (Maoist)*. Berghof Transitions Series No.3. Berlin: Berghof Research Center for Constructive Conflict Management.

Pahari, A. K. 2010. 'Unequal Rebellions: The Continuum of 'People's War' in Nepal and India.' In *The Maoist Insurgency in Nepal: Revolution in the Twenty-First Century*, edited by M. Lawoti and A. K. Pahari. London: Routledge.

Panday, D. R. 2011. *Looking at Development and Donors: Essays From Nepal*. Kathmandu: Martin Chautari.

Pandey, N. N. 2005. *'Nepal's Maoist Movement and Implications for India and China.'* RCSS Policy Studies No. 27. Colombo: Manohar Publishers.

Paudel, N. P. 2005. 'Financial System and Economic Development.' In *Nepal Rastra Bank, Nepal Rastra Bank in Fifty Years in Fifty Years*. Kathmandu: NRB. https://www.nrb.org.np/contents/uploads/2019/12/Golden_Jubilee_Publications-Nepal_Rastra_Bank_in_Fifty_Years__Part-I___-Resource_Management_and-_Organizational-_Development.pdf.

Peek, J., and E. Rosengren. 2000. 'Implications of the Globalization of the Banking Sector: The Latin American Experience.' *New England Economic Review*, Federal Reserve Bank of Boston, September, pp.45–62.

Polanyi, K. 1933. 'The Mechanism of the World Economic Crisis.' Translated by Kari Polanyi-Leavitt. *Der Osterreichische Volkswirt* 25: 2–9.

Polanyi, K. 1944 [2001]. *The Great Transformation*. Boston: Beacon Press.

Polanyi, K. 1945. 'Universal Capitalism or Regional Planning.' *London Quarterly of World Affairs* 10 (3): 86–91.

Polanyi, K. 1947. 'On Belief in Economic Determinism.' *Sociological Review* a39 (1): 96–102.

Polanyi, K. 1957. *Trade and Market in the Early Empire*, edited by M. Arensber and H. Pearson. Chicago: Henry Regnery.

Prebisch, R. 1984. 'The Global Crisis of Capitalism and its Theoretical Background.' *CEPAL Review* 22: 159–178.

Rankin, K. 2004. *The Cultural Politics of Markets: Economic Liberalization and Social Change in Nepal*. Toronto: University of Toronto Press.

Regmi, M. 1971. *A Study in Nepali Economic History, 1768–1846*. New Delhi: Manjustri Publishing House.

Regmi, M. 1977. *Land Ownership in Nepal*. Delhi: Adroit.

Regmi, M. 1978. *Land Tenure and Taxation in Nepal*. Kathmandu: Biblioteca Himalayica.

Regmi, M. 1999. *Imperial Gorkha: An Account of Gorkhali Rule in Kumaun 1791–1815*. Delhi: Adroit.

Schneider, G., and B. Nega. 2016. 'Limits of the New Institutional Economics Approach to African Development.' *Journal of Economic Issues* 50 (2): 435–443.

Seddon, D. 1987. *Nepal: A State of Poverty*. New Delhi: Vikas.

Seddon, D., G. Gurung, and J. Adhikari. 2002. 'Foreign Labor Migration and the Remittance Economy of Nepal.' *Critical Asian Studies* 34 (1): 19–40.

Selwyn, B., and S. Miyamura. 2014. 'Class Struggle or Embedded Markets: Marx, Polanyi and the Meanings and Possibilities of Social Transformation.' *New Political Economy* 19 (5): 639–661.

Seppälä, T. 2014. 'Biopolitics, Resistance and the Neoliberal Development Paradigm.' *Journal für Entwicklungspolitik* 30 (1): 88–103.

Shakya, M. 2016. 'Labor Militancy in Neoliberal Times: A Preliminary Comparison of Nepal with South Africa.' In *World Anthropologies in Practice Situated Perspectives, Global Knowledge*, edited by J. Gledhill. London: Bloomsbury Academic.

Shneiderman, S., L. Wagner, J. Rinck, A. L. Johnson, and A. Lord. 2016. 'Nepal's Ongoing Political Transformation: A Review of Post-2006 Literature on Conflict, the State, Identities, and Environments.' *Modern Asian Studies* 50 (6): 2041–2114.

Shrestha, M. B., and C. Khorshed. 2007. 'Testing Financial Liberalization Hypothesis with ARDL Modelling Approach.' *Applied Financial Economics* 17 (18): 1529–1540.

Stein, H. 2008. *Beyond the World Bank Agenda – An Institutional Approach to Development*. Chicago: University of Chicago Press.

Tamanaha, B. Z. 2015. 'The Knowledge and Policy Limits of New Institutional Economics on Development.' *Journal of Economic Issues* 49 (1): 89–109.

Thapa, D. 2012. 'The Making of the Maoist Insurgency.' In *Nepal in Transition: From People's War to Fragile Peace*, edited by S. von Einsiedel, D. M. Malone, and S. Pradhan. New York: Cambridge University Press.

Thapa, G. B., and J. Sharma. 2009. 'From Insurgency to Democracy: The Challenges of Peace and Democracy-Building in Nepal.' *Institutional Political Science Review* 30 (2): 205–219.

Uprety, P. R. 1980. *Nepal-Tibet Relations1850–1930: Years of Hopes, Challenges and Frustrations*. Kathmandu: Puga Nara.

Vasily, L. A. 2009. 'Struggles Against Domination: Forms of Nepali Dalit Activism.' In *Governance, Conflict, and Civic Action: Ethnic Activism and Civil Society in South Asia*, edited by D. Gellner. New Delhi: Sage.

Veracini, L. 2015. *The Settler Colonial Present*. London: Palgrave Macmillan.

Waller, W. 1988. 'Radical Institutionalism: Methodological Aspects of the Radical Tradition.' *Journal of Economic Issues* 22 (3): 667–674.

Waller, W., and A. Jennings. 1991. 'A Feminist Institutionalist Reconsideration of Karl Polanyi.' *Journal of Economic Issues* 25 (2): 485–497.

Waller, William, and Mary V. Wrenn. 2019. 'Feminist Institutionalism and Neoliberalism.' In *Paper Presented at International Initiative for Promoting Political Economy, Envisioning the Economy of the Future, & the Future of Political Economy Conference*. Panel: Neoliberalism's Divergent Cultural Outcomes: The prosperity Gospel, Right-Wing Conservativism, and the Other's Vision, Lille, France, July 3–5.

Whelpton, J. 2005. *A History of Nepal*. Cambridge: Cambridge University Press.

World Bank. 2019. 'Nepal Gross Domestic Product Time Series.' *Development Indicators*. Accessed: https://databank.worldbank.org/source/world-development-indicators.

Yadav, P. K. 2016. *Social Transformation in Post-Conflict Nepal: A Gendered Perspective*. New York: Routledge.

Zharkevich, I. 2019. *Maoist People's War and the Revolution of Everyday Life in Nepal (South Asia in the Social Sciences)*. Cambridge: Cambridge University Press. doi:10.1017/9781108609210.

Index

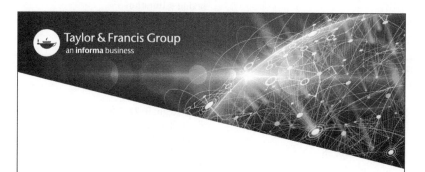

For Product Safety Concerns and Information please contact our
EU representative GPSR@taylorandfrancis.com Taylor & Francis
Verlag GmbH, Kaufingerstraße 24, 80331 München, Germany